, SEDET AD DEXTERAM PATRIS. ET ITERUM

ORTUOS, CUIUS REGN　　　　　　　　　　IN

QUI EX PATRE FILIOQ　　　　　　　　　　JM

ATUR: QUI LOCUTUS E,　　　　　　　　　ET

ECCLESIAM. CONFITEOR　UNUM BAPTISM　IN

RECTIONEM MORTUORUM, ET VITAM VENTURI

NIPOTENTEM, 42 FACTOREM CÆLI ET TERRÆ,

NUM DOMINUM IESUM CHRISTUM, FILIUM DEI

ÆCULA. 76 DEUM DE DEO, LUMEN DE LUMINE,

M, CONSUBSTANTIALEM PATRI: 78 PER QUEM

ES 93 ET PROPTER NOSTRAM SALUTEM 100

PIRITU SANCTO 115 EX MARIA VIRGINE, 121 ET

NOBIS 163 SUB PONTIO PILATO; 174 PASSUS 178

83 SECUNDUM SCRIPTURAS, 191 ET ASCENDIT

T ITERUM VENTURUS EST CUM GLORIA, 209

N ERIT FINIS. 234 ET IN SPIRITUM SANCTUM,

FILIOQUE PROCEDIT. 254 QUI CUM PATRE ET

QUI LOCUTUS EST PER PROPHETAS. 263 ET

ECCLESIAM. 268 CONFITEOR UNUM BAPTISMA

TO RESURRECTIONEM MORTUORUM, 284 ET

, PATREM OMNIPOTENTEM, FACTOREM CÆLI

IN UNUM DOMINUM IESUM CHRISTUM, FILIUM

SÆCULA. DEUM DE DEO, LUMEN DE LUMINE,

UM, CONSUBSTANTIALEM PATRI: PER QUEM

T PROPTER NOSTRAM SALUTEM DESCENDIT

EX MARIA VIRGINE, ET HOMO FACTUS EST.

The Creed in Slow Motion

The Creed in Slow Motion

Martin Kochanski

**HODDER &
STOUGHTON**

First published in Great Britain in 2022 by Hodder & Stoughton
An Hachette UK company

I

A CIP catalogue record for this title is available from the British Library

Hardback ISBN 978 1 399 80154 6
eBook ISBN 978 1 399 80155 3

Typeset in Sabon MT by Hewer Text UK Ltd, Edinburgh
Printed and bound in Great Britain by Clays Ltd, Elcograf S.p.A.

Hodder & Stoughton policy is to use papers that are natural, renewable
and recyclable products and made from wood grown in sustainable
forests. The logging and manufacturing processes are expected to
conform to the environmental regulations of the country of origin.

Hodder & Stoughton Ltd
Carmelite House
50 Victoria Embankment
London EC4Y 0DZ

www.hodderfaith.com

This book is dedicated to
Dom Mark Pontifex (1897–1991), monk of Downside,
who delighted in rational argument.

Contents

Introduction   I

I

BEING: God the Father

1   I believe   11
2   I believe in   14
3   God   17
4   One God   23
   The parable of the cube   27
5   The Father   31
6   Almighty   42
7   Maker of heaven and earth   48
8   Of all things visible and invisible   58

II

ACT: God the Son

a.   Creation
   The parable of the shadows   69
9   I believe in one Lord, Jesus Christ   71
10   Born of the Father before all ages   76
11   God from God   78
12   Through him all things were made   85

b. **Intervention**

13 For us men   93

14 And for our salvation   100

    The parable of the scissors   109

15 He came down from heaven   112

16 Was incarnate   115

17 Of the Virgin Mary   121

18 And became man   133

c. **Rescue**

    The parable of the signpost   147

19 He was crucified   150

20 For our sake   163

21 Under Pontius Pilate   174

22 He suffered death   178

23 And was buried   181

24 And rose again   183

25 In accordance with the Scriptures   191

d. **Fulfilment**

26 He ascended into heaven   199

27 And is seated at the right hand of the Father   204

28 He will come again in glory   209

29 To judge the living and the dead   217

30 And his kingdom will have no end   234

Contents

III

LIFE: God the Spirit

31 I believe in the Holy Spirit, the Lord   239

32 The giver of life   242

33 Who proceeds from the Father and the Son   254

34 Is adored and glorified   260

35 Who has spoken through the prophets   263

36 I believe in one, holy, catholic and apostolic Church   268

37 I confess one baptism   277

38 For the forgiveness of sins   280

39 I look forward to the resurrection of the dead   284

40 And the life of the world to come   287

Further reading   291

Introduction

We are told that our house is built on a rock. But even a house on a rock needs some kind of structure to hold it together. We are part of the mystical body of Christ, but even a mystical body needs bones, for without them it will be as shapeless as a slug. The Creed is those bones.

It is to keep the building together and to keep the body in shape that we regularly recite the Creed in church and recommit ourselves to it. At least, recommitting and reconnecting to the foundations of our faith is what we ought to be doing, but in practice, all we do is recite.

Because think about it. Suppose I have a moment of enlightenment – an instant when I don't just say the words, but hear what I am saying and understand what I am hearing. You can never predict when the Spirit will strike. Let's suppose that the words are the 'for us' of the Incarnation and that at that moment I am filled with awe that the Infinite should have taken on finiteness for my sake. That moment might only last a heartbeat. But even a short time takes time. From then on I will be one heartbeat out of step with everyone else in the relentless forward march of a congregation all saying the same words. That cannot be allowed. Imagine if everybody did the same as me, and tried to mean the Creed while they were saying it. Imagine the chaos.

And so we all march on, watching our neighbours out of the corners of our eyes. We succeed in keeping step all the way to the end, but at the price of not looking where we are going: at the price of not going anywhere.

The only way to engage properly with what one is saying when one says the Creed is not to say it right through and all together, but to take it slowly and reflectively by oneself, phrase by phrase or even word by word.

That is what this book is for. It both does it and encourages you to do it – because ultimately it is *your* mind that counts. Your belief can only be an act of your own mind: nobody else's.

The Creed is the bones of faith, and only with living bones can we have a vertebrate and living faith, growing naturally in the right shape and proportion and bearing fruit at the end. And we do need such a faith. We need it first of all for ourselves because a faith glued together out of mixed bone-dust and incense is not a faith but a mere cultural identity: it makes Christ just a badge that we wear, nothing more. That is not faith at all. It has no roots, and it will be blown over by the first storm that comes. And life is full of storms.

We need a living faith for another reason as well: because others need it. They know we have the words of eternal life and they come to us for them: sometimes diffidently, sometimes defiantly and confrontationally, but secretly hoping to be convinced. At the very least they may want to understand exactly what it is that they are not believing in. To say to them about a doctrine, 'Oh, that's just one of those things that Christians say because they are Christians,' is a betrayal and a blasphemy. To say 'It is true because it says so in the book' is not much better: it feeds the sheep on silage instead of living grass.

Things are *never* true just because the books say they are true. This applies to science, mathematics, history – any human activity – and not just theology. The pianist does not play the notes because they are printed on the page but because they are the right notes. Things are true because they are true, and only a truth that is in the heart can reach the hearts of others.

We have help. The Spirit is the life-giver. If you let him give life to the ideas in your mind then you will be alive and able to give life yourself. The Lord commands us to love him with the mind and the Lord gives no commandment in vain. So we know that he is lovable-with-the-mind – that is, the effort of trying to understand will not be fruitless – and that he has given us minds so that we can love him by using them.

The method of this book is this: to take the Creed one phrase at a time and to pursue its meaning and its message in many lights and from many angles. Every angle has something to give, and all of them together add up to bring us closer to the solid truth. Even the detours will turn out to have been part of the journey.

Every light illuminates. In this adventure, anything that human beings know or experience can be a source of light. God made us whole and the world whole, and every aspect of it illuminates every other.

A defence of lay theology

This is not a catechism or a theological manual. Such books exist. It is not written by a professional theologian. Such people exist. The books are valuable and the people are valuable, but what I am doing here is different: and it is valuable as well. So is what you are doing when you read this book.

If you decide to call the theology of the theologians 'high theology', then this book could be called 'low theology'. Low theology ought not to need naming or defending: but in a world professionalised to the point where soon you won't be allowed to breathe without first getting a breathing certificate, it unfortunately does need to be named and defended.

Yes, you can always look up the doctrines in a reference book. Yes, the teaching authority of the Church, who has been researching these subjects with thousands of people for thousands of years, is supreme. When we make mistakes we go to her for correction. But the same sorts of things could be said about mathematics, and yet we find it worthwhile trying to prove theorems. The same could be said about the physical sciences, but doing experiments other people have already done is still not a waste of time.

The defence of low theology is simple: if the Creator of All had wanted a hierarchical universe in which one half of it did exactly what the experts in the other half said should be done, he would have arranged it that way while he was here with us. He would have commissioned the scribes and doctors in the Temple to enlighten the world from above, instead of picking up a ragtag of fishermen and other amateurs to illuminate it from below.

Julian of Norwich was not a scribe or a doctor, but her twenty years of meditation on the vision she had been given of the Passion produced a work that still knocks one flat today, 630 years later. Dante Alighieri was a poet, not a theologian, but the *Divine Comedy* established a theology of love which has never been surpassed. Thérèse of Lisieux had no doctorate, but she herself is a Doctor of the Church.

I am not any of these people. I am me, just as you are you. Our value is shown by the fact that God could have made a splendid and glorious universe that didn't give rise to you and me, *but he didn't*. He chose not to. He chose to make *this* universe instead, the one with us in it. That has to count for something.

And again: if God hadn't meant us to think, he wouldn't have given us minds. But he has.

So let's get going. If what I write rings true, thank the One who shows us truth. If you find I have missed out something important, laugh, for laughter is from God. And if you see that I have made a complete hash of things and got hold of the wrong end of the stick, then rejoice because you have found the right one.

Why have a creed at all?

There are verses in the Gospels that lurk in the background for centuries doing nothing, and then come suddenly to life and change everything. That is why nobody edits the Gospels down to 'What you need to know'. One example is the exchange between Jesus and the rich young man. 'If you want to be perfect, go and sell all you have and give it to the poor.' As we know, the young man went away sorrowing, because indeed he was very rich.

There are comforting interpretations of this episode which reassure us into not going away sorrowing when we hear the story. A delicate emphasis on 'If you want to be *perfect*' is one way of doing it. But, basically, the whole story depicts a failure.

Except that about 230 years later, the landowner Anthony of Egypt heard these words and *did* want to be perfect. He obeyed them and went out into the desert: one of the first monks.

Except that almost a millennium after that, a young man called Francis, son of the prosperous Assisi merchant Pietro Bernardone, heard the same words and went out and turned the whole world upside down.

I mention all this because there is another little exchange in the Gospels that has been almost forgotten. The evangelists themselves find it so uninteresting that they can't quite remember who spoke the important words, Jesus or the man he was talking to. The words are these:

> You must love the Lord your God with all your heart, with all your soul, with all your strength, *and with all your mind.**

This looks like a quotation of the first of the Ten Commandments, but if you look, it isn't. Jesus has expanded it. (He did tell us he had come not to abolish the Law and the Prophets but to fulfil them and bring them to perfection: and here, unnoticed by almost everybody, is an example.)

Those words 'with all your mind' are not in the law of Moses.† They are new. They change everything. They make theology possible. Indeed, they make all science possible, since in practising the physical sciences we are praising God by celebrating his works.

'With all your mind' changes everything in two ways. First of all, it says that the love of God must be not just a feeling but an act – an act of the whole person, which includes an act of the mind. A religion based on nothing more than feelings of holiness is no religion at all.

The second consequence of 'with all your mind' is more radical. God will not demand the impossible. If we are commanded to love God with our minds, then it must be *possible* to love God with our minds. In other words, God must be lovable-with-the-mind – that is, comprehensible. This makes theology a rational activity, but it does more: it places a constraint on the activity of God. If God is to be lovable-with-the-mind, then he *cannot* act arbitrarily, because whatever God does must be accessible to

* Luke 10:27, JB, italics added.
† Deuteronomy 6:4–5.

5

reason (and so must the world he creates, which is why physical science is possible).

The mind is not often thought of as an organ of love. This is a consequence of the Enlightenment idea of the mind as a cold, calculating machine powered solely by logic. Romanticism completed the equation: if the mind has no feelings, then feeling can have nothing to do with the mind. But 'love with all your mind' disproves all that. The mind is every bit as much an organ of love as the heart is.

The way we love with the mind is by understanding. The way we agree about what we understand, and communicate it, is by finding words to express it. And the words work both ways: forwards and backwards. Understanding gives rise to the words to express it, and the words give rise to understanding. And so the idea of a Creed begins to take shape.

The next step is this. Man is a rational animal but also a fallible one. We make mistakes. More than that, when we are taught something we find hard, or puzzling, or simply don't like, we find ourselves turning it into something we *do* like or understand; or else we just push it into a corner and forget about it.

That is human nature, and it is why, sooner or later, every science needs not just its words but its textbooks and its agreed statements of what is true. The science of being (which we call 'theology') is no exception. We need a Creed.

A Creed tells us who we are. It reminds us of truths we have forgotten (or would like to forget). It steers us away from mistakes people have made in the past, which is a good thing because we are people too and quite likely to be making the same mistakes. The mistakes may be attractive, but they are not true: and in the end truth is everything.

That is the reason why the Church has a Creed. The Nicene Creed (called by dismal pedants the Niceno-Constantinopolitan Creed) was born at the Council of Nicaea in AD 325 and reached its final form at the Council of Constantinople in AD 381. Everyone agreed that it expressed the truth. Again the process works both ways: the fact of agreeing on that expression of the truth defines what the Church is.

6

Introduction

As a confessor once cheeringly told a friend of mine, it doesn't matter if you disagree with every bishop you've ever heard from and think that every priest you have ever met is an idiot: if you believe what is in the Creed, you are a Christian (a turbulent Christian, perhaps: but then so were half the saints).

People learn, and understand, and believe – but they also forget. So the Church in her wisdom has not let the Nicene Creed sit around in books about fourth-century Church history. For the last thousand years we have all said it at Mass every Sunday. Every week, the words come out of the history books and come alive as we speak them.

I
BEING

God the Father

Credo in unum Deum,
Patrem omnipotentem,
factorem cæli et terræ,
visibilium omnium et invisibilium.

I believe in one God,
the Father almighty,
maker of heaven and earth,
of all things visible and invisible.

I

I believe

I said, casually, that we say the Creed at Mass. Of course, that isn't really true. WE don't say it: I do. This is important, and it matters; there have been fights over it; and for the moment the right side has won.

In most of the Mass it really is WE, and no doubt about it. It is good and right that it should be so. WE give glory to God in the *Gloria*, WE ask the Lamb of God to take pity in the *Agnus Dei*. In the prayers addressed to God by the priest, even in the Eucharistic Prayer itself, it is WE.

If I have counted rightly, there are three places in the Mass where this is not the case.

The first time is when I proclaim out loud that I have sinned excessively and it is all my fault. That is called a 'penitential act', but it is more: it is a tremendous affirmation of myself as a responsible agent endowed with free will by God. You probably don't notice me doing this at the time because you are at the same moment engaged in doing exactly the same thing: my sins are my business; yours are yours. (My friend Christina tells me she omits 'greatly' from the words, 'I have greatly sinned': all I can say in reply is that I suppose she knows what she is doing.)

If at this point we were to say WE had sinned, then it could mean one of two things. 'WE' means 'we': the obvious, grammatical meaning if I say 'we' is that I am saying that *you* have sinned greatly and so has your neighbour on the other side and so has that man sitting over there in the corner whom neither of us likes very much. I can't possibly know any of this. I am saying something I do not know. That is, I am not saying anything with a meaning, but only making noises with my mouth.

The alternative interpretation of 'WE' is that by saying it I am asserting some sort of corporate sin. But it is a general rule that that which belongs to everybody belongs to nobody in particular. The 'WE' takes all the meaning out of what I am saying.

'We have sinned.'

'You mean, *you* have sinned?'

'No, of course *I* haven't, but *we* have.'

That is the first time we say 'I'. The third time is when we quote the centurion with the sick servant: 'I am not worthy to receive you under my roof'.* The second time is when we say the Creed, and that is what this book is about.

When the persecutors, the torturers and – worst of all – the deriders corner me and accuse me of holding weird beliefs (for instance, that a man sits on the throne of God), how liberating it would be to get out of it by explaining that a Jew reigning over the universe is what *we as Christians* believe. That amounts to saying 'I don't believe' without having to say those particular words – just as saying 'I forgive her *as a Christian*' is the polite way to say 'I don't forgive her at all.'

To summarise: whenever 'we believe' replaces 'I believe', it lets me off the hook. The verb 'believe' is no longer an act but an identity, a part of the Christian brand: that is to say, it is nothing.

The framers of the liturgy don't want to let us off the hook: that is not what hooks are for. But you can see how that nice Canon Screwtape† smoothing things over in committee would try to convince everyone that 'we believe' would be kinder all round. Screwtape has another motive as well. If he can get the most dangerous people in the world to spend five minutes every Sunday standing up in church together and saying, 'I, personally, don't believe anything in particular,' how much better it will be than having them saying, 'I hereby commit myself to God.' Better, that is, for the devil rather than for us.

---

* The Order of Mass, citing Matthew 8:8.

† *The Screwtape Letters* by C. S. Lewis (1942) is a collection of letters of advice from a senior devil, Screwtape, to his nephew Wormwood, a junior tempter who is beginning his first assignment.

The same story applies at the other end of time. If God welcomes me one day into the joys of heaven, he will be welcoming me because I am *me* and because I have done what *I* have done and loved in the way *I* have loved, not because I am part of a WE and God lets me in on some kind of bulk entry ticket.

The gates of heaven are not open to A Christian. God says, 'I call you by name and you are mine,'* and nobody is called 'A'.

The world has been trying to deny this recently. It is just too much bother to treat a person as a person. So the policy is to ignore the individual and see only the attributes. You are A *this* or A *that*, and the 'this' and the 'that' come with moral judgements attached. One 'this' may make you so inferior that everyone has to be condescendingly nice to you; another one may make you unclean or guilty, and if you dare to ask what it is you are guilty of (as my philosophy tutor asked in 1980 when he was being deported from Czechoslovakia 'for being guilty'), that only doubles your guilt. What you as the guilty person have missed is the principle that you are *nothing* other than the sum of your attributes, nothing but 'A this' plus 'A that'. If you dare to assert that you are 'I', not 'A', then you deserve to be crushed; or re-educated.

So 'I believe' is not just (as it might once have been) a liturgist's device for keeping me firmly on the hook as I recite the Creed. It has become a cry of liberation and an assertion of existence. Of course, there is a price to pay, because now I am not able to get out of awkward clauses in the Creed by WE-ing away their meaning. So it is more important than ever to find out what *I* am committing myself to when *I* say the words, 'I believe.'

* Isaiah 43:1.

13

2

I believe in

Credo in

If I look through the Creed to see what I am committing myself to by saying it, I see a strange thing. I'm not saying 'I believe *that* this or that fact is true,' but 'I believe *in* someone or something.' It happens over and over again.

Linguistically, there are times when you can say 'I believe in . . .' and mean nothing more than 'I believe in the existence of . . .' Think of 'I believe in Father Christmas' or 'I believe in unicorns.' But that is not the only use of the words, it is not the most interesting use of the words, and it is not how the words are used in the Creed.

When I say 'I believe in you' to the turbulent teenager next door, I don't mean that I believe in his existence. I mean that I have belief in him, that I put my trust in him. And that is what I am doing when I say 'I believe in God.'

As far as existence goes, anybody can believe that God *exists*. Even pagans do, though they don't know him well enough to dare to believe *in* him. Even atheists believe in a principle that gives order to the world and prevents the laws of nature suddenly being different on Wednesdays.* That, too, is a seed which, if it is

---

* Primo Levi tells the story of a chemist who had to investigate why the X-ray films his employers were selling only turned out defective if they had been manufactured on a Wednesday. (This detective story is in the 'Silver' chapter of *The Periodic Table* (1975).) The important point is that never for one instant did the chemist consider the simplest explanation, that the day being Wednesday was the direct cause of the defects. To the extent that a physical scientist believes there is no such thing as 'Wednesdayness', he is implicitly putting his faith in a principle that says which kinds of physical laws are allowable and which kinds aren't. That is, he is believing in a principle behind the laws.

allowed to germinate, grows towards knowledge of the existence of God.

Just believing that God *exists* is an act of the pure detached mind. It is easy and it has no direct consequences. But believing *in* God, putting our trust in God, entrusting ourselves to God, is an act not only of the mind but also of the whole person. It is rare because it is hard, and it is hard because it really does have consequences.

To believe *in* is to make oneself vulnerable. If I believe in you then I am opening myself to you: I am deliberately failing to put up barriers against whatever you might take it into your head to go and do. If I believe in the teenager next door, I won't take care to lock up my silver every time he comes round.

By believing in you, I am giving you the power to let me down just when I thought I could trust you most. I could have protected myself against that – I could have locked up the silver – but by believing in you I have decided not to protect myself at all. Belief *that* God exists is an act of pure reason, but belief *in* God is an act of love.

'I hereby believe'

From time to time I am going to give a translation of the Latin of the Creed which is different from the one we use in church. This is not because I claim that my translation is better. The translation we use in church is about the best possible given the requirements of recitation and the circumstances in which it is done. But there are places where something significant in the Latin gets glossed over or left out because you can't say it in English, or at least you can't say it without footnotes. The Creed as recited has to be recitable, but it can happen that, when reflecting on the Creed in slowness and in quiet, the Latin says something that ought not to be missed.

Latin is a language with grammatical cases, like Polish and German but unlike English or French. Different cases mean different aspects of the same thing. The Latin *in thalamo* (with the ablative case) means 'in the bedchamber': that is, it means a position or a state. On the other hand, *in thalamum* (accusative case) means 'into the bedchamber': that is, a movement or an action.

The Creed uses the accusative, not the ablative. It says *Credo in Deum*, not *Credo in Deo*, so an absolutely literal word-for-word translation would be 'I believe into God.' That would be grotesquely bad English, but the point to take from it is that *Credo in Deum* is not a state of affairs I am describing, but an action I am performing. I am performing it here and now, right at the moment I am saying the words. I could say, without doing violence to the meaning or to the English language, 'I *hereby* put my trust in God.'

This pattern continues all the way through the Creed. The Creed is not a description but a declaration. It is not a sequence of statements, but an act.

3
God

God calls each of us by name, even the sparrows; but we cannot return the compliment because *God has no name.*

This is true not just in English and Latin but in every language, and not just in Christianity but in all the religions of the children of Abraham.

God, Deus, Dieu, Bóg, Gott – every one of them is just an ordinary word made special by writing it with a capital letter. In Greek, ὁ θεὸς just says 'the god'. In Arabic, *al-lah* just says 'the god', or 'the spirit'. The namelessness is universal – so what do we mean by it? Or rather, since all religion is from God, what does God mean us to mean by it?

Early in the history of revelation, God manifests himself to Moses in the burning bush on Mount Horeb and tells him to lead the sons of Israel out of Egypt. Moses thinks ahead to what the Israelites are going to say when he tells them to leave a land of abundance and go out to be tormented by hunger and thirst in the wilderness. They will ask what his authority is. They will ask who the god is who is telling Moses to tell them to do this. So, prudently and reasonably, Moses asks God for his name.

And God answers Moses. 'I am who I am,' he says. 'Say that WHO IS has sent you.'* That is, under the guise of giving an answer, God in fact avoids answering the question at all.

God refuses to answer because 'What is the name of God?' is not a valid question. It is as if Moses has asked, 'What colour is the number twelve?'

Naming cannot work when it comes to God because of what naming is and does. To make a high (but brief) philosophical

---

* Exodus 3:14.

analysis of it, when you identify anything, you do so in two steps. First, you say *what kind of thing* it is – for instance, 'It is a human being.' Next, you say *which*, out of all the possible things of that kind, the one you are talking about is – Edwin, say, rather than Eleanor. The act of naming is that second step.

With God, the naming (the second step) can't happen because with God the first step is impossible. There is no *kind of thing* that God is. God is not of any kind: God *just is*. So there is nothing that naming can do.

There is also a less abstract way of looking at it. Asking God, 'What is your name?' means asking, 'Which god are you?' But God is not a god. The pagans persecuted the early Christians as atheists because they said we had no gods, and they got our beliefs exactly right. We do not believe in gods. There are no gods. God is not a god.

In every religion with gods, a god is a spirit that is part of the world and has some powers over it. On the other hand, God is *not* part of the world and does not just have powers over it. God is more. God is the one because of whom it exists at all.

Although the term 'god' is wrong, it at least points in the right direction. That is why every language chooses 'god-with-a-capital-G' as the way to refer to God: although God isn't a god (there are no gods), at least the concept of 'godness' points in the direction of Godness. Think of it as a signpost: a signpost to a place is not that place, but it does point towards it. It tells us which direction to go in.

Unnameability

It all goes further than this. It is not just that God *cannot* be named: there is also a sense in which God *ought not* to be named.

Names give a degree of control and even power over whatever it is that is named. They summarise. They encapsulate a thing into a form we can handle. Nobody can encompass infinity, but the mathematical symbol ∞ wraps it up in a stroke of a pen and lets us talk about it. In a sense, it tames it.

I have noticed that this happens with diseases. Sometimes you hear about somebody suffering from an illness. The illness has facts about it. It has symptoms, it has times or circumstances when it feels better or worse; perhaps it progresses. Hearing all this gives you a feeling of helplessness: probably the same kind of helplessness the sufferer feels. It is unsettling. But if someone then ties that nameless set of symptoms together and gives it a name, our helplessness and disorientation vanish. 'Poor man,' we say to each other, 'he's got Brett's Palsy.' We do not feel lost any more. Perhaps the named disease is serious, perhaps it isn't; perhaps it is going to get worse, perhaps not – that isn't the point. The important thing about Brett's Palsy is that it has a name. Naming it makes it something we can talk about without worrying about the details every time. The name wraps it up safely and we never have to unwrap it unless we want to. It gives us a handle, a way of holding on to the fact, just as the symbol ∞ gives us the impression of being able to hold on to infinity.*

God cannot be wrapped up. God has no handle. It is not possible to be at a safe distance from God – and so God cannot have a name.

Human nature being what it is, knowing we mustn't name God and actually not naming God are two different things. The history of the Jews shows this. The mysterious four-letter word (the 'tetragrammaton') יהוה, or YHWH in our alphabet, which as far as I have understood means 'I Am' or 'Who Is', or both at once,

---

* You may think, 'Lucky bystanders, poor patient,' but it isn't necessarily so. Something named and determinate, however dreadful it may be, is easier to get to grips with than a looming cloud of symptoms – because you *can* get to grips with something that has a name, and you can't get to grips with fog. Luke Jackson makes this point emphatically. As a teenager with Asperger Syndrome, he wrote a book called *Freaks, Geeks and Asperger Syndrome* (2002) about how to be a teenager with Asperger Syndrome. He is absolutely firm about it: if a child is diagnosed with Asperger Syndrome, he tells parents, *tell the child*. Compared with, 'I'm just weird,' a named diagnosis is a liberation.

amounts to a refusal to give a name – but it ends up being used just as if it were a name.*

The Jews may have a streak of human disobedience, forever rushing off to worship foreign gods, but they also have a strong sense of the sacred. The 'name but not a name', יהוה, is too holy ever to be pronounced. It was spoken once a year by the High Priest when he was quite alone, and after the Temple was destroyed it was never uttered again. Nobody knows for certain what it sounded like (Hebrew did not write vowels until very late in its history), but the consensus is that the sound of YHWH was what we now write as 'Yahweh'.

This causes a certain amount of embarrassment. Every Jew knows that on seeing the word יהוה in Scripture, one does not utter 'Yahweh' but says the word *Adonai* ('Lord') instead; the uncircumcised, however, are not so intelligent. That is why, while the Jerusalem Bible scholarlily writes that the name of the Lord is Yahweh, to avoid the risk of that word being said out loud, in all liturgical uses of those texts the name is written explicitly as 'The Lord'. If it ever strikes you as absurd to be told that the name of the Lord is 'The Lord',† then reflect that it is entirely your fault for being one of the ignorant Gentiles. Or in a more elevated way, take it as a useful reminder of the unnameability and untameability of Ultimate Being.

The God of the pagans

Heretics and pagans are a help to us in understanding the Creed. Heretics, because while we have got used to the sacred words sliding past us, they have seen what startling things the words actually say; and pagans, because they show us a certain kind of foundation: what anybody at all can reasonably have come to know

---

* In Evelyn Waugh's *Black Mischief* (1932), a guide, being asked by the surveyors what a nearby bare hill is called, replies '*Laku*,' ('I don't know'). In due course, the town of Laku appears on the maps.
† Amos 9:6, and the song of triumph after crossing the Red Sea at Exodus 15:3.

without the benefit of any revelation. In his great *Summa Theologiæ*, 'Summary (or compendium) of Theology', St Thomas Aquinas regularly refers to the Greek philosopher Aristotle in precisely this way, as if to say, 'What I am saying just here is nothing special: even the pagans know it.'

Our God is nameless. Many pagans do actually believe in the existence of the nameless God who is the creator of all things. None of the gods they do name and talk about is identified as the source of all being. Their creation myths stop short of actual creation-from-nothing: whatever story they come up with, there is something already there. A cow licks a lump of ice into the shape of the world. Often the stories sound absurd, as if the narrator knows that they are answers to a question that ought not to be being asked because it has no answer.

The gods of the pagans are immensely powerful, they can act within the world for good or ill, they need to be persuaded or placated: but they are not the Creator. They are mere subsidiaries.

There is rather a good 'theological DNA' experiment which demonstrates this. One kind of real DNA analysis takes a sample of known DNA and a sample of unknown DNA and mixes them together to see which of the unknown strands match the known ones. The theological analogy is with the syncretistic religions of the New World – for instance, in the state of Chiapas in Mexico. These religions mix Christianity with the West African religions that came over in the slave trade. Like the DNA strands, the components of the religions mix, and where they are compatible, they match.

What is enlightening is what happens to the pantheon of the African gods. None of them pairs up with the Father, Son or Holy Spirit. Instead they match with what you might call 'one level down', so that each saint or apostle is identified with a god: a being endowed with supernatural powers. This living experiment shows that the original African religions saw God himself as not a god but as something above the gods, something beyond, something not to be talked about.

In this way, even the pagans are right about the God who created the heavens and the earth. God the Creator is the unnameable, the unsummarisable, the uncapturable, the inde-scribable, the God about whom nothing whatever can be truly said. And so, for the pagans, no one must attempt to talk about him or name him. To talk *to* him and believe *in* him, as the children and stepchildren of Abraham claim to do, is simply presumptuous.

In all this, paganism is right. God truly is an infinite distance away from us, and it truly is a distance we can never bridge. We can never enter into a relationship with God. Where paganism falls short is that it forgets that there are two sides to this infinite gulf. We cannot bridge the infinite gap – but God can. We cannot enter into a relationship with God – but God can enter into a relationship with us.

Salvation history documents this, and the Creed proclaims it.

4
One God

Unum Deum

Just as the 'God' in 'one God' is not really a name, so the 'one' in 'one God' is not really a number. The Unnameable is also the Uncountable.

St Thomas Aquinas tells us that in 'I believe in one God', the word 'one' is not an answer to a 'How many?' question – as if the lady had come along with her theological tea trolley.

'And how many Gods would we like this morning, dear?'

'Just the one, thank you very much.'

'How many is God?' is as meaningless as 'What is God's name?', and for the same reason. Both questions begin with the concept of a range of beings of the kind that God is. 'What is God's name?' tries to pick one out. 'How many?' tries to choose how many are picked. Both questions are meaningless because 'beings of the same kind that God is' has no meaning. God just *is*, and that's that.

You can tell yourself the same truth in a simpler way if you remember that God is the Creator of everything, the source of its being. To ask, 'How many Gods?' boils down to asking, 'How many everythings?'

All this means that when we talk about 'one God', we are not counting: we are finding a word to express how unique God is.

The Jews learned this. The history of their revelation is in part the history of their growth from belief in a counting 'one' to a non-counting 'one'. Or, as you might say, from a belief in one god to a belief in One God.

In the beginning, the Jews did have a god in whom they believed. All their neighbours did too. We had our god, you had yours. Our god helped us and your god helped you. If you and we did battle and we won, that showed our god was the stronger. If you and we did battle and you won, that showed that your god was the stronger. Or perhaps it showed that your god and our god were the same god under different names and he liked your name for him better than he liked ours . . . so let's try using your name for him from now on.

One can see this happening in Greece and the Near East. First everyone's local mountain and sky gods merge into Zeus, and then the Greeks conquer the Egyptians and the Egyptian god Ammon becomes Zeus-Ammon.

At the beginning of our own history, the only slightly unusual thing about the god of Abraham and Isaac was that he refused to say what his name was. Apart from that, the Jews started from the same place as everyone else, with 'We are the best because our god is the best.'

What happened next was unique. The purely utilitarian business of having a god to look after them (and if he doesn't, sack him and employ another) grew into an enduring and deepening relationship and, amazingly, the usual performance clause faded away. 'Our god is our god even if he lets us down.'

The history of the Old Testament is the history of the Jews' relationship with their god, with all its ups and downs, and it was a relationship that continued to grow in times of defeat as well as times of victory. That is why the Old Testament has carefully preserved so much history, from the family stories in Genesis to the more 'historical' history of the later books, because the history was the story of that relationship. Preserving it meant that one could reflect on it and understand it better and better as time went on: like rereading one's early love letters or having a special affection for the really terrible music that was playing when you and I first met.

The critical moment came when the Jews definitively lost everything, even their homeland, and were deported to Babylon. That, if anything, was the moment to invoke the performance clause, sack their god and take on the gods of the victors. Instead, the Jews did the exact opposite.

The early books of the Bible received their final form during the Babylonian exile. In the opening chapter of Genesis, where

God creates the world, the Sun and Moon appear on the fourth day. For the Babylonians, the Sun and Moon are gods, but in Genesis they are nothing more than objects God has made: useful objects.

In their forced period of reflection, the Jews came to a shocking discovery: 'The creator God is the same thing as the god of the Jews, the god whom we have known, and served, and disobeyed, and argued with, for longer than anybody else.' This new realisation permeates the later books of the Old Testament.

None of this stopped people carrying on making the same old mistakes. Even at the beginning of the New Testament there were plenty who thought that 'our god is God' meant 'our god is the best god EVER!!!' and were waiting for him to come and crush their enemies. It took the coming of God the Son *and his dying on a cross* to teach them that the victories of God happen in a different way.*

How can we possibly relate to God if he is something so far above anything that we can experience or understand? How should we conceive of such an exalted being? How could we address it, even if we dared? The next word of the Creed is about to supply the shocking answer.

No other gods

We know there are no gods. We say so, if asked; but, backsliders that we are, we don't always behave according to our beliefs. The Creed comes to the rescue because it is a sequence of acts, not statements, so when I stand up in public and say, 'I *hereby* put my trust in one God,' I really am doing it. I am renouncing slavery to all the little might-be-gods such as horoscopes, racial purity, cultural hygiene, economic progress, personal fulfilment and the rest.

---

* Monsignor Ronald Knox even adds that Jesus 'could have accomplished the salvation of the world even if he had seen fit to ascend to his Father from his cradle at Bethlehem' (*A Retreat for Lay People* (1955), Chapter XIII). I think Knox is wrong: but more of that later.

These little synthetic gods are not real, they are ghosts, and if I put my trust in them, I too will be a ghost and not real. Only God can give me life and make me human. It is true that being human is less comfortable than being a rule-following machine: but it also means being alive.

'You shall have no other gods but me'* is more than just an instruction. It is there to show us where true life is.

* Exodus 20:3.

The parable of the cube

It is time to pause for a moment and bring out a general point about method. In this book I will be using many analogies with other sciences. That needs a justification, so here it is.

The three great sciences are mathematics, physics and theology. Between them they cover the whole spectrum. Mathematics is about nothing, physics is about something, and theology is about everything.

Mathematics* is the science of truth. It does not depend on being, or on facts. Whatever may exist or not exist, the truths of mathematics are always true.

Physics† is the science of facts. It is the study of things as they are, and in that way it depends on being, and presupposes it. If there were no universe, there would be no physics. If the universe were different, physics would be different.

Theology‡ is the science of being. It studies being and it studies Being Itself, which is what we call 'God'.

A note for the atheists: saying the word 'theology' is not an underhand way of putting words into your mouth and making you say you believe in God. 'There is no God' is a well-formed statement in theology, to be discussed using the methods of theology. We claim that 'There is no God' is well formed but false, like '2+2=3'. You claim that 'There is no God' is well formed and true, like '2+2=4'. Very well: we agree on what we are arguing about, which is the first step towards a constructive encounter.

---

* Mathematics includes logic, because logic is the foundation on which all mathematics is built.
† Physics includes everything that is built on a physical foundation: chemistry, biology and all the exact sciences.
‡ I have chosen a broad definition of theology here, which includes a lot of what some people will call 'metaphysics'.

The science of theology provides us with a battleground upon which we both agree, and an agreed set of weapons and ways of using them to settle disputes.

The point of bringing the sciences together like this is that they have more in common than you might think. Each has different themes and methods, but they all have their experts and their non-experts. They all find some things easy and others hard. They all rest on faith of one kind or another. And pursued far enough, each of them ends up pointing beyond itself, towards ultimate truths it can indicate but not grasp. Properly seen, having to say 'thus far and no further' is not a sign of frustration but of enlightenment.

Each of the sciences illuminates the others. It may be that in studying the Creed one comes across a problem or an embarrassment that makes one lose confidence in the whole theological enterprise. Looking sideways and finding that another science has the same kind of problem will remove the embarrassment and bring new confidence. Or again, if theology ever gets too abstract (this is always a danger, because *being* is something one cannot see or touch), a more down-to-earth science can sometimes provide a concrete analogy and make things clearer.

I am going to pick an example from mathematics because that is the science that everyone respects (although not everyone loves it). Here it is.

Seeing the cube

It is a perennial problem with theology that I say one thing and you say another and . . . what do we do next? The things we say can't both be true, so what is it to be? Compromise, anathema or despair? Here is a down-to-earth, practical example from mathematics to show how sometimes two eyes can be better than one. It is best done with a friend, but if you are on your own then you only need to use a little imagination.

- On the table in front of us there is an object.
- You pick it up and hold it up to the light and you say, 'It has four sides.'

- I pick it up in my turn. I hold it up to the light and I say, 'It has six sides.'

Where do we go from here? How many sides does the object really have? You say four, I say six, so which of us is wrong? Who wins and who loses?

If you leave the maths out of it and think about disagreements in general, you will know the kinds of answers that people give at this point. Some will say we ought to be respectful of diversity and I am being needlessly confrontational in talking about 'right' and 'wrong' at all. Politicians might encourage us to split the difference and agree that the object has five sides. A broad-minded churchman of a certain kind might tell us that *in a very real sense* four and six are the same thing.

You and I both listen politely to these answers, but none of them makes sense. We may not agree on everything, but we do definitely agree that four is not six, six is not four, and neither of them equals five. We may have got hold of opposite ends of the stick, but at least we know that it is a stick, and the same stick, and that sticks matter. These easy ways out are not ways out at all: on that, we most definitely agree.

There is another way of dealing with this disagreement without sinking into meaninglessness. It is not a way *out*, but a way *through*. It will enlighten us both.

In my initial statement of the story I carefully withheld one vital fact. Here is the story again, with that fact put back in.

- On the table in front of us there is a cube.
- Pick up the cube and hold it up to the light with its face towards you. Squint at it with one eye shut, and you will see a square silhouette against the light. That makes it four sides.
- Now hold the same cube at a different angle, this time with one corner pointing directly towards you. When you squint again, you will see a hexagon: six sides.

We are both right, and we have both won. That is not because we have given in to 'four equals six' or 'they both equal five' or whatever other nonsense the spectators have been urging on us. We have won not because we both see exactly the same but because our observations, though different, are observations of the same thing. It is a thing that cannot be summed up in one single silhouetted view. A cube, which is a three-dimensional object, makes one shape if you project it one way onto two dimensions and another shape if you project it another way.

Mathematically, this enlightenment has come from discovering that there is a geometry beyond the two dimensions of silhouettes and shadows. The 'four' and 'six' of our individual experiences are only shadows of the true cubical reality, which is a solid object, not a bare outline. It is a solid object with six faces, eight corners and twelve edges.

The moral of the story is not just mathematical. What it has just told us is this: *No eye has ever seen a cube and no eye ever will*. That is not a paradox, but the strict and precise truth. The eye cannot see the cube in itself, the cube in its full glory of cubicality. All the eye can see is shadows, not realities.

Given those shadows, our minds can put together what two eyes have seen, to give us knowledge of something the eye alone cannot see. Or, to put it another way, the eye without the brain is as blind as the brain without the eye. Or to put it another way still: we see the world best, in its solidity, in its reality, when the left eye and the right eye see it in different ways.

As with mathematics, so too with theology and with the Creed. If in this book I show you something from a direction that you don't expect, I am not saying that the direction you are seeing it from is wrong, and I am not claiming for my own point of view anything more than the status of a shadow. All I claim is that my shadow is a truthful one. I am saying that if we can somehow perceive the truth from two directions at once, we have a chance of perceiving it better. 'Four sides' and 'six sides' are both equally wrong, but they both equally lead us towards the truth.

5

The Father

Once, a long time ago, I received a circular inviting me to a service at St Ebbe's Church in Oxford. It offered a special attraction. During the Creed, everyone was welcome to remain silent for any parts of it they happened not to agree with. It would have been worth turning up just for that, with microphone and graph paper, to conduct an exercise in Statistical Theometry; but being a very new and brainless undergraduate, I didn't. So I can't say how it all worked out in practice, but in an alert and intellectually honest congregation I wouldn't be surprised to find it all getting a bit quiet right now, at this moment in the Creed, at the word 'Father'. In fact, some people might even get up and leave at this point. The Creed is getting serious.

Up to now, we could all agree because we were declaring our shared faith in ultimate Being – one that is so ultimate it cannot even be named, so we call it 'God'. This is the God of everyone. It is the God of the pagans (who is too far above the world to be talked to or talked about). It is the God of the scientistic atheists (which is the principle of coherence behind the laws of nature). It is the God of Abraham and the God of Isaac; and it is our God too.

But that still leaves two big questions open. What or who is God? And whatever the answer may be, *what do we do about it?* Now the Creed starts to give answers. The first answer is the word 'Father', and it is outrageous.

Who, or what?

The distinction between 'who' and 'what' can seem a subtle one, but it is a help towards understanding the ways in which different religions approach the fundamental question of being; so it is worth taking a moment to see what the distinction actually means.

Looking around us at everything we ever encounter, that 'everything' is made up of two kinds of entity. One kind is WHO – other people are the obvious example. The other kind is WHAT – for instance, objects or machines.

The point about WHO and WHAT is that we see them differently and interact with them differently, and that is because they *are* different.

When I interact with you as a WHO, you are someone, not something. I can make a picture of you in my mind as 'like me, only different', and although that picture may be wildly inaccurate, it is never nonsense. We are both the same kind of thing, both WHOs, and what happens between us is communication, not causation.

On the other hand, when I interact with something as a WHAT, I am acting as a cause. When I get into a lift and press button 3, I set in train a sequence of causes and effects, of which arriving at the third floor is the final result. I do not say 'please' as I press 3 because there is no WHO there to say 'please' to.

The trouble with deep distinctions of the WHO-or-WHAT kind is that they can swing rapidly from 'too obscure to grasp' (before they are explained) to 'too obvious to be interesting' (afterwards). All I can really suggest is to hold on while the distinction unfolds itself in our relationship to Being. But if you want a quick extra guide, consider that the creepiness some people feel when they are expected to talk to a machine comes from having to treat a WHAT as an imitation WHO; and the injustice that other people feel about being treated as units of labour, units of consumption or units of diversity comes from being a WHO but being treated as if they were a WHAT.

So which of the two is God? A WHO or a WHAT? Is God (or Being Itself, if you want to call it that) a 'Who Is', to whom we can apply our WHOish categories of thought, or a 'What Is', for which any attempt at WHOing is a misconception?

There certainly have been WHAT religions. There still are, and Buddhism is an extreme example. In Buddhism, 'Being Itself' is so very WHAT that it is unspeakable and indescribable.

Answering 'WHAT' to the WHO-or-WHAT question has immediate practical consequences. It is universally true that man is made in God's image, and this means that in a religion where God is a WHAT, people turn out to be WHATs as well. Our duty to others is then shaped by this fact: they are WHAT, not WHO. Finally, our duty to ourselves is to let go of our own illusions of WHOness and become pure WHAT also.

The scientific religions of the more civilised parts of the early Americas also believed in WHAT, but in a more instrumental sense. What we call their 'religion' is more a matter of laws of nature than anything. For them, 'Being Itself' operates according to determinate laws, so that we can manipulate it just as we can manipulate the physical world around us. If, for instance, the laws of nature say that the spilling of lifeblood is necessary to provide the life force that makes the sun shine, then lifeblood must be spilt: and so it is. First the blood of the kings and the priests, then the heart's blood of suitable numbers of captives.

This is quite different from the petitionary sacrifices that Old World pagans directed towards their gods when they were invoking or bribing them: it is a straightforward matter of cause and effect. 'Being Itself' in this case is again a WHAT: not the 'beyond-WHO' of the Buddhists this time, but rather a 'beneath-WHO', a mechanism to be operated. And once more the WHATness of Being WHATifies *us*; or at least that part of the human race whose purpose is to be sacrificed to make the world go round.

The scientific religions of the twentieth century operated in the same way. Their WHAT-God was a future ideal state of the human race, and to starve or liquidate millions of subhuman WHAT-elements for the sake of that God was accordingly not a crime but a duty.

The religions of Abraham and Isaac – Judaism, Christianity and Islam – are firmly on the opposite side. They are WHO religions. God, 'Being Itself', is a WHO, not a WHAT. This has immediate and far-reaching consequences. Since the practical difference between WHAT and WHO is that one *uses and manipulates* WHATs but *interacts and communicates with* WHOs, this means that as we go through life and (by existing at all) somehow relate to Being, our relationship with it must be a WHO-to-WHO, 'I–thou' relationship and not a WHO-to-WHAT, 'I–it' one. This is good not only because it is true but also because of its effects: if we treat God as a WHO then we will not be able to treat one another as WHAT. Humanity is preserved.

Someone said once that all good theology is dangerous. WHOing God certainly fits this pattern. It says something definite about God and us. It is good because it is true. It is dangerous because WHO brings all the temptations of anthropomorphism with it.

For instance, fools take it upon themselves to say that God is *angry* with this or that person, or *hates* these or those people. What the fools really mean by 'God' is 'I', or, more precisely, 'I-with-a-very-loud-voice-and-if-you-disagree-with-me-then-you-are-not-just-wrong-but-damned'. This is truly taking the Lord's name in vain. In fact, it is heresy, and if you and I mimsily refrain from identifying it as such then we are collaborating in it. If we allow these people to call themselves 'Christians', then we are blaspheming the name of Christian. By remaining silent when we hear things like this, we libel our own faith.*

To WHO God is risky; but we cannot get away from the fact that God, from the first call to Abraham, is consistently telling us to do it. He is always telling us to see him as 'Who Is'. So we have no choice: we have to take the risk. Just as the best antidote to disease is health, so the best antidote to heresy is clear, true and firm faith. Let's see how far we can get.

Before starting, it is good to listen to Dionysius the Areopagite:

> The universal Cause is not a material body, and therefore does not possess outward shape or intelligible form, or quality, or quantity, or solid weight. IT has no local existence which can be

---

* 'I saw soothfastly that our Lord was never wroth, nor ever shall be . . . I saw truly that it is against the property of His Might to be wroth, and against the property of His Wisdom, and against the property of His Goodness.' Julian of Norwich, *Revelations of Divine Love*, chapter 46.

perceived by sight or touch . . . IT is not soul, or mind, or endowed with the faculty of imagination, conjecture, reason, or under-standing; nor is IT any act of reason or understanding. IT cannot be described by the reason or perceived by the understanding, since IT is not number, or order, or greatness, or littleness, or equality, or inequality. IT is not immovable, nor in motion, nor at rest. IT does not live, and is not life . . . IT is not any kind of thing such as we or any other being can have knowledge of. IT does not belong to the category of non-existence or to that of existence. Existent beings do not know IT as it actually is . . . nor can the reason attain to IT so as to name IT or to know IT. No affirma-tion or negation can apply to it; for IT transcends all affirmation and all negation.*

This is what is called *apophatic theology*: that is, theology that works by emphasising that our existing categories and concepts *do not* work with God because God is beyond them all. It is part of the 'Way of Negation', which brings us closer to God by strip-ping away anything that stands in the way. (Its opposite is the 'Way of Affirmation', which leads us to God through such things as goodness, beauty and love.)

It sounds odd that a science should base itself so firmly on not being able to talk about its own subject, but in theology this is a widely accepted principle.† St Thomas Aquinas, who in many ways is the greatest theologian who ever lived, cites Dionysius more than a thousand times in his magisterial *Summa Theologiæ*, and himself says, 'Because we cannot know what God is, but rather what he is not, we have no means for considering how God is, but rather how he is not.'‡ These are good words to engrave on our hearts before we go round telling people that we know better

---

* Dionysius the Areopagite, *The Mystical Theology*, chapters IV–V. 'Dionysius (or "Denys") the Areopagite' is the pseudonym of a Syrian writer of the late fifth or early sixth century who had an enormous influence on theology for a thousand years.

† In mathematics too; but that is a subject for another book.

‡ *Summa Theologiæ*, I, q.3, prologue.

than them: we have a duty to bear witness to the truth, but not to do it with off-putting certainty.

Bearing Dionysius in mind, when we refer to God as 'Who Is', we are not actually daring to label or describe God. What we are saying is what is important and relevant to us as human beings: that a right relationship for us to have with Being is a WHO-to-WHO one. Nobody can really, definitely *know* anything deeper about God than that.

If you think about it, the same limitation applies to our knowledge of human beings as well. We don't really know who anyone else is. Our 'knowledge' of the people we meet isn't really knowledge at all: it is nothing but an approximation. We make the approximation by constructing 'someone just like me plus a few differences'. We do this automatically (some people with autism are said to be able to do it only consciously and explicitly, which is harder). The fun and the frustration of getting to know someone come from having to adjust our understanding and expectations as time goes on, because as time goes on we encounter the other more and more *as truly other*, unique and not representable by approximations. We start by thinking we know someone, and only gradually do we get to know them – you might say, from the inside. Some theologians (from Dante onwards) describe the process and goal of love as 'in-othering'.

Our WHO-to-WHO relationship with God works in the same way as our relationship with people: an initial encounter with the other *as truly other* followed by a progressive in-othering. The story of salvation history, from Abraham onwards, is a journey from 'our god' to 'our God' and finally to 'God': a journey that starts with an intensely anthropomorphic God and progressively reveals him as someone who is truly and wholly other than us.

> My thoughts are not your thoughts,
> my ways not your ways
> – it is [the Lord] who speaks.*

* Isaiah 55:8 (JB).

Isaiah is not saying, 'Don't think,' but he is telling us that our thinking must be a way of encounter, not of capture or encapsulation. Its aim is the beginning of a relationship, not the completion of a research project.

The outrageous doctrine

Before going on, it is worth paying our respects to the sincere people at St Ebbe's who didn't just fall silent at this point of the Creed but actually walked out. If we don't know what it feels like to want to walk out of the Creed, then we need to learn. If we don't, our staying in is not a conscious decision or any sort of commitment; it is simply inertia.

We should always be grateful to people who disagree with us. At the very least, they sharpen us as a stone sharpens a knife. At best, they wake us up to how stunning the beliefs we profess actually are.

God is infinite, ultimate Being. Whatever exists, God is behind its existence: every sea, lake, hill and mountain; every planet, star and supernova; every galaxy; the whole universe. These things are beyond us in their strangeness and alienness, in their power and size. Many of them we cannot fully understand.

By rights, we ought to be dazzled by this and squashed flat by the greatness of it all. We ought to be bursting with a desire to make litanies like the great praising psalms or like the song of Daniel's friends in the burning fiery furnace: cold and heat, frost and snow, lightning and clouds, bless the Lord!

When we are flattened by the tininess of us compared to the greatness of creation and the still greater greatness of the Creator, we will realise the complete absurdity of thinking of the Power Behind Everything as a 'someone' that we could interact with in a WHO-to-WHO relationship. This is a necessary stage. We *have* to see it as absurd and impossible, or we aren't really seeing anything. We have to see the absurdity and feel it until the only thing that could stop us walking out of the church at once (like our principled friends) would be a direct command from God himself.

Because we have, in fact, received that command.

The call to Abraham (with all that came after) is not just one of mankind's occasional self-propelled steps in the direction of enlightenment. It is not a step by us towards God but an invitation *from him to us* to go WHO-to-WHO with the Infinite. It is by God's initiative and command that we are allowed to call God 'You'. There is no other way in which this could have happened. We could not have done it ourselves. A finite creature cannot make infinite leaps.

When we as Christians catch ourselves trying to be nice and ordinary and unalarming to our pagan friends, 'as ordinary as you but just that little bit nicer', we should stop, because it isn't true. There is nothing nice or normal or ordinary about saying 'You' to the power behind the universe; still less about claiming to have received a divine command to do so.

The indecent word

So far this has all been about the Old Testament, about Judaism. When it comes to the finite being respectful to the infinite and the created being respectful to the Creator, the Jews are already bad enough, calling God 'You' – but Christians are worse.

Whenever you are in a relationship with someone, that relationship has to be of some kind. That is logical. The relationship could be domineering or subservient, formal or informal, distant or intimate, equal or unequal. If I habitually call you, 'You over there,' things between us are one way. If I bow low every time and address you as, 'O King of thirty-six parasols, lord of a thousand elephants,' they are another.

If God is not a WHAT but a WHO, then it follows that I have a relationship with God. The question is: what kind of relationship is it?

The Jews worked this out as well as they could. God is far above us and far above anything one can conceive. The highest human beings we have anything to do with are kings and queens (the Near East was full of them), and God is far above even the kings. So it is not surprising to find more-than-royal modes of address in the Old Testament. Rather charmingly, they often come with the wheedling blackmail one has to employ when persuading an absolute monarch to do something: 'You have done such great things for us in the past; do not fail us now.' This kind of Scripture passage shows roughly what one might expect: a proper and decent relationship between highest and lowest. It shows that we know our place and God knows his.

Nevertheless, now and then something else shines through. For instance, there is that knotty passage of Ezekiel which is read at the Easter Vigil,* in which a prickly and legalistic God takes pains to make it absolutely clear that *the only reason* he doesn't abandon the house of Israel once and for all (which is what they deserve)† is that God has his own reputation to think of and is worried about what the neighbours might say. The speech is ridiculous, almost satirical, but then suddenly it is as if the sun has come out from behind a cloud: 'I shall remove the heart of stone from your bodies and give you a heart of flesh instead . . . You shall be my people and I will be your God'.‡ You can't hear that without tears in your eyes – that is, if you really do hear it. The power of the WHO relationship has broken through the court ritual and expressed itself in the only way that is valid for us: as love.

There are other loving images in the Old Testament. We are like a weaned child on its mother's breast,§ or God is like a husband who has abandoned us, his wife, but has had a

---

* Ezekiel 36:16–28.

† '. . . because of the blood they shed in their land and the idols with which they defiled it' (Ezek. 36:18, JB).

‡ Ezekiel 36:26, 28 (JB).

§ Psalm 130(131):2. There are two numberings of the Psalms: one is Greek in origin and the other is Hebrew. To over-simplify somewhat, the Greek numbering is used by the Vulgate and tends to appear in more liturgical, English, Catholic contexts, while the Hebrew numbering tends to be more biblical, American, Protestant. In this book I will give both the Greek and Hebrew numbers. For instance, the 'Old Hundredth', *All people that on earth do dwell*, would be Psalm 99(100).

change of heart: he promises to take us back and love us for ever.*

The Old Testament points the way, but none of these things is a definitive piece of doctrine in itself because, although the Bible is inspired, it is still the work of human minds. The prophets themselves may be inspired, but they, too, are still only human beings.

It took God the Son to tell us, once and for all, how we should conduct our relationship with God. It was something he alone knew, because man is not God and God is not man. Only he, incarnate, was both. And when his disciples asked him how to address God, he told them, 'Call him "Daddy".'†

To say 'You' to God is bad enough, but this is intolerable. If you find Jesus' answer to his disciples acceptable, then you have been numbed into complacency by hearing it too often. You are charmed by the sound and don't think about the meaning. Imagine how you would feel if a slug crawled up your arm and called you 'Uncle'. That would be disgusting and slimily inappropriate, and yet slugs are a lot closer to us than we are to God (we have much the same biochemistry as the slug and a lot of the same DNA). How much more indecent it is for us to address pure eternal perfection, the source of all being and all matter, as 'Daddy'.

The fundamental indecency of Christian belief is something that we forget when we comfortably repeat the same phrases day after day and week after week. We need to remember it:

First, because sometimes the difference between sincere non-Christians and us is just that they see the indecency in our doctrines and we no longer notice it. If we wake up and agree with them about that, they may one day end up agreeing with us about everything else.

Second, because by *not* seeing the indecency we forget why it is that we address God as our father, and why it is that we believe

---

* Isaiah 54:5–14.
† It is only fair to add that scholars disagree on the exact degree of 'daddiness' of the word *Abba*.

that God *became* a creature one step up from a slug. It is not because we have been clever enough to work it all out ourselves. It is because *God has told us* to call God a father, and because *God the Son chose* to become incarnate as one of us. These are God's acts, not ours.

Either Christianity is nonsense or it is divine. There is no middle way. If we think that Christianity does not affront what we (in simple human terms) see as the dignity and glory of God, then we do not understand it at all. It *does* affront them. The only excuse it has for doing so is that it does so by divine command.

If I could be properly conscious of God's dignity and glory, I would be conscious of how little he values them. Then – who knows? – I might value my own dignity and glory a little less.

6

Almighty

Understanding that there was no limit to the power of their god was what took the Jews to the discovery that their god was not a god at all, but God himself. The psalmist sings that God does whatever he wills.* This theme soaked into the mind and culture of the Jews, so that when they came to think about it philosophically, the only possible conclusion was that what they had thought of as their god was really God the Creator.

The logic works the other way as well. Being the creator of something automatically makes you omnipotent as far as that creation is concerned, because you are the one who decides what shall and shall not exist. Being the creator of everything similarly makes the Creator omnipotent over everything. It is not a question of a magic imp poking its finger into the mechanism of the world and fiddling with the gears to make X or Y happen. A creator can contemplate 'the universe in which X happens' and 'the universe in which Y happens' and decide which of them shall have existence. Omnipotence is not some kind of extra, but an integral part of being the Creator.

Strictly speaking, therefore, whoever has said 'God' has also said 'almighty'. The framers of the Creed put the word 'almighty' in anyway. If you are not a philosopher, the word tells you something important that you need to know. If you are a philosopher then you may be asleep or forgetting to think, in which case you need reminding. (After all, it has been said that the human mind is a machine for making every mistake that could conceivably be made.)

Being reminded that God is almighty is a useful protection against sliding back into thinking of God as being a god: just like

* Psalm 113B(115) and Psalm 134(135).

the gods of the pagans, only better. This is because gods are never almighty: they are superhuman beings, yes, with immense powers over the world, yes, but always, in every pagan mythology, they are within the world rather than behind it, and they are constrained by the rules of that world. Zeus has power over the lightning and hail, Poseidon has power over the storms and winds of the sea, but both of them are bound by Fate. By contrast, God is not in the world; he is the cause of the world, so he is the cause of everything within the world, and in that sense his power over it has no limits.

If you are ever tempted to slip into thinking of God as just a super-god, that one word 'almighty' will protect you.

The Almighty Father

All enlightenment has risks and all truth is open to misunderstanding. Thinking of God as the Almighty Father stirs up childish memories of 'My Daddy is stronger than your Daddy,' and unfortunately some people find the childish image more attractive than the adult truth. They treat God as 'almighty' in the sense of being a dispenser of miracles on demand, and as 'father' in the sense of someone who will provide miracles if he is nagged enough. These people demean themselves and the whole human race. According to them, they (and we) are no longer co-agents and co-rulers with God, but whining children who get what they want not by using their God-given intelligence and ingenuity, but by pestering. They are the kind of people who are capable of saying to their doctors, 'Thank you very much, but I think I will refuse your life-saving treatment: I will pray instead,' and even of telling other people to do the same. God does not work like that and prayer does not work like that: you can certainly pray for the crops to grow (indeed, you ought to) but you are at least expected to sow the seeds before you start praying.*

There are many things we have to be intolerant of, and this is one of them. It is bad enough that these people should rot their

---

* Like the Jewish joke about the man who prays to win the lottery until God answers, 'Meet me half way! At least buy a ticket.'

own minds with their 'pull the lever and get a wish', but they call themselves Christians while they do it, and the pagans we are all surrounded by might easily think that they *are* Christians. We ourselves demean Christianity if we do not stand up at this point and say loudly to anyone who will listen, 'These people are not Christians, but presumptuous fools.'

Jesus has already shown us that omnipotence isn't like that, both at the beginning of his ministry and at the end. In the wilderness the devil told him that God could turn the stones into bread: Jesus did not disagree, but he did not make the miracle happen. In the vision on the pinnacle of the Temple the devil told him that God would send his angels to hold him up if he jumped: Jesus agreed, but refused to jump. And at the other end of it all, in Gethsemane, Jesus both acknowledged that his Father could save him from his coming Passion and (although he stated his own preference) did not ask him to do it.

We need to get a better understanding of omnipotence, for ourselves and for the people who need to know what it is that we believe. The theory of 'the almighty wish machine' is self-evidently nonsense.

It is time to look at omnipotence more closely. Paradoxical though it may sound, this means looking at what an omnipotent being cannot do.

Non-omnipotent omnipotence

Being omnipotent does not mean that one can do absolutely anything.

First, and obviously, one can't do logically self-contradictory things. I cannot write a four-letter word with five letters in it. God cannot create a six-sided triangle. These things are impossible because they are nonsensical.

Some logical self-contradictions are subtler than this. A classic one is related to love. Love potions have always been a favourite theme in literature. They demonstrate the paradoxes of love and freedom, because if a potion were to do what it said, it would end up not having done what it said but the exact opposite.

Love potions are a logical impossibility because love is an act of free will. To coerce a person's will is to deprive that person of free will, and thus to deprive that person of the ability to love.

If, by administering to you the philtre given to me by an evil crone at the price of my soul (or whatever other price the story-teller has chosen), I receive from you all the external fruits of love, I still have the doubt gnawing at me: do you *really* love me? Yes, I have a simulacrum of your love with all its attendant benefits: but if I were to stop slipping those drops into your soup every day, would you still love me truly, or would you hate me? I long to know, but I dare not find out.

This is not mere literary amusement. As human beings, we are loving beings, and many of our hopes and prayers do turn out to be along the lines of, 'Lord, make him love me.' But to *make* someone love is a contradiction. It cannot be done.

So much for logical contradictions. The second limitation of omnipotence is subtler and it applies more widely. It is best illus-trated by an example.

Consider one of the world's great musicians: picking a name from the past, consider the pianist Wilhelm Kempff.* For the sake of argument we can take Kempff, in the world of music, to be omnipotent: that is, able to play anything he chose if he were to put his mind to it.

But now suppose that I tell you to imagine the night of his final public performance in Paris in 1981. The concert hall is packed; the audience are looking forward to the performance of a lifetime, one they have waited more than a year to hear. Wilhelm Kempff comes on stage. He acknowledges the applause. He sits down. He plays 'Three Blind Mice' with one finger. As an encore he plays 'Pop Goes the Weasel'. Then he gets up and leaves the stage.

You will refuse to imagine this because (you say) it is impossi-ble. I will adduce pianistic omnipotence on the analogy of divine omnipotence, and say that nothing is impossible for Wilhelm Kempff.

* 1895–1991. But any name will do.

Then you will reply that it is impossible for Wilhelm Kempff to do this *and still be Wilhelm Kempff*. And you will win the argument, because that is exactly the point: beyond the 'could' of mere mechanical capability, there is the 'could' of truth.

The 'could' of truth is the key. There are things that God cannot do not because they are logical impossibilities, but because God could not do them *and still be God*. The obvious ones are very obvious: God cannot will evil, or do it; God cannot hate.

Beyond that basic principle, exactly what particular acts would un-God God isn't something I can give a definite answer to, and neither can you, because we are fallible finite beings with finite perceptions. All the same, here are some suggestions to get you thinking further about omnipotence.

When I have mislaid my car keys and I am in a hurry to find them, I search for them where I think I might have left them. I do know that God is omnipotent, but all the same I do not waste time looking for my keys in places I know I haven't been, just in case God has miraculously transported them there. In terms of omnipotence, God is potentially capable of committing trivial and pointless miracles, but he cannot actually commit them and still be God.

When a doctor tells me what I must do to get my health back, I do not decide *not* to do it but to pray instead, because I know that that is not how God operates. This is the truth Jesus worked out for himself in the wilderness. This is what the 'pray-and-you'll-get-it' people do not understand.

If I pray to be cured of a besetting sin, such as an addiction to drink, I know that God will answer my prayer in some way, because answering prayers is what God does. But I also know that he will not answer it by just flicking a switch somewhere in my head and making me all right in an instant. That would make me an object, not a subject, and I know from salvation history that God's greatest care is to avoid violating the integrity of his creatures.

This intrinsic limitation of omnipotence is our best defence against the 'child's wishful thinking' objection to our belief in God as our almighty Father. We are God's children, but not children whose father spoils them by magically giving them everything they want. Our relationship with God is far deeper than that, and at the bottom of everything God is and does, there is not only love, but also reason.

After all, God the Father can't love us any more than he loves God the Son: but when the incarnate Son walked on this earth, look at what he did for him *and what he did not do*. Could God have cancelled the Crucifixion and still have been God?

7

Maker of heaven and earth

Factorem cæli et terræ

If God is omnipotent, then God has to be the Creator. It follows. But the Creed is not like a logical system where the game is to find the minimum set of indisputable 'axioms' that will let you deduce everything you want to deduce.* The Creed's job is to specify, yes; but also to remind us of the truth when we forget to reason properly. It reminds us of what is important. 'What goes without saying' does still need to be said.

God is not a god, a cause *within* the world. He is God, and the cause *of* it. 'Maker of heaven and earth' is there to rescue us when we get lost. Heaven above us and earth all around remind us, every moment, of their Creator. And 'maker of heaven and earth' is a reminder of something else it is possible to forget: God is good and creates nothing that is not in itself good,[†] nothing that is pointless.

This is more or less all that needs to be said directly about 'the maker of heaven and earth' because the rest was covered quite thoroughly in the last chapter. On the other hand, now is a good moment to address the conflict between 'Science' and 'Religion'. I use those 'scare quotes' because the 'Science' in that phrase is not real science and the 'Religion' is not real religion. I should have

---

* Euclid started it, with geometry, which is why he was still a textbook in schools twenty-two centuries later – not because of the geometry, but because of the way he reasoned from first principles. The question whether the statement, 'Given a line, you can always draw another line parallel to it,' was truly an axiom took millennia of argument to sort out, and the final answer was far more interesting than either 'yes' or 'no' would have been.

† Aquinas, *Summa Theologiæ*, I, q.5, a.3, '*Utrum omne ens sit bonum*'.

48

put scare quotes round 'conflict' as well, since there is no real conflict. Science has progressed very largely through believers with a direct religious motivation. Newton (gravity and mechanics), Mendel (genetics) and the Jesuit priest Lemaître (the expansion of the universe) are just three examples. That is just what one would expect. When you believe that everything makes sense, even Being itself, then that inspires you to celebrate the fact by discovering what sense each thing makes: 'Mountains and hills, bless the Lord!'* – stars and planets, bless the Lord!

There are people who get thoroughly rattled by the whole science-and-religion thing. Some of them buy books about it which (fortunately) they don't read. If you are not one of these – if the question doesn't interest you – then you can skip to the next chapter now.

On the other hand, if you fear that a formless mass labelled 'Science' is looming just out of sight behind your shoulder, ready to explode your beliefs and even you yourself – now is the time to turn and face the monster and watch it evaporate like the meaningless smoke it is.

Internalised theophobia

When you live in a society, you find yourself absorbing the thought-forms of that society even if you are utterly opposed to them. Of course, seeing the other side's point of view is important for constructive engagement, but this absorption goes further. You think more and more the way your enemy thinks until you *become* your enemy.

So, then: if you live in a theophobic society, then you absorb theophobia through your skin. (This can also happen when there are only a few theophobes but they make ten times as much noise as anyone else.) You end up looking at your own beliefs as if through the eyes of someone who hates God and doesn't want belief in God to exist. In other words, you look at yourself from the outside as if you had no inside. You put yourself in a state of

* See Daniel 3:75 (Vulgate); Psalm 148:9.

permanent defensiveness, of always being about to be criticised. It might be called 'the Christian cringe'.

All this applies more or less to any minority stuck in the middle of a hostile or uncomprehending majority. But too often we Christians seem to take it one step further. We let our enemies tell us what we believe. We let *them* tell *us* who we are.

The pattern is like this. We listen to the noisy people who call themselves 'scientists'. We let them tell us what it is that we believe, and we obediently believe what they tell us. Then they tell us that the 'beliefs' they have ascribed to us are nonsense, and we obediently believe that too. It makes us feel proper fools – which was the point of the exercise from the beginning.

Putting it like this makes us sound like victims. We aren't, and nobody should pity us. The whole thing is our fault. We are paying the price of sheer culpable laziness.

You can try to make excuses if you want. Being a victim is nice, and you don't want to lose that valued status. It's not your fault, you say. Religion is taught to children, you say, whereas religion is really for adults because religion is about how to live. (Children don't yet know what living is.)

Fine. But explanation is not exculpation. You are not a child now. If you want to know about something, you think about it and learn about it. A toddler can just about put one wooden block on top of another, but a bricklayer does not rely solely on memories of what he knew back then. He has thought and learned and studied and practised, which is why his house stays up.

We need to be like the brickie. His job is to make houses that don't fall down. Ours is to make lives that don't.

That concludes the exhortation, more or less, with what I hope is the right combination of 'You need to do something' with 'You are free to do it.' Now is the time for an example to pull it all together.

The aim is not to demolish the whole perverse conspiracy that unites great-scientist-worship on the one side with passivity-docility-and-guilt on the other. It is to give one clear example of the enemy's ploy (which can be summarised as, 'This is what you believe, and it is nonsense, therefore you are believing nonsense'). If you see through this ploy once then you will be aware of it wherever it appears in the future. You will see through it every time, just as your immune system, once it has seen an alien life form once, will notice it more quickly next time and be ready for it. Think of all this as a vaccination of the intellect.

That sales talk was needed because the example I am going to give is ridiculous, trivial and uninteresting.* I am sorry it is so but I have to use it because if I don't, you will think I am avoiding it. It is the old story of the six days of creation.

The 'them telling us what to think' version of the story goes like this:

> Genesis says the world was created in six days.
> Christians believe that the world was created in six days.
> Christians are wrong because the world was not created in six days.

Every one of those statements is false.

Science and myth

The Book of Genesis begins with a creation myth.†

A myth is not a lie. A myth is a way of telling the truth in terms of story, and story is one of the ways in which people communicate. It is one of the best ways. It is a powerful and enduring way, since a theory is soon forgotten but a story lasts for centuries. The parables in the Gospels are as alive today as they ever were.

To drive this point home, here are a handful of myths from the physical sciences. They will show what I mean about a myth being a story that tells the truth.

We get taught at school that an atom is electrons orbiting round a central nucleus. But electrons in an atom don't orbit. They don't move at all.

---

* Though not as much so as Stephen Hawking's story of how he saw through religion once and for all at an early age by noticing how many of the sentences in the Old Testament begin with 'And'.
† Actually it begins with two, which contradict each other to some extent (the second one starts at Genesis 2:5), but let's not complicate matters.

Later on, we get taught that the electrons in some atoms such as gold and mercury orbit so fast, so close to the speed of light, that they become more massive and the properties of the elements are subtly changed: this explains why gold is softer and yellower than you might expect, and why mercury, although a metal, is liquid. But the electrons still aren't orbiting. They still don't move, and in any case the concept of 'mass' in Special Theory of Relativity is subtler than one would expect.

Once, when I was building a radio, I read an explanation of a tuned circuit, the part of the machinery that makes the radio listen to one station and ignore the others. The explanation said that when the frequency is wrong, 'the current, as it were, takes fright'. I did not feel impelled to campaign for the setting-up of a Home for Terrified Currents. But I understood what the story was getting at and I have never since had difficulty with tuned circuits.

In a respectable article about evolution aimed at high-school students, I found the statement that 'caterpillars have learned' that eating the leaves of a certain plant makes them poisonous and distasteful to predators. That is obvious nonsense. 'The bird who ate me didn't like my taste' is not a sentence any caterpillar is going to utter, and anyway, as far as learning is concerned, there is no such thing as a collective, reasoning entity called 'caterpillars'.

Taken literally, each of these myths is false; but if it is interpreted in the right way then it is a good way of encapsulating a truth which, if spelt out in deeply technical terms, would puzzle everyone and captivate no one. Saying that the 'position' and 'momentum' of an electron obey the relativistic Schrödinger equation is exactly true and perfectly incomprehensible (and the equation can't be solved exactly in any case). The 'electron myth' is comprehensible and the story it tells is memorable. Even if the literal details of the story are false, *the truth the story tells* is true.

The point of a story is not in the literal details of it. If a painstaking historian were to discover that Samaritans were prohibited from using the main roads in first-century Palestine, would that make the parable of the Good Samaritan untrue?

The six days

Nobody *needs* to know whether the fishes came before the fruit trees.

The first creation myth in Genesis is set against the background of the best contemporary science, with 'the waters above the vault of heaven' and all the rest of it. Good, solid Babylonian cosmology. If it were written today, God might start by creating the Higgs bosons and the gravitons, or the Ricci tensor. But, written then or written now, the myth is not endorsing any particular physical theory. It does not make scientific assertions but simply takes contemporary science as the background. What the myth is saying is not this or that about vaults of heaven – or about bosons, come to that. It is saying that everything is made by God. It is saying that the existence of everything is not a random accident, but is intended.

Story works by progression, so of course the first Genesis myth labels the progression by means of days. But those are not meant to be literal days. St Augustine in the fourth century is already saying that these are not twenty-four-hour days: indeed, that they are not even time at all, but stages of dependency. The point of the story is not to say what you would have seen if you had been there with a stopwatch, but to show that everything is organised, ordered, structured.

That there is a sequence and a structure is important, but the exact sequence in which the structure works is not part of the message. Either the fishes come before the fruit trees or the fruit trees before the fishes. I don't know because I can't quite remember and I haven't bothered to look. I intentionally haven't bothered to look because I don't care what the answer is: I don't need to know. It is the *fact* of order that is important, not where every little thing fits into that overall order.

There is one more part of the myth that says something important about the creation, something we mustn't forget but quite often do: some of the world's most vicious heresies come from forgetting it. It is God's judgement on the creation as it happens. What God has created is good, good, good ... and finally, very good.

To pull all these threads together, what the first Genesis myth really says is this:

> The universe and everything in it is intended, dependent, ordered and good.

Everything else about the story, the evenings and the mornings and the next days and all that, is not *what* the myth says: only *how* it says it.

The approach I have demonstrated with the six days of creation is universal. You can use it whenever you engage with Scripture. It amounts to the fearless use of reason. You apply all your skill to distinguishing what the text is telling you from how it is telling it: all your skill and all your knowledge too, so that if new knowledge comes to hand, you can rethink the whole thing and (such is your faith) get a clearer picture of what it is all about. Knowledge and reason do not destroy faith, but they do sharpen it.

In the course of history, many new ideas have appeared to challenge what we believed, or thought we believed. We have dealt with them best when we have been able to apply reason to the problem without hesitation or fear.

An outstanding example is the rediscovery of Aristotle in the thirteenth century. Aristotle was the greatest philosopher of the ancient world. He was interested in everything and wrote about everything, and about everything he had something interesting to say. His wisdom and intelligence towered above ours. (They still do.) So the question arose: what if Aristotle contradicts what we believe? For instance (returning to the theme of creation), Aristotle said the world had been going on and on the same for ever, and we Christians appeared to be saying that it had a beginning. If you think about it, this is a far more important question than how many days it all took.

The correct approach was the one taken by St Thomas Aquinas. Aquinas took the time to work out in detail what Aristotle actually meant and also what *we* actually meant: not just the bottom line of Aristotle's reasoning, but what his arguments actually were; and on the other side, not just the words of Scripture and the Fathers of the Church, but what those words said.

As far as creation was concerned, Aquinas found that Aristotle had no real argument for an infinite age of the universe, only for 'There was no time at which the creation began.' And indeed, we also believe that the Creation was a creation *of* time. Even the Big Bang (if it happened) is *outside* time. So we are all agreed. And equally, on the scriptural side, an infinite age is still compatible with what Scripture is saying, which is that the whole creation is intended, ordered, dependent and good. So we are all agreed again.

Even now, the Big Bang may not be the last word. The universe may turn out to have been there always. The Polish cosmologist Martin Heller has theories of that kind but, as he says, if they are true then our faith in God will not need to change in the slightest.*

Un-learning how to read

All this is beginning to sound rather clever, and that is always a suspicious sign. Christianity is meant for the simple, you will say. You may also remember that although I have said that Scripture should be read with the mind, many people really do believe in the literal truth of every word of Scripture (irrespective of whether it makes sense or not), and you may ask, if that belief of theirs is wrong, where did it come from?

This inability to read Scripture properly is a new phenomenon, historically speaking.

The Jews are not capable of misreading Scripture because they do not read it, not in the sense that we mean 'read'. They do with the word of Scripture what their ancestors did with the word of God when it was addressed to them directly: they treat it as the start of a conversation. Having heard what God in Scripture says, the Jews reply, react, agree, argue, obey and disobey. Remember God telling Abraham that he will spare Sodom if there are fifty just men in it, and Abraham reverse-auctioning him down from

---

* Heller's model is based on the non-commutative geometry of Alain Connes.

50 to 45 to 40 to 20, and finally to ten.* God's actions are treated in the same way as his words.

There is a story of a group of Jews putting God on trial for breach of covenant for permitting the Holocaust. I haven't looked into the matter enough to know whether it really happened, but as a story it has truth. No one else could have done that with God, because no one else has exactly that kind of relationship with him.

We Christians are children of Abraham too (or adopted children, perhaps), and Christianity takes up the Jewish tradition. Scripture exists to be made sense of. Our job in 'loving God with the mind' is to understand what the sense is that it is making. I have already mentioned St Augustine and the six days of creation, but this tradition of understanding lasted for another thousand years. The great achievement of the thirteenth-century revolution in human thought – of Aquinas and his contemporaries – was to take cutting-edge reason and science wherever it comes from (even from pagans and infidels) and apply it to the understanding of Scripture and to doctrine. Given faith, this can be done without fear. If you have true faith then you have faith in your faith, and you know that reason and science cannot weaken your belief in the truth but only make it deeper and clearer.

If reading Scripture involves reading with the mind, the Reformation was the moment when a large part of the human race un-learned how to read, because an important theme in the Reformation was the rejection of reason. Luther condemned all Greek philosophy, especially that of Aristotle, as being pagan and therefore damned, and human reason as being as corrupt as the rest of human nature and consequently incapable of attaining the truth. Since the scholastic philosophers of the high Middle Ages had harnessed the power of Aristotle in a Christian cause, they too came under the ban. Christianity, hitherto a unique Semitic–Greek hybrid, was to swing firmly to the Semitic side, excluding reason as a mode of discourse.†

---

* This comedy is at Genesis 18:22–32.

† The theme of Semitic and Greek thought will be covered in detail in Chapter 19.

Authority was all, the authority of the Spirit and the authority of the written Scriptures, and, since reason was excluded, this meant the authority of whoever was deemed to possess the Spirit or was set above the people to interpret the Scriptures for them. Sometimes this move away from reason seems to have gone so far that one feels that the less sense a given passage of Scripture makes, the better, because the overwhelming power of God would be all the more magnified thereby.

Lutheranism has, of course, ended up with a theology that is much more rational than this, but it is extremes of this kind that are seized on by our enemies: the theophobes and the promoters of scientism.

If we let our enemies tell us who we Christians are, they will tell us that we are fundamentalists who believe every word in the Bible in its most literal sense. Anyone else, they say, isn't really a proper Christian at all but an evader or a backslider.

I can see why our enemies want this to be true: it gives them a nice easy target to attack. What I can't see is why we believe what they tell us about ourselves; but all too often it seems as if we do. Why should the anti-Christians be the ones to lay down what Christianity is and is not – or who is a good Christian and who is a not-properly-believing Christian? In using our brains, we are not evaders and we are not backsliders. On the contrary, we are loving God with all our mind and working hard every day to do it better. We are doing that because he told us to, and he told us to do it because it is right.

If you have endured to the end of this chapter, take one moral away from it. The next time your enemy puts you in a position and then attacks you for being in it – it doesn't only have to be religion, the principle works in politics as well – before starting to defend a position, take a moment to decide whether the position your enemy says you are in is where you really are.

8

Of all things visible and invisible

Visibilium omnium et invisibilium

There are times when the Creed sounds so splendid that for a moment nothing else about it matters. One of those times is now. The sound of *visibilium et invisibilium* sloshes from end to end of a resonant church like water in a good hot bath. These sensual pleasures are not to be neglected. God made them.

Nothing in the Creed, however, is there purely for sensual reasons. Every phrase is there because it says something that needs to be said and has not yet been said, or not yet been said clearly enough. We have come at last to the final part of the three-part affirmation of God's omnipotence. Why is this part needed? We have already said that God has created the heavens and the earth, which are visible things: so it must all hinge on that word 'invisible'.

A scientific motive

Physics provides an example of the necessity of believing that God is the creator of all things visible *and invisible*. It demonstrates the chaos that follows from avoiding or denying that truth.

If you throw a sack of potatoes out of the window, it will fall 16 feet in the first second, 48 feet in the second second, and 80 feet in the third. You could equally throw a rock or a cosmologist, and the result would be the same. A speed that increases by 32 feet per second in each second of the fall is characteristic of every falling object on earth. That '32' is a fact about the world. As such, we are entitled to ask 'Why?', and the answer can only be 'Because things are the way they are.' There isn't any deep mathematical reason for the speed to have to be exactly that number. Theologically, 'Because things are the way they are' points to the fact that God created not only all created *things* but also the *laws* they obey and all the *numbers* that go into those laws.

This example is easy to comprehend and confirm, but by itself it is not very important. If that '32' were '40' instead, then everyone would be that little bit heavier, and we would need legs that little bit thicker to hold us up: mildly interesting, at best.

Here is a similar example, except that this time it stretches across the whole universe and puzzles every scientist who ever thinks about it. There is a number called the Fine Structure Constant. It is roughly 137.* It is a kind of exchange rate between two kinds of atomic force. Unlike the force of gravity (which is different on Mars, say, or on the Moon) the Fine Structure Constant is the same throughout the universe, and it is exactly the same now as it was ten billion years ago.

Moreover, the Fine Structure Constant is genuinely interesting. It really matters. If it were much bigger, atoms would not be attracted to one another enough to make stable molecules, so there would be no chemical reactions. Since biology is made of chemical reactions, that means there would be no biology: and since we are biological organisms, that means that we would not exist. If the Fine Structure Constant were much smaller, atoms would be so attracted to one another that once they met, they would never part. No atom would ever leave one molecule to join another, so again there would be no chemistry, no biology, no us.

If the number were not what it is, we would not exist. So the question 'Why is it 137?' is an important and interesting one. And the question still has no answer, other than, 'Because it just happens to be that way.'

For Christians, this is no problem. We believe in the omnipotent Father, maker of all things invisible, and that includes the laws and the numbers that go in the laws: 'Constants of nature,

---

* If you are a physicist then you will notice that I am simplifying matters for the general reader by giving the name 'Fine Structure Constant' to the *reciprocal* of the Fine Structure Constant. That is because it is most often quoted as its reciprocal, which has been measured as 137.03599908.

bless the Lord!' We don't just stop there, because we must love the Lord our God with all our mind. We carry on doing science, but our belief means that we start from a sound foundation. If a number can be explained, we explain it; if it can't be, we accept it for what it is: a gift from God.

For theophobes, who erect what they call 'Science' as a wall against any hint of He Who Must Never Be Mentioned, the situation with the Fine Structure Constant is one of utter, utter terror. They fear that any appearance of 'Because it just happens to be that way' opens a crack in their defences through which, 'Because God made it that way,' can easily enter.

Not being able to talk any sense on the subject of 'Why?', they erect towering fortifications made of nonsense instead and hope that, awed by the authority of 'Science', we won't notice the difference. But we do. Here are two samples for your delight and derision.

One defence is called the Anthropic Principle. It has been invented out of thin air. It is a kind of super-law which says that laws and numbers of nature are illegal *unless they make human life possible*. Inventing a magic principle like that sounds like wishful thinking, and it is.

Another defence is sillier still. It is called the 'multiverse'. It says that there are infinitely many universes, none of which we can see. In each of them there is a Fine Structure Constant and in each of them it is a different number. The aim is to make the question 'Why 137?' as uninteresting as 'Why do I live at 137 Acacia Avenue rather than (say) number 11?' You may well think that inventing infinitely many invisible universes is too high a price to pay for theophobia.*

And meanwhile we, who know that God made 'all things invisible', are calm and safe and can carry on doing real science instead of losing ourselves in fear-induced fantasies.

---

* Not that God couldn't have made other universes if he wanted (the Bishop of Paris was already insisting on this in 1277), but the way the 'multiverse' works makes science itself impossible.

The good and the bad God

The Creed keeps us safe from cosmic insanity, but that cannot have been its purpose. In evolution, nothing appears because it may be useful one day in the future. We did not start to walk on two legs or grow big brains because one day they would make us masters of the world. Adopting an awkward gait or enlarging an already expensive organ could only have been done because it was a good thing to do *at the time*. Evolution cannot make long-term investments. It operates in the present, not the future.

Exactly the same applies to the evolution of doctrine. The fathers assembled at Nicaea in AD 325 cannot have been thinking about twenty-first-century follies but about something that mattered in the year 325. So what was it?

An answer may lie in the problem of evil. This can be either moral evil or physical suffering: the same kind of question arises. Can a good God create evil? Why does God permit suffering?

True answers are hard. Attempts at an answer tend to become the kind of theoretical answer that seems to be perfectly convincing until one takes one's eye off it for a moment, at which point the whole thing feels artificial and over-complex and all the thinking has to be done again. For this reason, a simple answer has emerged time and time again through history. It is called dualism, and it is entirely wrong.

Dualism explains everything by saying that there are two powers governing the universe, not one. One of those powers is God, who is infinitely good and is responsible for all the good there is. The other is his opposite, who is infinitely evil and responsible for all the evil there is. The world is a battleground between the two.

This is a parody of the truth, and all the more dangerous for being a parody rather than a simple falsehood.* Dualism demotes

---

* The devil has sometimes been raised to the status of 'anti-God' by careless minds, never with good results. The devil is just another created being – of angelic status, we are told – who happens to have used his free will to turn to evil.

the Creator of all things from being the creator of everything to being just one of two contestants. If you think about it, this leaves us with no particular reason for choosing one side rather than the other, nor even (really) for deciding which of them is right. The choice is left to convenience, and to circumstances, and perhaps to whichever side offers the better bid.

Some dualisms decorate their fundamental distinction in other ways – for instance, identifying the evil god with the Jehovah of the Old Testament and the good god with the loving Father of the New. An even more common decoration is to label spirit as 'good' and matter as 'evil'. Zoroastrianism provides an important example, not least because it has more to do with the beginnings of our own religion than we usually remember.

Zoroastrianism, as preached by the sixth-century-BC Persian prophet Zarathustra (latinised as 'Zoroaster'), began as a radical monotheism in which everything is made and ruled by the One God. This belief may well have helped the Jews along their path of discovery that their god was God. Other Zoroastrian beliefs found their way in as well: for instance, belief in judgement and life after death. The Wise Men who came from the east to worship the baby Jesus were probably Zoroastrians.

But Zoroastrianism had a fatal flaw. Just beneath God the Creator in the hierarchy of being, it believed in two spirits created by God: a good spirit and a bad spirit. As the centuries went on, people began to forget God the Creator, who receded into the infinite distance where paganism usually places him, unreachable from this world. All that was remembered was those two spirits, the good and the bad, with the world as their battleground. Some people even chose to worship the evil god rather than the good one, either to placate him or because in this world he had the more obvious power.

There are plenty of such cults around today.

We Christians are saved from all this because the Creed wipes it all away. It wipes away the equation 'spirit good, matter bad' because we believe in a God who created matter, which means that matter is in itself good, and not an evil thing or an unfortunate accident.

As for the idea of an evil anti-God, we believe in a God who created *all invisible things*, and therefore any 'anti-God' you could possibly imagine can only be a thing created by God and dependent on him. Indeed, there is no point in even thinking about such a being, because God tells us to talk to *him* as our father, and why should we want to talk to a subordinate monkey when we have been invited to talk directly to the organ-grinder? Unlike the later Zoroastrians, we have God near us and with us always.

I am not slinking past the problem of evil. It is a problem, just as free will is a problem. The psalmist asks God why he does not destroy the wicked. We do right to apply our minds to the problem – but it is not our duty to find a solution to it as a condition of our salvation. Jesus did not come to preach theological theory. He came to teach us how to live in this world and be ready for the next. What he preached, he preached openly, clearly, to anyone who would listen. He told simple stories that everyone could understand and remember and reflect upon. He taught little children, and he told us that we need to be like little children.

We are human, so we like understanding things. That is not bad. When we do understand something, we are happy, and that is not a bad thing either, because the mind is made by God and understanding is what the mind is for. But we must never think that understanding deep truths makes us gooder or more saved than anyone else. They do not. Salvation ultimately comes from doing, not knowing; and the only truths necessary for salvation are the ones that a little child can understand.

II
ACT

God the Son

II.a

Creation

Et in unum Dominum Iesum Christum,
Filium Dei Unigenitum,
et ex Patre natum ante omnia sæcula.
Deum de Deo,
lumen de lumine,
Deum verum de Deo vero,
genitum, non factum, consubstantialem Patri:
per quem omnia facta sunt.

I believe in one Lord Jesus Christ,
the Only Begotten Son of God,
born of the Father before all ages.
God from God,
Light from Light,
true God from true God,
begotten, not made, consubstantial with the Father;
through him all things were made.

The parable of the shadows

On the gravestone of Saint John Henry Newman there is the motto *Ex umbris et imaginibus in veritatem*, 'Out of shadows and images into the truth'. It sounds rather as if Newman was against shadows, but if he was, he was wrong. There are shadows and shadows: and faithful shadows can tell us the truth. Sometimes nothing else can do it.

Stand on a high place and look out at the view. A shadow moves swiftly across the landscape. Its shape tells you what it is a shadow of. You look up, and screw up your eyes to see if you can see the plane. The shadow was a shadow – it was not the plane itself – but it was telling you something at least, and that something was true.

I walk along a path in the afternoon with the sun behind me. My shadow stretches in front of me. It moves when I move and when I stop, it stands still. It goes without saying that the shadow is always where I am and never where I am not. Looking at it more closely, it is curved where I am curved and straight where I am straight. It is a faithful shadow and it tells the truth.

Shadow is not always truth and it is not always truth in every sense. The shadow accompanying me on my walk is 13 feet long and I am not. It is flat and dark grey and I am not. The shadow of a plane flying over a range of hills writhes, leaps and bounces while the plane itself goes serenely on. So it is necessary to use discernment. The right kind of faithful shadow shows one those aspects of the truth that it is able to show and thus indicates truths one might not be able to perceive in any other way. The wrong kind of shadow, or the right kind looked at wrongly, makes no sense at all.

To take an example from the Creed, when we call the Son 'the Son', we do not mean that God the Son is a literal son in our sense. As Dionysius and Aquinas both tell us, nothing we say positively about God can be literally true. What we do mean in the Creed is that the unknowable relationship between the Unknowable and the Unknowable is such that when its shadow is cast onto the landscape of human thought (just as the plane's shadow is cast onto the hills), that relationship has a 'shape' that we recognise as 'father and son'. This shadow is a faithful shadow of the truth of God, just as my shadow on the path tells the truth about me.

We need sense and discernment when it comes to interpretation. I am not flat and grey, the plane above the hills is not bouncing all over the sky, and (to take a simple example) the Father is not older than the Son. All these are obvious errors and no one risks falling into them. Other potential errors are subtler and we need to take care.

All the same, there is no need to feel ashamed of shadows. Shadows can be faithful, and faithful shadows can tell us the truth. The Creed is full of them.

9

I believe in one Lord, Jesus Christ

Et in unum Dominum Iesum Christum, Filium Dei Unigenitum

When we first hear in the Creed about God being the Father, it is about God's fatherhood of all that is created: God is the 'father' of the universe and of everything that is made. That concept is present in any religion that has any idea of God at all. Even for the pagans (whose gods are not God), *Iuppiter*, 'Jupiter', has the word *pater*, 'father', hidden inside it. This is quite clearly a metaphorical fatherhood, combining notions of authority, power and paternal care: it is human language, shadow language, communicating a richer reality.

When the Creed turns from God the Father to God the Son, things get more difficult because the implications of the word 'father' change. As long as we were thinking of God as *our* father and the father of everything, we were tying something unknowable (God) to something knowable (the universe and ourselves), and this helped us to learn a little about the Unknowable. Now suddenly we have God the Father being the Father of ... God. When God the Father is on one side and God the Son is on the other side of the father–son relationship, both sides are unknowable and indescribable, and we are left bewildered.

This is the moment to seek comfort in the words of Jesus, because the whole language of Father and Son comes from him. It is not Jesus as God who matters here, but Jesus as man. God the Son had spent thirty years being one of us and thinking like us, understanding words the way we understand them, before he started to tell us anything at all about the relationship between these two persons of God. As God and as one of us, he decided that talking about 'the Father' and 'the Son' was the best way for us to understand what needed to be understood. Since he was God he knew the truths that had to be conveyed, and since he was also a man and knew how men think, we should have confidence in his choice. The Church he founded has followed him and so, naturally, does the Creed.

The choice of 'Father' and 'Son' is the best choice, but it is also a hazardous one. This can be seen in the fact that no sooner has the Creed introduced the word 'Son' than it sets itself to cutting away the misconceptions that might come from the use of father-and-son language. This purification of the image is hard work but it has to be done, because although no language can completely describe what God is, 'Father and Son' is the best language we have.

The God of cod

God created the universe. He loves the universe and works to bring it to its culmination in glory. In our case this includes bringing us to comprehension (as far as is possible) of the nature of God himself.

If we are the only ensouled and intelligent species in the universe, then that is all that needs to be said. There are people who think that we are alone: the eminent cosmologists Barrow and Tipler, for example, claim that there can't be aliens because if there were, they'd already be visiting us.* I rather prefer the Vatican astronomer Guy Consolmagno, who sees God's love of life and joy in creation as being so abundant that it could not possibly result in a universe that *didn't* teem with life in every corner.† Some of it could be in a form we can't even recognise as life.

If there were another intelligent race in the universe, then it would have a different view of God from ours, simply because it would be starting from a different place and would be seeing the reality of Reality from a different angle. Its thoughts would 'float on a different blood'.

---

* John D. Barrow and Frank J. Tipler, *The Anthropic Cosmological Principle* (1986), chapter 9.
† Guy Consolmagno, *Brother Astronomer: Adventures of a Vatican Scientist* (2000), Part One, 'The Vindication of Mars'.

So let's suppose that one day we have visited aliens, or communicated with them by radio or laser or something: it would be a strange conversation, with every question and answer taking a hundred years to travel across space. Let us look ahead to the day when the Pope's traditional blessing *urbi et orbi* in St Peter's Square has become *urbi et orbibus*, 'for the City and the worlds'. On that day, what will we be talking to the aliens about?

Not about physics, because that is the same everywhere. Not about technology, because whatever one of us may have invented, the other will sooner or later have invented it as well.

It is the aliens' theology that will be truly fascinating. The moment *any entity at all* is self-aware – which means being able to say 'I' truthfully and to say 'you' and mean it – it has a relationship with Being Itself: that is, with God. So the aliens clearly will have such a relationship, conscious or unconscious, implicit or explicit. What kind of relationship? That will be the fascinating thing.

Our first question to the aliens will be, 'How was it for you?' Are they fallen, or unfallen? If fallen, have they been redeemed? If so, how? If not, when and how will it happen? Or is the act of redemption which has been performed for us through Jesus Christ on this earth definitive not just for us but for the entire universe? 'God so loved the *worlds* that he sent his Son . . .'? That would be a truly humbling discovery.

Like us, the aliens will see God through shadows: truthful shadows, but as their nature is different from ours, so will their shadows be. And that, for both sides of the conversation, will be the delight and the joy. Two shadows are better than one; two eyes are better than one.

The reason for considering all this at this particular moment is that we are considering God as the Father of God the Son. For us, who have fathers, this is a good way of looking at God: it is a truthful shadow. But what if the aliens don't have fathers? It is an idea worth exploring.

Consider the fish of the ocean, which have no fathers or mothers. As P. G. Wodehouse tells us:

Unlike the male codfish, which, suddenly finding itself the parent of three million five hundred thousand little codfish, cheerfully resolves to love them all, the British aristocracy is apt to look with a slightly jaundiced eye on its younger sons.*

The cod's millions of fertilised eggs float away on the ocean current, never to be seen again. Infant cod have no fathers. And so, although God is the same always and the same everywhere, throughout the universe and on every planet, aliens in the form of ocean fish will *not* be able to call the first and second Persons of the Trinity 'Father' and 'Son' because the words will have no meaning for them. The language will simply not be available.

The poet Richard Church has a charming illustration of the unavailability of language. He is writing about his childhood in 1900 and the sycamore tree in his garden:

> My brother and I learned to expect, every autumn, the winged seeds that could be thrown into the air, to come helicoptering down, *though in those days we could not describe that enchanting movement, for the word had still to be coined to describe an invention undreamed of.*†

If the aliens we communicate with are fish, the words 'Father' and 'Son' will mean nothing to them, and yet they will (such is God's love and generosity) have *some* concept of the being and nature of God, and consequently of the Trinity. They will have understood them in terms of ideas that make sense to them just as we have understood them in terms of ideas that make sense to us. When you and I argued about the number of sides a cube had, putting our 'four-sided' and 'six-sided' views together brought enlightenment to both of us. The same will happen when we exchange with the aliens our respective understandings of God. Both sides will

---

* P. G. Wodehouse, 'The Custody of the Pumpkin', in *Blandings Castle and Elsewhere*.
† Richard Church, *Over the Bridge*, Chapter 5, 'The Age of Bliss' (italics added).

be able to understand the truth more fully. It will be one of the joys of that interstellar conversation, if it ever takes place. (If it doesn't, it will certainly be one of the joys of heaven.)

Even in this world, when we go missioning in far-off cultures, it is a challenge but also a delight to discover the way the culture thinks and understands, and to adjust our own thinking so that it makes sense in that culture. In doing so, missionaries receive the other culture's understanding of the things that matter, and thus deepen their own.

The truth of the Trinity is more mysterious and wonderful than any language we can use to describe it. As Dionysius the Areopagite says, our words cannot define or circumscribe God. They can only point.

To come back to the Creed: the best possible language *for us*, the human race, is the language of fatherhood and sonship. Our created nature has determined it and the incarnate God has verified and guaranteed it. So now let us watch the Creed as it develops that language while at the same time it clears away our misconceptions and purifies our ideas.

10

Born of the Father before all ages

Et ex Patre natum ante omnia sæcula

There are two ways of making a sculpture. One is the Rodin method. You take a lump of clay, you slap on a leg here, a nose there, until you have the finished work in front of you ready to be cast in bronze. The other is the Michelangelo method. You take a block of marble which you know has David in it, you chisel away the parts that are not David, and there you are.

The Creed here is working like Michelangelo. It has taken a solid block called 'fatherhood and sonship' and now it is taking a chisel to it, hacking away the bits that aren't part of the truth of God. Once the process is complete, what remains will be the pure truth.

For many of the 'parts that are not David', it is obvious to anyone that they need discarding. For example, you can think of all the father-and-son clichés that have been used in comedy through the ages. But some aspects are trickier because they are not *obviously* inappropriate. Here are a few of them. Human parents have any number of sons from zero upwards. Human sons have two parents. Human sons have a date of birth: before it, the father is alone; after it, the son is younger than the father.

So now the Creed sets to work with its chisel.

Unigenitum – the one Son: Like the oneness of God, the oneness of the Son is not really numerical. It is not a question of God the Father having N sons, with N happening to be equal to 1. God the Father is unique and not countable, and it is exactly the same with God the Son.

Et ex Patre natum – born of the Father: Looking at it from the opposite direction, from Son to Father rather than from Father to Son, the relationship is also unique. God the Son comes *entirely* from God the Father and from nothing else. Whenever this is misunderstood, confusion follows. For instance: God the Son is eternal, and eternally related to the Father; when he takes on matter or flesh as an incarnate human being, he does so by being born as the son of Mary. You can't conflate the two into one and turn the story into 'God is the son of Mary'. However beautiful it may be as a poetic idea in hymns and so on, it is not literally true. So the Creed takes care to protect us from it.

Ante omnia sæcula – **before all ages:** Finally, human sons are younger than their fathers, but the Father and the Son are co-eternal. There is no time at which one of them exists and the other doesn't. The relationship between Father and Son is outside time in any case, because time itself is created by God.

The Creed has denied a lot. It needed to, to make it clear what 'Father' and 'Son' mean as far as God is concerned. With the next phrase, it will turn from denial to assertion, talking not about what the Son isn't, but what he is.

God from God

*Deum de Deo, lumen de lumine, Deum verum de Deo
vero, genitum, non factum, consubstantialem Patri*

A remarkable thing about what you might call the big questions, the questions that are not about particular things but about everything as a whole, is that whenever anyone has sat down to think them through, they have always ended up having what you might call the same basic 'shape'. It doesn't matter when or where it is done, or which science is involved. A thinking theologian or a thinking physicist begins to notice the same pattern in the background: things seem to arrange themselves into pairs of opposites, and those opposites are, in some kind of abstract sense, infinitely far apart.

The necessary and the contingent, I: whetherness. Things exist, or they do not exist. Sticking to the things that do exist, some of them exist *necessarily*: they cannot *not* exist. You could say that they 'just are'. Other things exist *contingently*: they do exist, but they might not have done. If you believe in God, then God is an example of a necessary being. If you don't, then something like the truths of mathematics could be your example. As for a contingent being, you and I are both contingent. We might not have existed, but we do.

The necessary and the contingent, II: whatness. Given an existent thing, could it have been different from what it is? Physical examples are the simplest. It is possible to believe that 'speed increasing as time goes on' is a necessary fact about falling objects: it could not have been otherwise. On the other hand, nobody can seriously believe that the particular rate of increase in speed that we observe here on earth is necessary. It could have been different. So that is an example of a different kind of contingency, not in *whether* a thing exists but in *what* exactly the existing thing is.

The permanent and the changeable. This third example is less fashionable than it once was, but it is also the easiest to see. You can see it by looking up and then looking down. When you look up you see the sky, and you see permanence. The stars and planets are the same this year as they were last year and a thousand years ago, and their motions (simple or complicated according to their nature) go on for ever. Look down here, and all around you you will see wind and weather. You will see decay. Things left to themselves rot or shrivel or die. Motion itself is not for ever, and each thing that moves will stop moving sooner or later.

There are other pairs of opposites, but these will do to be going on with. The first thing they have in common is that in each of these examples, the opposites really are completely opposite. If you think of them as the opposite ends of a stick, it has to be an infinitely long stick.

The important and suggestive point follows on from this. If you take the stick made out of 'whetherness' and the stick made out of 'whatness' and the stick made out of 'permanence versus changeability', they naturally line up in parallel. In the bundle of sticks you have made, one end has necessity, permanence, perfection, the One, and God if you believe in God. The other end has contingency, change, imperfection and the Many; and also us.

This alignment of opposites is common to the whole human race. The sticks are parallel, and they are infinitely long, and the deepest yearnings of the human spirit are tied up with finding a way of connecting one end of the sticks to the other.

The infinite gaps: a tour

Let's make things clearer by making a picture, one not that dissimilar to the world view that prevailed literally until the ideas of Copernicus and Newton were accepted, and metaphorically ever since. 'Down here' you have all the imperfections, and 'up there' you have perfection and even a certain kind of timelessness. Putting it in astronomical terms, people associated 'down here' with everything up to the orbit of the Moon, so the charming old word 'sublunary' can be used to describe it. 'Up there', far away, the place of inaccessible and airless perfection, has no such simple name, but 'supernal' works rather well.

The key insight is that the supernal is infinitely far above the sublunary. The question is then, 'What do we do about it?' All the world's religions and thought systems have some sort of answer. What follows here is a swift, summary and superficial tour of the landscape. A proper study would take a lifetime, but even a brief contact with the ideas is enlightening.

Paganism is resolutely sublunary. An infinite distance cannot be bridged by finite beings, and sensible pagans do not make the attempt. The supernal is remote and unreachable, we cannot know it and it cannot be interested in us. So it is not worth considering. We are stuck 'down here' and we have to deal with what we find down here: spirits, gods, demons. We placate some and bribe others, or we invoke the friendly ones against the ones that hate us. By ritual, invocation and sacrifice we do whatever is necessary for our own survival.

Buddhism is a mirror image of paganism because it also sees the infinite distance as unbridgeable but it views it from the other end, the supernal end. It sees the sublunary as having no enduring value or meaning or even existence. The unchanging and self-contemplating supernal is the only reality.

Some learned people say that Buddhism is a selective part of Hinduism with the pagan parts etched away; or perhaps that Hinduism is made out of a core of Buddhism with enough sublunary gods added to give the common people something to hold on to. Whichever it is, the gap between sublunary and supernal is infinite and cannot be bridged.

Neoplatonism is an attempt to bridge the unbridgeable. It is the esoteric belief system that grew out of some of the more mystical themes of Plato's dialogues. In a sense, it is only of historical interest because it is no longer alive; but it fascinated people for a thousand years and continues to influence Christian thought today. Neoplatonism is aware of the gap between the motionless, eternal, unchanging, self-contemplating One and the sublunary world which is in every way its opposite.

The fascinating thing about Neoplatonism is that it actually tries to tackle the gap. It does this by introducing intermediary beings to link the One to the Many and to connect the Unchanging with the world of change. There are layers upon layers of these beings – Powers, Forces, Aeons, whole hierarchies of them. You could think of them like the piers of a bridge spanning a wide river such as the Ganges.

That same river image shows why Neoplatonism cannot work. You put piers into a wide river to make a number of narrower streams, each narrow enough to be bridged. But if you have an *infinite* river and put a pier in it, then wherever you put the pier, it is going to be infinitely far from one of the banks. So there is still an infinite gap to bridge, and the pier has been no help at all. You might as well not have bothered.

Islam goes the opposite way to Neoplatonism. If it is born in a superstitious world full of djinn, afārit, and other spirits, the very first thing any true religion of God has to do is to tidy them all away in the cause of monotheism. This is a necessary piece of hygiene. The space between God and man, so full of intermediaries in Neoplatonism, becomes in Islam a pure vacuum in which nothing can breathe – not even human reason. God is all-powerful. All things are the way they are because God has decreed it so. The whole duty of sublunary beings is not to question the supernal but to worship and obey.

Scientism

Scientism deserves a section to itself because it surrounds us on all sides. It is not that it is explicitly preached, as such: it doesn't make enough sense for that. It just seems to soak into us so that we risk believing it without even realising that that is what we are doing.

Scientism is a belief system founded on the idea that 'science' has the answer to everything, from the questions of existence downwards. What that word 'science' means is a little vague. It starts off as something like 'school physics', full of simple certainties, but it quietly morphs into 'whatever the people who call themselves "scientists" tell us to believe'.

Of course, science can't really be self-certifying in this way (not even mathematics is), so in practice scientism boils down to a religious belief that denies it is a religious belief. Indeed, it bases its entire authority on that denial, claiming somehow to be certainty, not belief. Scientism is mostly a disease of over-clever undergraduates, but occasionally it is not grown out of and persists into adult life. The basic problem with scientism is that while science can tells us *how* things work and *how* to do things, it cannot tell us *what* to do. The outcome is a monstrous hybrid in which the personal prejudices of the scientist (or scienticist?) are robed in the absolute authority of 'Science Itself'.

Scientism tells us that everything is all right as long as 'Science' tells us to do it. Thus Arthur C. Clarke in his novel *2010: Odyssey Two* has a scientific super-race cruising the galaxy, observing here, intervening there and, as Clarke genteelly puts it, 'sometimes, dispassionately, they had to weed'. Even genocide is all right as long as it is scientific: above all, if you don't enjoy it.

This is not the place to confute scientism, but I am mentioning it here because it is another example of the way in which humanity tries to deal with the infinite gap between sublunary and supernal.

The first possible scientistic approach to 'Why are things the way they are?' is to say that there is no other way they can possibly be – for instance, because of some deep mathematical truths that we haven't discovered yet. This amounts to saying that necessity rules everything: in other words, the supernal is the only reality. Mathematics imposes its 'cannot be otherwise' on everything, so that in a purely mathematically based universe even free will becomes logically impossible.

There are other attempts to account for the gap in scientistic terms. I touched on both the Anthropic Principle and the 'multiverse' a few chapters ago and that ought to be quite enough for anyone. I mention them here just to say that even these fantasies can be located in terms of the universal problem: the problem of the infinite gaps.

Back to the Creed

The purpose of this chapter so far has been to show how everyone everywhere always agrees on the basic problem of existence, which is that there is a gap between one end of Being and the other (you can call it 'necessary versus contingent', 'unchanging versus changeable', or by many other names), and the gap is infinite.

Christianity can't deny that gap, so it doesn't. It can't deny, either, that the gap is unbridgeable, so it doesn't. So far, Christianity is just like any other religion or philosophy.

But then Christianity makes a unique and outrageous claim: that the infinite, unbridgeable gap *has been bridged*. More than that: the Creed is about to take us step by step through the story of that bridging.

If you look at it from our end, the human sublunary end, what the Creed is going to narrate is simply impossible. From the other end, the supernal divine end, it is not actually impossible, because God is omnipotent, but nobody with the slightest respect for the dignity of deity could imagine for a moment that the Perfect and Eternal would stoop to muddy itself in imperfection and transience. It would be more than indecent: it would be obscene.

But that is what we say happened, and in the Creed we are about to go through it step by step. We are about to make some huge claims. We are by implication saying that our God is a God who does not live up to our own high standards of divine dignity and appropriateness. Perhaps we ought not to be surprised – 'my thoughts are not your thoughts', after all – but if we aren't at least a little bit shocked by the goings-on the Creed is going to reveal, we haven't fully understood the point.

Now we see the reason why the Creed is, as it were, drawing breath now before plunging into the story. The fabric of doctrine is about to be subjected to some pretty severe stresses and, just like in a ship with a storm approaching, everything needs to be battened down or it will get loose and break things. Any decently pious person will want to disbelieve the story, or reinterpret it, or take it in any sense other than the literal. One way or another, people will want to explain it away. Anti-Christians want it all to be false, either out of disdain for Christianity or out of respect for the One. Christians who dedicate their lives to keeping their heads down and seeming normal to everyone else will want it all to mean nothing ('But aren't the words beautiful?').

This is why, at this point, the Creed puts away the chisel and takes out a bunch of nails, to nail everything down so that it can't blow away. *Deum de Deo* – bang, God from God: Jesus is not just a messenger or a sort of archangel on steroids. *Lumen de lumine* – bang, Light from Light: the Son, like the Father, is a cosmic force. *Deum verum de Deo vero*, true God from true God: there is no getting away from it, the Son is as truly God as the Father is. *Genitum, non factum*, begotten, not made: the Son's relationship to the Father is not that of a tool being created for a specific purpose, and birth is the best analogy that we have.

To conclude it all, *consubstantialem Patri*, consubstantial with the Father. 'Consubstantial' is a horribly technical term, and now and then people have tried to elbow it aside in favour of something that sounds nicer and means less. I am sure they meant well. There is always trouble with technical terminology. Jesus was right to talk about sheep and harvests instead of using intellectual terms.

If you delve into the meaning of 'form' and 'substance', you will get a good, reliable answer about 'consubstantial': 'of the same substance'. But terms like those are forever changing their meaning,* and for those of us who don't have the lungs for the rarefied air of high philosophy, let me tackle the 'consubstantial' phrase in another way. *Whatever* technical terms you currently use to help your understanding, and whichever of those terms you choose to apply to the Father, if you apply the same terms to the Son then you will get the same answer. That is how same the Father and the Son are.

Given that the Father and the Son are so same, what is the point of having the two of them? The Creed is about to make that clear.

---

* They have nearly swapped meanings since the high Middle Ages.

12

Through him all things were made

Knowledge is an all-at-once thing: timeless. So is understanding: once you have acquired it, the whole thing is present to you all at once. But we are beings in time, not outside it, so although knowledge is all at once, coming to know happens in time and not in one mystic flash.

The Creed as we recite it is spread across time and so it suits our temporal nature. In that sense, it works like a story. But that brings us up against the paradox of storytelling, which is that *the thing told* is timeless but *the telling of it* is an activity in time, and while it is going on it is only half done. You can't properly follow a story unless you have a feel for where it is going, but you can't know where it is going until it has got there.

If you think of knowledge as a tower built on secure foundations, the paradox comes out like this: either you start from the bottom and learn about pile-driving and concrete-pouring without knowing what they are for, or you start from the top and find you need scaffolding round the structure because there is nothing to hold the thing up.

In many ways, it is better to look at coming-to-know in terms of painting rather than architecture. When you paint something, you don't paint each inch of it perfectly before you go on to the next. You apply a coat of primer to the whole object at once and let the primer dry. Then you paint it all again, from end to end, with undercoat, and when that's dry you sand it down and rinse off the dust. Finally, you go over it a third time, applying the top coat – and that is the way to get an enduring result.

This is how education works. It is also the experience the Apostles had. The primer was the centuries-long relationship which they as Jews had been having with God the Father. The undercoat was their short years of being with the incarnate Son. And, without being too precise about it, the sanding and rinsing and top-coating correspond in some sort of way to the 'Emmaus time' between the Resurrection and the Ascension and the 'time of the Spirit' which started at Pentecost.

When the Creed affirms eternal truths, it has to do so in a temporal process – first one phrase, then another. It has exactly the trouble you might expect with the storyteller's paradox, and now is the moment to confront that trouble. The Creed has carefully introduced the Son as 'just the same as the Father, only different', which seems logically coherent but pointless on its own, like poured concrete. Now it tells us the point of what it has been doing, by saying, 'Through him all things were made.'

I suppose there must be philosopher–grammarians to whom this contrast of prepositions – a creation *by* the Father and *through* the Son – will tell them everything they need to know: but I am not one of them and I will assume that you aren't either.

The storyteller's quandary here is this: the Father and the Son are properly understandable in the context of the Trinity, but we can't get to the Trinity until we have gone all the way through the Father and the Son and have arrived at the Spirit. So it seems that we are stuck. We can't start until we have arrived, but we can't arrive until after we have started.

What we need is something that gives shape to the whole before the true shape is fully revealed. We need a rough sense of what the doctrine of the Trinity is going to be, to take us through to when we can look at what the doctrine of the Trinity actually is. If you are still thinking of painting, this 'something' corresponds to the undercoat that will (later on) help the top coat stick. If you are thinking of architecture, this is scaffolding: it will be superseded by the building itself once the building is complete.

Some people find it possible to manage on something as simple as, 'The Father is the father and the Son is the son and the love between them is the Spirit.' I can't quite do that, so here is an outline of a different way of looking at the Trinity. It is meant to be a way to make the 'Binity' of the Father and the Son comprehensible enough for us to follow the story until it is time for the whole Trinity to appear. It really is an outline, and the whole thing will be gone into again later in this book, once the Creed has got as far as mentioning the Holy Spirit by name.

The structure of creation

God is the omnipotent Creator and we are made in God's image, so one way of approaching the reality of God in the Trinity is to look carefully at the reality of ourselves as omnipotent creators. Fortunately, this is an experience that each of us can have.

Take a blank piece of paper and put it in front of you. Then, *with respect to that piece of paper* you are omnipotent: you are in the place of God.

You, the creator, have an **idea** of what you are going to paint or write or draw. You take up your brush or your pen and you perform the **act** of painting or writing or drawing. Let's narrow down the example for a moment and suppose you are writing a story. In a good story, the characters do not say and do what you tell them to: they say and do what they want to say and do. They have **life**.

Idea – Act – Life represents the triune nature of artistic creation. Indian mysticism has a parallel in *sat, cit, ānanda*: 'Being, Awareness, Bliss'. The parallel for us Christians is the Father, Son and Spirit.

This is not intended to be a definitive statement. Whole books have been written about the nature of these parallels, especially in terms of mysticism: I will quote one of them later. But even in its present form it should be enough to get us through the story told by the Creed. The basic attributes of Father and Son come naturally out of it: the Father self-contemplating, timeless, eternal; the Son acting and implicated in the world and in time.

It is also encouraging to us as Christians to see that the three-ness of the Trinity is not purely a Christian invention. The innovation of Christianity is not about threes. The innovation is that because we have a relationship with Being Itself in terms of *persons* – a WHO-to-WHO relationship – this triple structure of Being and the creative act finds its outcome in the three Persons of God.

II.b

Intervention

Qui propter nos homines et propter nostram salutem
descendit de cælis.
Et incarnatus est de Spiritu Sancto ex Maria Virgine,
et homo factus est.

For us men and for our salvation
he came down from heaven,
and by the Holy Spirit was incarnate of the Virgin Mary,
and became man.

Into time and place

So far, the Creed has been purely concerned with universal truths. Now it changes gear. It starts to talk about events rather than truths, which means that it moves from the universal to the specific. A truth is true always and everywhere, but an event happens at a specific time and in a specific place.

A few chapters ago we touched on the theology of aliens. It is time to revisit them for just a moment. The last visit showed that truths have to be expressed in words and images, and that however universal and eternal the truths themselves may be, the means of expressing them must depend on 'the blood that your thoughts are floating on'. A race without fathers would have to be told about the relationship between God the Father and God the Son in a different way – and (by his goodness) God will have told them that truth by now, in a way that suits their nature. They will have learnt exactly the same thing we have, but from a different direction.

If we and the aliens tell each other our doctrines, then, like two people looking at a cube, we will have a better understanding of True Being than either of us on our own could have been capable of attaining. Leaving all thought of aliens aside, even we here on earth have many different human cultures. The best missionary activity has as much listening in it as it does preaching, and the missioner learns as much from it as the missioned.

That last time the aliens were mentioned, it was all about universal truths. This time it is something different. This time the Creed is going to be talking about events rather than truths. An event is the exact opposite of a truth. A truth is true always and everywhere: it is true (if you think about it) even before times and places exist, even before there is such a thing as 'when' or 'where'. An event, on the other hand, necessarily has a specific 'when' and 'where' attached to it. It wouldn't be an event if it didn't. A truth is universal; an event is specific.

It could be that those aliens are cleverer than us, or know the universal truths better than we do. It could be that they are holier than us or closer to God than us. They might be unfallen while we are fallen, and be walking daily with God in their equivalent of the Garden of Eden. As far as the eternal truths go, we might have to do nothing more than listen to the aliens without speaking; or just be near them, as one does when one meets someone exceptionally close to God.

All that: yes. But there is one thing we know and they don't, one thing we can tell them, however wise they are, and they will have to sit and listen. It is the events. *It is what God did here, for us.* The events that are about to be narrated in the Creed are events that happened to us and no one else; happened here on earth and nowhere else. And they are events that matter. However low we may be, and however high the creatures may be that we are bringing this news to, they will not know the news until we tell them, and it is our duty to tell them, for their enlightenment and for the greater glory of God.

This is both something to be proud of and also something not to be. 'What wonders the LORD performed for us,' says the psalmist, 'indeed we were glad.'* But also, 'What wonders the LORD *needed to* perform for us,' so that somehow we need to be glad and ashamed at the same time. As I once heard in a special class at school, taught by a philosopher of international reputation, 'You are all here because you deserve it' (a calculated pause), 'or because you need it.'

What God has done for us has universal value and gives us another way of getting close to the universal truth that is God. Because we ourselves are beings embedded in time and place, salvation history has come to us not in ready-made visions but by way of a sequence of events, each one with a 'here' and a 'now' attached to it. Now the Creed is starting to take us through them.

---

* Psalm 125(126):3.

I3

For us men

Qui propter nos homines

When I go to an art gallery, there comes a point when I stop being able to see. To the first few paintings I give my full attention, but then the attention begins to run out. Later paintings get barely a glance and, unless I am careful, by the time I am in the second or third room I find myself reduced to reading the label and only glancing up at the painting for a moment to check that they haven't hung something else in its place. That is not right. Those later paintings are just as much works of art as the first ones. They have been painted by artists who are just as good, with just as much passion and inspiration. They would be just as nourishing to the spirit, if only I could see them.

The same kind of thing can happen with the Creed, because the Creed is long. The first few phrases are arresting, enlightening, stirring; but nobody can be arrested and enlightened forever, and soon the attention fades. Eventually the successive phrases start to come across as nothing more than '[INSERT HOLY WORDS HERE]'. That is as bad as what happens in the gallery. Worse, because behind the mist of '[INSERT HOLY WORDS HERE]' there are deep truths that people have died for: truths for us all to live by.

With a cultured and intelligent friend, I worked out how to cure the gallery problem in a refreshing and effective way. Now I recommend our method to everyone. It is theft.

Go to the gallery not intending to admire but to steal, and everything changes. You stop looking at each picture as an object of admiration or a unit of culture power. You look at it as something you might want to have in the house – or not want to have. One painting may be admirable up on the wall of a gallery but impossible to live with close to. Another may be unspectacular at first sight but able to give you something more to appreciate every time you pass it.

Try it for yourself. On your next visit, go round each room the way you always do – 'three paces, admire, three paces, admire' – but before you leave that room, look quickly round and identify the one painting you would most like to steal. In that moment you will be looking at the painting from the point of view of a prospective patron (if that is the right word), and this will strip away the barrier of vacuous awe that has been standing between you and it.

The same kind of exercise works with creeds. It peels away the hallowedness from the hallowed phrases and lets one hear what they are actually saying.

The idea behind this exercise is remembering what a creed is for. A creed is not just any old list of true statements. We do not stand up solemnly in church and proclaim that water is wet, or that pigs can't fly. It is obvious why we don't do it. Why waste our breath saying what nobody can not believe? The whole point of a creed is to state truths that *not everyone* believes.

The cure for art-gallery hypnosis is centred on desire. It remembers that paintings, as well as being art, are desirable, and the exercise is to feel that desire in the purest way possible. The cure for creed hypnosis centres round belief. It remembers that the statements in the creed, as well as being true, are *disbelievable*, or they wouldn't be there. The exercise is to try to perceive that disbelievability.

I don't mean that we should ourselves try to disbelieve. That is not the point. What I mean is that we should be like the woman in one of G. K. Chesterton's essays who loved going to the zoo to look at the rhinoceros, because he existed but looked as if he didn't. This was not an attempt to disbelieve in the rhinoceros's existence but to rejoice in the fact that he does exist. When we recite each phrase in the Creed, we should delight in it in the way the woman delighted in the rhinoceros: believing it, but knowing that a perfectly reasonable person might not.

This isn't a paradox. It works with zoology and theology, and it even works in physics. Newton's First Law of Motion states that unless a force acts on it, a moving body carries on moving in the same direction and at the same speed for ever. This is an important law, and the foundation of modern dynamics. Teachers teach it, children memorise it; but for most of them it is not much more than '[INSERT SCIENTIFIC WORDS HERE]'. You don't truly understand the significance of Newton's First Law until you have found the motives for disbelieving it. It isn't hard because there are plenty of them. In fact, it is more than just disbelief: out in the real world, Newton's First Law is *obviously not true*. Kick a football – it won't go on for ever but will slow down and stop. Drive a car – and watch what happens when you take your foot off the accelerator. In our everyday, real-world experience, things need constant pushing to keep them going, and only in the heavens does motion go on forever.

It is only when you realise this that you can see that the First Law is not just nice words but something revolutionary. The First Law says things don't stop even though experience says that they do. To make the law fit the reality, new forces need to be conjured out of thin air: forces such as friction and air resistance. You can't believe in the First Law without turning everything else upside down to fit it. And this is the Newtonian revolution.

It is the same with the Creed. Every statement in the Creed is capable of being rationally disbelieved, or it would not need to be there: and believing it turns our view of the world inside out. That is the Christian revolution.

The problem with 'on account of us'

You can't properly appreciate a painting until you get close enough to it to be able to steal it. In order to discover what believing in *propter nos homines*, 'on account of us men', means, it is necessary to imagine how someone could seriously and rationally disbelieve those words.

It's a lot of weight to put on to three Latin words. But I think that it is worth doing, and that it can be done.

The first motive for disbelieving in *propter nos homines* is dry and philosophical, but still a good reason.

Aristotle studied causation in all its forms. He concluded that there must be a First Cause – something that acts on other things but is not itself acted upon by anything. Aristotle was a pagan and had no concept of God, but when his thought was rediscovered in thirteenth-century Europe, St Thomas Aquinas saw that Aristotle's First Cause must be identical to what we call 'God'.

The First Cause acts on everything and nothing acts on it: that is the definition of what it means to be a first cause. And yet to say (as we do in the Creed) that God did something 'on account of us' amounts to saying the exact opposite: that *we* have caused *God* to do something. We have acted as causes affecting the First Cause. That is absurd, so it needs sorting out.

For the English, there is an additional motive for disbelieving in *propter nos homines*, or at least not thinking about it. It is a cultural one. Among some people (some sincere English Protestants are like this, or at least look like it when seen from the outside), petitionary prayer is rather frowned on because it sounds as if one were telling God what to do. God (they feel) knows perfectly well what ought to be done without us needing to tell him, and as well as being unnecessary, it is impertinent of us to do so because it is *simply not our place* to give advice to God. (To be English is to care a lot about what it is and is not one's place to do.) The corollary is that if it is not one's place to make God do things by asking for them, then it isn't one's place either to make God do things by needing them.

These philosophical and cultural motives are understandable and not in themselves unreasonable. They are not self-evidently wrong any more than the pre-Newtonian ideas of motion were wrong. But although they are reasonable, we know that they *are* wrong. We know this because Jesus told us. Jesus repeatedly told us to ask God for anything and everything, to nag him the whole time, the way you would nag an indolent judge into taking the trouble to hear your case.* We trust Jesus well enough to know that he would not insist on our doing something pointless.

* Luke 18:1–8.

Consequently, we know that in this sense we are authorised and encouraged to 'act as causes' with respect to God, the First Cause. Either through our petitions or by our need, God can find himself doing things 'on account of us'.

Believing that God can act on account of us is the beginning of the Christian revolution. Making sense of how this is possible is when the revolution will really get under way.

So standing up in church and saying 'on account of us men' really does say something that could be disbelieved and is therefore something that needs to be said. We are saying something about God. We are saying that God has no sense of divine dignity and no sense of scale or proportion. God values human beings on the same scale as ten-a-penny sparrows, and he loves each one of them.

As Christians, we shouldn't stop there. We have to go further than solemnly proclaiming our belief in the disbelievable. We have to try to believe in it *for a reason*. We are created with minds and Jesus commands us to use them, so 'I believe it because it's in the Creed' is not allowed. At best, it is intellectual laziness. At worst, it makes outsiders think that the only reason for our belief is that we believe in it, a circularity that deprives our religion of any rational foundation and reduces it to just another lifestyle option. That is a libel against Christianity and a grave sin.

'Jesus said so' is a route by which we can arrive at belief; but the rational ground of our belief must be more than just a divine command. So what is it?

Love as reversal

The earth is a speck in the vastness of the universe, and, compared to the infinity of God, even the universe is a small and short-lived thing:

> Also in this He showed me a little thing, the quantity of an hazel-nut, in the palm of my hand; and it was as round as a ball. I looked thereupon with eye of my understanding, and thought:

What may this be? And it was answered generally thus: *it is all that is made.* I marvelled how it might last, for methought it might suddenly have fallen to naught, from its littleness. And I was answered in my understanding: *It lasteth, and ever shall, for God loveth it.**

Just like the word 'person', the word 'love', when we use it in connection with God, is a shadow of something too rich and multidimensional for us to comprehend. All the same, it is a faithful shadow. If we listen to it rightly, we will hear the truth. And, indeed, love explains the whole puzzle of causation.

The first part of the puzzle is the disproportion between us and God. Love explains it. You can never be too small or unimportant to be loved by me: that is in the nature of love itself. And so the question of whether God loves us at all has nothing to do with size or status or significance, or anything else about us. There is only one thing we need to do before God is able to love us: we need to exist. Nothing else is required. Nothing else is relevant.

The second part of the puzzle is the apparent contradiction by which the creatures affect the creator and caused things affect the First Cause. Love explains this too. Think of your own experience of love. Where love is concerned, it doesn't matter how grand you are or how insignificant I am. If you love me, I can make you happy just by being happy and sad just by being sad: your love has given me that right, that power. Not to put too fine a point on it, by loving me you have conferred on me the ability to give you sleepless nights.

Not only does loving me make you have feelings because of me, it also makes you do things because of me, on account of me. Transposing all this from human love to divine love, God's love for us is what justifies the *propter nos homines* of the Creed.

To summarise: *propter nos homines*, 'on account of us men', is an outrageous thing to claim about God. It would be possible to

* Julian of Norwich, *Revelations of Divine Love*, chapter 5 (italics original).

disbelieve it, which is why it is in the Creed. Trying to find a way to see how believing it could be reasonable has led us straight to the notion of love, and to consideration of God's love for us.

In many ways, God's love for us is still more outrageous than the phrase that led us to it – and the Creed isn't half over yet: there are more outrages on the way.

14

And for our salvation

The word 'salvation' doesn't see much use outside a churchy context. The trouble with words that isolate themselves like that is that with time they come to forget what they mean. We sort of remember that 'salvation' has something to do with rescue, but not exactly what, and the odd survivals of it in the outside world don't help because they are simply rescues of a melodramatic kind: from sinking ships, things like that.

It doesn't take many hours of isolation in intensive care for a patient to forget what is real and what isn't. Isolated in a sacred space, the word 'salvation' forgets reality and fades away into a touch of drama accompanied by a faint whiff of incense.

Since salvation is central to what God did and central to what Christianity is all about, the word 'salvation' itself needs rescuing. The way to rescue it is to go back to its beginnings and the concepts it was born with.

Saving 'salvation'

The word 'salvation' comes to us from and through Latin. The first difficulty in getting a grip on it is a general one: words in different languages have what you might call different widths. A good example is mushrooms. French has no word for 'mushroom'. The French word *champignon* covers mushrooms and toadstools and fungi in general, so that a Frenchman with (say) athlete's foot is suffering, literally, from mushrooms: a charming if surreal picture. But the charm evaporates when you realise that translating the word *champignon* into English is impossible unless you have first found out exactly what the original French writer was talking about.

And for our salvation

The Latin word *salus* is a *champignon* kind of word. Its range of meaning includes what we call 'safety' in English and what we call 'health'. The trouble is that English has no word that means both. The closest way I find of conveying that meaning is 'being all right', which is certainly not dignified enough for a Creed.

Still, having started with *salus*, let's follow the story forward.

When you possess *salus*, you are *salvus*, you are safe. (Indeed, our word 'safe' comes indirectly from *salvus*.)

The verb *salváre* means to cause someone to be all right. If you think about it, there are two ways of causing someone to *salvus*, to be all right. One way is when people are all right to start with and we want to keep them that way. So in Night Prayer there is a line which says *salva nos dormientes*, keep us safe while we sleep. The other way of 'causing someone to be all right' is when they aren't all right and we want to make them all right again. In other words, they need to be saved.

That gets us to *salvátio*, which is the act of *salváre*: the act of causing someone to be *salvus*, causing someone to have *salus*. And as we know, *salus* itself means being all right.

Finally, *salvátio* gets naturalised into English, and so at last we reach 'salvation'.

Looking back on all this, there are two points of ambiguity. The first is because we don't know what sort of all-rightness is meant – where is it located, in the wide range of safety and health? The second is because salvation could be about *keeping* us all right when we are, or *making* us all right when we aren't.

I am inclined not to worry too much about the business of safety versus health, and just to accept that being all right is what is meant. The second ambiguity is resolved by looking back at the broad sweep of history from Eve to the second Eve (Mary) and from Adam to the second Adam (Jesus). The conclusion is inescapable: 'salvation' means to rescue us. It means making us all right because we aren't.

In fact, for those who are amused by words, 'salvation' has an ugly twin. Exactly the same parentage is shared by another word that started its journey through history with *salus*. It is salvage.

There is no way one could rewrite the liturgy to include that word. But just sometimes, when the incense gets too thick and 'salvation' seems too high and noble, give a thought to salvage. There is nothing high and noble about salvage. It smells of oily water in flooded engine rooms. It sounds like 'ullage' and 'sludge'. The occasional touch of salvage will keep us from getting too far above ourselves.

We could even revert to plain English monosyllables that will never float up and away out of sight. Think about the Son coming down from heaven *to put us right*.

The trouble with salvation

Why should 'salvation' even need clarifying? The answer is that when people are uncomfortable with the concept conveyed by a word, failing to understand the word at all is a clever way of soothing the discomfort. The truth behind the story of this particular word is that, at bottom, we just don't like the idea of needing salvation.

Not everyone is as honest about this as my friend who admits to leaving out the 'greatly' from 'I have greatly sinned' at the beginning of Mass. I haven't asked her, but if she were as honest later on as she is at the beginning, she might take refuge in a discreet mumble at *salus* or salvation – because WHAT DO YOU MEAN, I'M NOT ALL RIGHT? What is unusual about my friend is not that she is uncomfortable with the notion of her not-all-right-ness, but that she admits the fact openly.

There are plenty of ways of justifying feeling uncomfortable about 'salvation' and 'not being all right'. For one thing, the few uses of 'salvation' outside church are of the panic-emergency-peril kind: being in battle or in a city under siege, rather than being caught out in the rain without an umbrella. Most of the time, most of our lives have very little in the way of panic and emergency and peril, and this makes the idea of salvation sound so ridiculously disproportionate that it is hard to take it seriously.

There are other kinds of disproportion that also push us away from thinking about salvation. Did God the Son really endure the indignity of becoming incarnate (I might ask) just so as to free me from an embarrassing chocolate habit?

Old-fashioned devotional works used to tackle the question something like this: my sins and vices, individually tiny though they are, are a stickle on a prickle on a twig on a branch of the Crown of Thorns, and are purified (like all such) by the blood of our Saviour who wore it. This answer works, but it demands access to a state of mind most of us have not got any more. It is one of those turns of phrase that can reinforce what you already know; but if you don't already know, it can't teach you.

Finally, the sense of disproportion can be applied not to me but to the whole human race. Look at the world now and compare it to the world in the first century BC. Leaving aside material things like dentists, is AD really much better than BC? Are we any gooder now than we were then?

The existence of such a number of objections reveals the truth. When so many objections to a doctrine or an idea pop up at once from so many different directions, it is a sure sign that they are not what the real trouble is. What is happening is that people are so afraid of the doctrine that they will throw anything at all at it, suitable or unsuitable, just to make it go away.

It is time to put all the individual objections to one side and dig deeper to find the real trouble. The same thing happens in gardening when you chop the top off a weed and new shoots sprout up all around: you have to take out your spade and dig the whole thing up. It happens too in psychiatry, when people are repressing a fear or trauma instead of facing it. All sorts of bad things pop up in the psyche, wearing all sorts of disguises, and it takes skill to discern the underlying cause.

We have trouble with salvation (or being salvaged or put right) because we have trouble with love. The trouble we have with love is twofold. We aren't good enough at loving ourselves; and we aren't good enough at letting ourselves be loved.

The duty of self-love

Self-love is a duty which is recognised in the Commandments. The commandment to love your neighbour as yourself cannot mean anything unless you love yourself in the first place. Moreover, love of self and love of neighbour are cousins. The more you understand one of them, the more you understand the other; and the better you are at one, the better you become at the other.

The stern old books talk about 'self-love' as a bad thing. The reason for this apparent contradiction is that the 'self-love' they are talking about is not really love at all. The easiest way to see this is to start by looking at the analogy in love for others. When you let your children stay up all night or rot their teeth with sweets, you can call it love if you want, but it is not love at all. It is laziness at best; at worst, it is selfishness, sacrificing their health and happiness to build up a picture for yourself of yourself as indulgent and kind. The last thing this so-called love really aims at is the good of the so-called beloved. Indeed, it makes the object of that 'love' just that: an object and not a person. You are treating the child you are spoiling as a WHAT, not a WHO: as something that exists as an accessory to your own wishes and not as a real, living good in its own right. Calling this selfishness 'love' is a lie.

Now, transpose this whole fake love from 'love towards others' to 'love towards self' and you get an exact picture of the 'self-love' the books warn you against. It is not real love at all.

There is another way of getting love wrong apart from the spoilt-child route, and it is the one that matters most here. You could call it 'love *if*'. Self-love contaminated with 'love *if*' is poison, and it is at the root of the trouble people have with salvation.

'I love my love with a B because she is beautiful,' is not love. Neither is, 'I love my love with a C because she is clever.' Beauty and cleverness are delightful things but they are not a person, only an attribute of a person. If I love your beauty, I am not loving *you* – I am merely loving you *if* you are beautiful. If I love your cleverness, I am not loving *you* – I am merely loving you *if* you are clever.

If you insist on expressing sentiments through the letters of the alphabet, the only valid expression of true love is the letter Y: 'I love you with a Y because you are YOU.'

This is not just a theory. The marriage service is built on it and proclaims it in that terrifying series of 'rejections of the attributes'. Loving with a B is banned, loving with a C is banned, 'loving if' is excluded: you take each other 'for richer, for poorer, in sickness and in health'.

Love is not love if it is *if*.

Transposing back from love of others to love of self, if I love myself with an S because I am strong or with an H because I am heroic, that is 'love *if*'. It is not love.

This distinction is one that the stern old books get exactly right. If I have sinned, then to regret and repent the sin so that God can heal me is one thing. To be unhappy at not being able to look up to myself any more is quite another. It is not repentance, only the emotion of a disappointed idolater.

The problem with being loved

We all want to be loved truly, loved for ourselves. That goes without saying: but is it true? Think of my self-respect! If you love me, I want to *deserve* to be loved by you. Yes, I know that deserved love is 'love *if*' and therefore not real love, and yes of course I want real love not fake – but all the same, couldn't I please deserve it too?

> Darling, if you danced like an elderly elephant with arthritis I would dance the sun and moon into the sea with you. I have waited a thousand years to see you dance in that frock.*

. . . but isn't there a tiny bit of her that would have liked to hear, 'Darling, how beautifully you dance'?

I know intellectually that to love truly is to love 'for better, for worse, for richer, for poorer, in sickness and in health'. I

* Dorothy L. Sayers, *Have His Carcase* (1932).

know it intellectually, but intellection is not feeling. My whispering devil tells me that if you insist on loving me for myself alone, that must be because I am too bad, or poor, or sick to be loved for any other reason than just being me. Which is pretty humiliating.

Moving back to salvation: intellectually, I know that God's love is unconditional, but knowing is one thing and feeling is another. I can't help feeling that it really needs to be deserved love: love *if*. In that warped state of mind I have to believe one of two things. Either I believe that God loves me, which means that God has found me worthy to be loved *if*, which means that I don't need salvaging. Or I believe that I do need salvaging, which means that God can't love me *if*, which means that God does not love me at all, which means that I will not be saved.

All this reasoning sounds pretty irrational – and so it should, because it is. The semi-conscious thinking we do when we aren't paying attention often turns out like that. We only half-listen to our shoulder devils. If we listened to them properly, we would know that what they are saying is nonsense. If we turned and looked at them, they would dissolve.

In the end, there is only so much arguing that can be done. The real answer about love is going out there and doing it – practising love of others and practising self-love, each of them reinforcing the other, until at last your picture of God's love for *you* is no longer contaminated by the devil of 'love *if*', and you graciously accept the idea that you need saving.

It can take a lifetime – but then, a lifetime is what we have.

The problem with trust

That brings us to the final problem with salvation and being loved, which is insecurity.

In every human love, you love me today – but will you love me tomorrow, when perhaps I will need your love? Here lies the great advantage of the fake love that comes from looks and money: if I am rich today then I am pretty likely to be rich tomorrow, so if you love me for my riches today, then (fake though that love is) you are pretty likely to love me in the same way tomorrow. It may be fake but at least it won't be going away.

On the other hand, if today you love me truly, in other words, for myself, *what if tomorrow you change your mind?*

God is not that whimsical. God is faithful and eternal and sure. But I am human, and my fears are still there. I anthropomorphise God in ways I shouldn't. That is why I would be much happier if I could tabulate my virtues, add them up and look at my balance at the Bank of Good and Evil and say to myself, 'I deserve God's love.'

Don't get me wrong. I know the theory and I know the principles and I believe in them implicitly. I know that God loves everybody, because God cannot not love. I know that if I am full of sin, and I admit it to myself and throw myself on the ground, defenceless, saying, over and over, 'God, have mercy on me, a sinner' – well, the gospel tells me that God's infinite mercy will be poured out on me.

Trust God, trust in the gospel, and all will be well. But can I trust in my own trust? Yes, I am confident that the gospel is right, but I am confident in it *today*, and what if I lose my confidence tomorrow? Then I will still be a sinner in desperate need of rescue (there is no going back on that, once I have admitted it), but I will no longer be able to believe that rescue can come. I will be the most miserable of men, and there will be no way out. I would have been far better off if I had stayed believing that I deserved love and had no need of salvation. It would have been a lie, but a reassuring one.

The answer is not so much intellectual as practical and spiritual. Perfect love casts out fear. The saints are happy because they know they are sinners. What the rest of us need in order to attain that happiness is love, much more love.

It is all very well to say that we need more love. What is missing is a good way to get more of it. So let me suggest a 'love fitness workout plan'. Bit by bit, day by day, by graduated stages, work on loving more. Remember that loving doesn't mean liking, and you can (you must) love even someone you actively dislike and wholly disapprove of.* Do it badly, because later on you will begin to do it well. The more you love, and the more people you love, the easier the logic of love becomes to understand. Unless you live in a cupboard, you will have plenty of material, and as you get fitter in the field of love, more opportunities will naturally appear. As with anything, from the flute to martial arts, the more you practise, the easier it becomes, until one day you will find that you can even love yourself. And then at last you will be able to trust in God's salvation.

---

* Do not, however, be tempted to try this on public figures. A public figure is not a human being but a fictional character created by publicity, press and media. It bears little relation to the actual person who shares its name.

The parable of the scissors

The Father's thoughts are not our thoughts: we are told this by Isaiah.* The Father's thoughts are not the Son's thoughts either, or not exactly: Jesus tells us this.† We are told to 'love with the mind', and being told to do it means that it can be done; but at the same time there does seem to be a point beyond which our thoughts just cannot go. The Father's logic seems to be above and beyond ours.

This is a hazardous thing to be thinking. Saying, 'What makes sense to God needn't make complete sense to us,' sounds very close to, 'What makes sense to God needn't make sense, full stop.' That second sentence abolishes all possibility of 'loving with the mind'. It makes faith irrational – which makes faith-haters happy and makes pious reason-haters happy too, but should make us very unhappy indeed because it is a lie – and a harmful one.

There are two mistakes one can make about the Father's logic, about 'logic beyond'. One is to think that we can grasp it ourselves and encompass it with our reason, which leads to arid argument that never gets anywhere. The other mistake is to think that 'logic beyond' is so completely inaccessible that it's possible to invent any random nonsense at all and defend it by saying, 'God's thoughts are not our thoughts.'

The true answer is this: the Father's logic is 'fingertip logic'. We cannot grasp it, but we can at least touch it.

My aim here is to show that 'fingertip logic' is not something cleverly invented out of thin air to get us out of an embarrassing situation, but a real thing: a pattern that appears over and over again in human thought. 'Can't grasp but can touch' is a regular way for the human mind to climb beyond itself.

* Isaiah 55:8.
† 'But as for that day and that hour, they are known to nobody, not even to the Son; only the Father knows them' (Mark 13:32).

This story is all about boundaries, because you can think of 'can't grasp, can touch' as being on the exact edge between 'inaccessible to the mind' on one side and 'accessible' on the other. As always, the best place to start is with an analogy from the real world. In this instance, the easiest one is a pair of scissors.

Scissors can go wrong by being too loose, so that they can't cut because the blades don't touch. If you have the kind of scissors that are tightened with a screwdriver, you tighten them; if not, you throw them away and get another pair.

Scissors can also go wrong by being too tight, in which case the blades collide before you can shut them. In this case, too, the scissors are useless.

But there is a boundary between the blades colliding and the blades not meeting at all, between 'colliding' and 'not colliding', and when the scissors are adjusted exactly to that boundary, something completely new happens. The scissors move above and beyond simple questions of collision. *The scissors cut.* The impossible boundary between colliding and not colliding is not a contradiction, but the whole point of having scissors at all.

Let's follow this with a mathematical example, since mathematics is a science and, love it or hate it, a science with authority.

We all know numbers. We count with them. I have two hands and two feet and ten fingers, and one pen in my hand. We count and add and multiply: these numbers are entirely within our grasp. (Mathematicians call them 'the natural numbers'.)

A simple question: if I have eight sheep and I give you three of them, how many sheep do I have left? We both know the answer. I don't have to say it here.

Another simple question: if I have three sheep and I give you eight of them, how many sheep do I have left? The answer this time is that there is no answer: the question is an impossible one. And yet children are taught the answer to this question that has no answer: 'Three minus eight equals minus five.'

The minus numbers are weird things. They are self-evidently impossible, because you can't have a field with minus five sheep in it. At the same time as being impossible, they are possible, because when we do sums with them, those sums work (as anyone with an overdraft will know).

The boundary between 'possible' and 'impossible' has taken us beyond the natural numbers to 'numbers beyond'. We can't grasp those 'numbers beyond' – we can't use them to count sheep – but we can touch them. Touching them, we can make a logic that will deal with them, a 'logic beyond' – it is a fingertip logic, a logic of touching rather than grasping.

'Logic beyond', fingertip logic, comes from boundaries. We have had a physical analogy with the scissors and a mathematical analogy with the sheep, and now it is time to get back to thinking about God.

One boundary that points towards 'the Father's logic' concerns omnipotence and causality. We know God is all-powerful and the cause of the existence of everything, which must make God responsible for everything that ever happens. But, at the same time, God has given his creatures free will, so that it is the creature who decides what that creature does: not God. So is God responsible or not responsible? The boundary between 'responsible' and 'not responsible' points above and beyond itself, towards a logic of the Father that we can touch but not grasp. The 'problem of evil' is one manifestation of this almost-contradiction, but there are many others.

Another boundary is more fundamental than this. God is One: there can be nothing that is not God. And yet the very act of creation is an act of bringing into existence 'something that is not God'. Again this is *almost* a contradiction but not quite, and, again, reflecting deeply on it brings illumination. It is one pointer towards the doctrine of the Trinity.

With experience, the patterns of 'the Father's logic' become easier to recognise. There *are* patterns in it, and gradually one begins to be able to touch them – or almost touch them – or at least touch them with the fingertips. Divine reason is above our reason, but it is never *un*reason: to think, as some people do, that 'illogical' and 'religious' are in any way compatible is simply wrong.

15

He came down from heaven

Descendit de cælis

I can live with being martyred, but I can't bear to be laughed at.

As a weapon against belief, derision is more powerful than either argument or persecution. Persecution makes you a hero, against argument you argue back; but if someone says you are silly there is nothing more to be said.

There is certainly a comic aspect to the stage-setting in this part of the Creed. We can't and mustn't hide from that. The One through whom all things were made bounces up and down through his creation like a child on an escalator in a big shop: 'First floor, ladies' fashions.' Christmas: DOWN. Holy Saturday: further DOWN. Easter Sunday: UP. Ascension: UP again. And there is still the Second Coming to be considered.

Fortunately, our enemies don't stop at ridicule but go on to say that all this is impossible. And they are right: it is. How can the creator of everything find himself *within* his own creation? It would be like me finding myself inside a computer program I have written. It is impossible, so it can't have happened – so our enemies say.

Contradiction is better than ridicule, because at least one can engage with it. So let's do that. Our answer is: it is impossible, and it did happen.

It is necessary to be very, very careful at this point. It is the mark of a cult that its members like to believe impossible things. It is the ultimate way of 'knowing things that other people can't know' and feeling the warm glow of possessing an inner secret incomprehensible to the multitude. There is a pitying superiority that comes from looking down on the common herd who have not received the revelation that two and two make three. This distinction between insiders and outsiders is what keeps a cult in existence.

The relevance and danger of all this is that there are people who want their Christianity to be a cult. They want their beliefs to make no sense because they think that is how they can put their trust fully and completely in their faith. People who behave like this let themselves down, devalue us and, worst of all, they leave people outside the Church hungering helplessly for the sanity that comes from rational belief. Sometimes your friends are your worst enemies.

The parable of the scissors is the way out of this maze. There is a boundary here between the possible and the impossible: between 'God is everywhere' and 'God has visited a specific time and place'. There is a logic behind all this – the Father's logic – which we can touch, but not grasp.

Coming down to here

The 'up and down' doubt with which this chapter started is easily answered. The Creed is not a textbook: it talks in pictures because when we understand, we understand in pictures. We say 'down from the heavens' because, although heaven isn't 'up' in any space–time kind of sense (it isn't anywhere), in our *mental* universe, 'up' is a good place to put it.

Beyond the literal 'up and down' there are two real sources of discomfort. One is this business of God being somewhere inside his own creation. That, as I have said, is a matter of the Father's logic, and touching it with our fingertips is all we can reasonably hope to do.

The other discomfort is this. 'Coming down from heaven' does not only involve being somewhere. It also involves being somewhere in particular. History tells us that this is located at 35° East in longitude, and in the second half of the reign of the Emperor Augustus. The discomfort comes from the very specificity of that place and that time.

Intellectually, this isn't a problem. If God is to come and intervene in the world he created then he has to do it somewhere and at some time. That is logical; but all the same, there is no getting away from the feeling that it is unfair. What about all the people who lived and died before the coming of Christ? What about the patriarchs, or the virtuous pagans, or the pagans who couldn't be virtuous because no one told them how? And the same set of questions can be asked about place as well as time: why did Jesus come as a Jew, and why did he come in the Roman Empire?

Each of these questions can be addressed by the intellect and can open the path to new understanding. Each also has value as a spiritual reflection. After all, the question, 'Why the Jews?' is really just like when God is asking you to do something and you ask him, 'Why me?'

There comes a point when the intellectual answers, even if they are correct, do not satisfy the heart, and yet no other answers present themselves. Then we can only really fall back on saying that God is what God is and God has acted the way God has chosen to act: all our mysteries must point to that central Mystery.

This is uncomfortable and almost humiliating. But it does not just happen in theology. In every science there are moments when one simultaneously thinks, 'This is the truth,' and feels, 'The truth ought not to be like this.' The 'Why like this?', 'Why the Jews?' complaints about salvation have a parallel in the mind of a physicist who penetrates the intricacies of the natural world but cannot believe it is right for the laws of nature to be so complicated. Equally, a mathematician who finds that a theorem expressed in a dozen simple words* needs two hundred pages for its proof ends up with a deep and unanswerable feeling that *things ought not to be like this*.

Perhaps things aren't like this; or perhaps they really are. Perhaps physicists will find simpler theories and mathematicians shorter and more limpid proofs; perhaps in heaven we will be able to understand the Father's logic. But perhaps none of this will happen: as the Son himself has told us, there are things the Father knows that even the Son does not.

---

* For instance, 'Every map can be coloured using no more than four colours.'

16

Was incarnate

Et incarnatus est de Spiritu Sancto

There is no getting away from the meat. In every civilised language, 'carne' means meat. A carni-*vore* eats meat, a carni-*val* is when you say goodbye to meat at the beginning of Lent, and in Latin a carni-*fex* is a butcher. So meat it is. God the Son was in-carn-ated: put into meat.

Everybody has a picture of what religion is. We see it on the screen the whole time, so even the least religious of us know about it. The picture comes to us without any need of study or thought. Religion, 'proper' religion, is calm persons in pale robes, chanting or meditating. Religion, 'proper' religion, is dignified and ethereal. It transcends this muddy world of ours and leads us up and out from its cares and imperfections.

If that is what proper religion is, Christianity is a most improper religion.

You only have to look at the Church's rituals to see this. Far from leading us away from matter into pure celestial realms, the Church revels in matter in all its varieties. Wine, water and oil. Fire, smoke, ash and leaves. Salt, wax, bread. And meat.

The Church is serious about these things – you might even say, obsessive. For example, a priest in a Czech prison camp in the 1980s saved a few raisins from his meagre ration and soaked them in water and kept them warm for days until he could reasonably suppose that some sort of fermentation had taken place, and *only then* was he able to celebrate a furtive Mass. Not for one moment did he think he could do without the wine. He did not say, 'It's all symbolic, after all, and surely God will understand.'

Looking at the list of liturgical substances, they are so fundamental that, in English, every one of them (apart from water) is a one-syllable word. This shows how they all belong to the very bones of language and the foundations of our experience. It is a good exercise to go through the list and identify where each of them appears in the liturgy (I always need to remind myself about salt), but there is one substance you may be puzzled by. Where, you will ask, in Christian ritual is the meat?

Look at yourself in the mirror. The meat is *you*.

The Church is exactly as serious about the meat as she is about all the other substances. Here is an example. Suppose you read, in a guidebook or something, 'At this point in the ceremony the priest sprinkles the feet of selected persons with holy water to symbolise Christ's washing of his disciples' feet.' You would not think twice about it. If you considered it at all, you would say, 'How sensible, and how practical.'

Nevertheless, the Church does not see it like this. In this case, the Church is not sensible at all. Take the grandest cathedral, the most senior cleric, the most magnificent and valuable vestments: all that. None of this makes any difference. The heavy vestments that took so long to put on correctly are laboriously taken off again. The priest or the bishop, however grand, however arthritic, ties a towel round his middle and really does kneel down and wash the feet of each of twelve people. There is enormous symbolism in this meeting of meat with meat: of course there is. But the meeting itself is not allowed to be replaced by a symbol. It has to be real, because *meat matters*.

Or think of something you see more frequently: Holy Communion. An orderly Communion is a beautiful thing to watch. A line of people file out of the pews row by row and queue patiently to receive the Sacrament. To go from the beautiful to the practical, though: people (even orderly people) take up space, and there will be times when there are too many people and the church is too small. At a popular Mass they might end up standing shoulder to shoulder in the porch (I have done that) or outside listening to a loudspeaker (I have done that too).

Now the Church is usually a practical institution and you would therefore expect to find, for times when the flock is too big to feed in any dignified or practical way, some suitable substitute. There will be some specially solemn and efficacious blessing laid down in the rubrics to save a sacred occasion from degenerating into an undignified scrum. After all, you will say, it is the grace that counts, not the calorific value of a morsel of bread.

You might reasonably expect such an adapted ritual, but you would be disappointed. There is no substitute. We have to squeeze ourselves past hot sweaty strangers to be fed bread *literally*, because nothing else will do. Bread is the body of Christ, and our bodies are meat. Bread must meet meat, because both are matter, and matter really matters.

This liturgical obsession with matter is not a whim or accident. It is a direct reflection of Christian theology.

Rising above mere matter

Let's leave Christianity to one side for a while and look at the religious evolution of mankind on a grand scale, from prehistory onwards: a steady upward climb towards enlightenment.

In the beginning, we all simply wanted to stay alive. We wanted to eat and not be eaten. We wanted the crops to flourish and game to be abundant. To this period belong the mechanistic religions of the Americas, in which just as watering the ground makes the seeds grow, so spilling human blood makes the sun shine and the cosmos keep going. Other religions reckon that the world is controlled not by laws of nature but by beings more powerful than ourselves. They aim to placate them or persuade them by gifts: I'll scratch your back and you'll scratch mine. Some of this sense persists in the Old Testament. The special relationship the Jews have with God leaves room for some respectful blackmail, as when the Jews look up to the LORD and tell him, 'Back us, or everyone will say what a loser you are.'*

Once the question of how to stay alive has been addressed, human beings turn to wondering what life is. This isn't mere airy curiosity, because the meaning of life will surely tell us something about how life ought to be lived.

---

* For example, 'Look kindly on our faults, for the sake of your name. Why should the gentiles ask, "Where is their God?"' (Ps. 78(79):9-10).

When we look at life, the first thing we notice is that we seem to be under two influences. On the one hand, we are the plaything of powerful, irrational, animal urges. On the other hand, we possess a certain amount of reason, serenity and detachment. Plato has a picture in the *Phaedrus* of the soul as a chariot drawn by two winged horses, one immortal and the other mortal, the one striving calmly upwards and the other rampaging, uncontrolled.*

You could say that these two halves of us are the stormy waves and the deep unmoved ocean beneath, or that they are the sphere of earth (the region of change, decay and imperfection) as opposed to the heavens above (pure, clean, clear and, above all, rational). Whichever way you look at it, there are two sides to us: body and spirit, meat and mind, lower and higher.

Remembering our culture's picture of what 'proper' religion is, the choice seems obvious: higher, rather than lower; up, rather than down. Accordingly, one ought to rise to be ruled by spirit, not matter; reason, not impulse; by mind: by the high, not by the low. So if you believe in spirit being superior to matter, you seek ways of putting 'mind over matter'. You can go further and believe in spirit being good and matter being bad, or further still and deny that matter has any real existence at all – or even deny the reality of existence itself.

Our own lives are shaped by what we believe; but the life of the human race is shaped by it too. Man is made in God's image, and the image we have of God defines the image we have of man.

Dualistic religions, in which matter is bad and spirit is good, divide the human race into two as well. There are the elect, who possess secret knowledge and live the pure spiritual life, and the common herd who do not possess it and do not live it (but who work to feed and clothe the elect in this unspiritual world). Furthermore, since matter is bad, that means organic life is bad, and the elect of such religions frequently follow remarkable diets to avoid ingesting life into themselves and strange sexual practices to ensure that no more organic life is let loose on the world.

* Plato, *Phaedrus*, 246a–254e.

Hinduism shows what happens if matter is not evil but just an unfortunate mistake. There is not much to choose between living in one mistake and living in another, so reincarnation is commonplace, and the search for liberation from the mistake may take many lives. Consequently, in contrast to the desperate one-life urgency of the religions of Abraham, nothing that happens to anybody in any particular life matters very much.

Finally, in Buddhism, the flesh is left out altogether. Matter doesn't really exist, so the religion has nothing to say to it. Strictly speaking, *other people* don't exist either, since existence itself is an illusion. Sei Shōnagon, a court lady in tenth-century Japan, the highest of high civilisations at a time when we in the Christian West were all rain and mud, went for a walk one day and saw a poor lady who had fallen out of favour at court, starving to death in a hut. Shōnagon went home and did what had to be done: she composed an elegant poem on the mutability of fortune.*

This is not heartlessness in the face of human suffering. It is the logical outcome when matter and life are both illusions.

Looking back on this grand ascent: we started as material beings looking for some understanding of our existence. Spirit took us and led us upwards, raising us from our lower to our higher selves, shifting the balance of power away from matter and towards the spiritual plane. Spirit never stopped. It went on and on, upwards and out of sight, until matter was gone and spirit became the only truth. We climbed the mountain of enlightenment so high that there was no air left to breathe. Matter was left behind for ever.

How matter matters

The story of the ascent of the spirit into enlightenment is all very well, apart from one awkward fact. Whatever anyone may say, we are not pure spirit. We *are* made of matter. We *are* made of meat, and a religion that disappears off to the sky and refuses to talk to meat and matter is of no use to us. The thing is, once it has soared

---

* See Ivan Morris (trans.), *The Pillow-Book of Sei Shōnagon* (1967).

out of sight, we don't just stand around helplessly looking up after it. We jump back three millennia and return to our old superstitions. We go to magicians and soothsayers once more, except that now we call them therapists and practitioners. We no longer tear the hearts out of prisoners to keep the sun shining but we do smash light bulbs to keep the weather from changing. We identify people as unclean by reason of their caste or their way of life, and persecute them accordingly. In fact, we are exactly back where we started: down off the mountaintop of enlightenment and back in the bog.

Christianity is not immune to fashion and the winds of contemporary culture. It can't be, because it is made of us and we are human. But behind all these detours, Christianity has something that anchors it safely and for ever. It has a God who voluntarily came down from heaven *and united himself to meat*.

For Christians, it is impossible for matter to be evil or a mistake or an illusion. Not only did God intentionally create it and make it real and see that it was 'good, good, good, good, and very good', he also chose to inhabit it. As Christians, we are free to invoke the spiritual life to moderate the turbulence of the meaty life (more than just free – it is something we need to do), but we are never allowed to take that too far. We can't float serenely above the material world, never touching it, because that is not what God himself did. On the contrary, God plunged into it, made himself part of it and lived in it all the way through to the very end. His very first miracle was making wine. Whenever we seem to be about to get over-spiritualised, the fact of *what God did* rescues us and reminds us of our meaty nature. And so do the bread, the wine, the salt, the ashes and the oil.

God the Son became in-meated partly because we needed to be reminded of this, but even more because there is no other way to become human. There are obvious difficulties to *being* both body and spirit (what happens when we die and the body rots?), and a religion of spirits-imprisoned-in-bodies wouldn't have those difficulties: but such a religion would not be true, and the Incarnation reminds us of that. As for the difficulties of dying, the Creed will deal with those later on.

17

Of the Virgin Mary

Exactly two ordinary people are named in the Creed. They are the Virgin Mary and Pontius Pilate. It has to be this way because these are the people responsible for the two key events of the Redemption: the birth and the death of Jesus.

The Creed here is summarising exactly what the angel Gabriel said to Mary: 'The Holy Spirit will come over you, and the power of the Most High will cover you.'* This is just as it should be: there is nothing that needs to be added. Mary and Joseph's 'Yes' to the angel is the pivot on which salvation history turns. Indeed, the start of the year in England used to be on 25 March, not on 1 January, precisely to honour the Annunciation, the moment of the Incarnation and the salvation of mankind.†

Even when they were still believing in gods and not yet in God, people were aware of God's greatness and man's insignificance, of divine power and human weakness. Greek mythology tells the story of Semele, loved by the god Zeus in human form. Zeus's wife Hera persuaded Semele to make her lover show himself to her as he truly was. So she made him swear by the river Styx (an oath no god can break) to do whatever she asked, and then asked him to show himself in all his

---

* Luke 1:35.

† This is confusing for historians who do not expect January 1642 to be the month after December 1642. The first day of the year in England was changed from 25 March to 1 January by the Calendar (New Style) Act 1750. (That Act also introduced a system of leap years identical to the Gregorian Calendar instituted in 1584, without actually mentioning Pope Gregory VII, who instituted it.)

divine glory. He wept, but could not disobey, and Semele was a pile of ashes.*

Outside mythology, Moses also asked to see God as he truly was, but the loving LORD told him that no one could see his face and live: he covered Moses' face with his hand, and only let him see his back after he had passed by.†

Divine power and human weakness are the natural way of things, but salvation history stands it all on its head. The story is not about divine power and human weakness but about divine weakness and human power. (You might say that the theme is there in some form from the moment of creation, because the very act of giving free will to created beings means that they and not the creator are in charge.)

Since it is so upside down, this 'divine weakness and human power' is a fragile state of affairs. It is fascinating to see the efforts God is always making not to overturn it. The story of Dives and Lazarus is one example.‡ The rich man, in torment, begs Abraham that if he himself can't be saved, at least Lazarus should be sent to warn his five brothers of their peril before it is too late. Abraham says no, because they already have Moses and the Prophets to instruct them. Proclaimed from a pulpit, this can sound like the voice of a stern teacher saying, 'If you didn't pay attention and do your homework then you must take the consequences.' But it isn't that at all. It is simply that God knows that to be human is to be free, and that to overwhelm freedom (even from the best of motives) is to abolish humanity. It is the old love-potion paradox, repeated in another key.

When God *does* choose to intervene in human affairs, he uses the gentlest means possible: God is not in the whirlwind; he is in the still, small voice. The Annunciation is the greatest example of this. Yes, God is the same God who locks the sea behind closed doors; who is the master of lightning, wind and hail; the maker and master of Behemoth and Leviathan (the sea monster he made

---

* One version of this myth is told in Ovid, *Metamorphoses* III 273–309.
† Exodus 33:18–23.
‡ Luke 16:19–31.

just so that he could play with him) – but when it comes to the fate of the whole universe and the entire human race, the most important moment since the Creation, the God of power and might puts it all into the hands of a powerless young woman. He commands nothing. He simply asks her, 'Will you do it?'

Could she have said No?

Some people find this question shocking. How could the Blessed Virgin Mary, mother of God, Queen of the angels, and all the other titles we give her, have brought the entire course of salvation to a halt, just with one word? Surely a properly pious mind should revolt at the very thought. But if you think about it clearly, that is how it had to be. For consider: either 'Be it done to me according to your word' is a real statement and a real act, or it is not. If it is not, it is not just nothing but worse than nothing: a charade and a fake.

There is a basic and brutal philosophical fact about all human acts: if you couldn't *not* do it, then you didn't do it. If (as a neighbour of mine once did) you drive your car across a busy road and through the iron railings separating the lanes, demolish a garden wall and end up inside the front room of a house, which then needs to be propped up with scaffolding to keep it from falling down – and you do all this because you are having a heart attack and your body, in spasm, is pressing hard on the accelerator – you escape prosecution. That is a humane fact about the law, but it is the reason for it that is important. You escape not because people with heart attacks are allowed to do things like this, but *because you did not do it*.

Aristotle worked all this out in detail, and this means something to us because intellectually we are still Greeks ourselves. Aristotle in the *Ethics* teaches that the only acts with moral content are the free ones: the ones that could have gone the other way. If my foot kicks my doctor in the face when he is testing my knee reflexes with a hammer, it's all right, not because he deserves it ('He hit me, so I hit him back'), but because I didn't do it.

This means that if you go all pious and decide to believe that it was impossible for Mary to say No to the angel Gabriel, *then you also believe that she didn't say Yes.* If it was truly impossible for her to say No, she didn't *say* Yes: the sound that came out of her mouth sounded like 'Yes', but it was just like the sound a doll makes when you pull a string and it says 'Mama'. In technical vocabulary, it was a sound, but not a speech act. And if what you believe is really what happened, the hinge of the whole of salvation history is nothing but a fake.

But God did not fake the Annunciation. The Annunciation was reality, not theatre, because God is good and God does not lie. We have to conclude that Mary had a free choice between Yes and No, and that she freely chose to say Yes.

Settling the question of Mary's free choice opens up new questions, to be considered in all seriousness and all reverence: how was Mary able to make a decision of that magnitude? And what would have happened if she had said No?

What if she had said No?

Could the angel Gabriel have nagged or bullied Mary into accepting? No, because compulsion is not God's way.

Could Gabriel have radioed back to base, 'Sorry, boss, number 23 didn't bite. On my way to ask number 24'? No, because that would have meant that Mary's answer had never been going to make any difference, so that even asking her the question would have been a charade. For Mary's consent to the Incarnation to make sense, Mary had to have not only full freedom but also full power. Her response had to make a difference.

Some people try to have it both ways. They maintain that (a) Mary's No would have meant No but also that (b) God's infinite love for the world means that it would still have been saved by some other wonderful act of love. I appreciate the beauty of that sentiment, and it is indeed true that there are no limits to God's love. This idea comes close to denying that Mary's choice had any effect, but I think it stops just short of it. On the other hand, beautiful though it is, it brings in a complete invention of which we have no knowledge whatever (what would that 'other wonderful act of love' have been?) and it pushes aside the appalling definitiveness of every human act of love, even the smallest. So it is not really helpful.

Every time I do anything, however tiny, it means that I *do not* do something else: that is fundamental. And actions have consequences. All of them do. As I sit and write this, two potential universes are jostling each other in the hope that I will condescend to give reality to one of them rather than the other. One universe is the one in which I go out in a minute and have a cup of coffee. The other is the universe in which I don't. The fate of trillions of atoms hangs on my decision. When I make that decision, one of these would-be universes will receive the transcendent and incomprehensible gift of existence. It will never lose it. The other will never come to be, and all the glories it might have contained will never exist – it will be just as non-existent as the universe in which God said on the sixth day, 'Let us make unicorns,' or the universe in which the Virgin Mary said No to Gabriel.

'What if?' never works with God. We do not know what would have happened if Mary had said No, but because she said Yes, we don't need to: there is nothing to know about that other universe which might have come into being at that moment but never did. Even the Father knows nothing about it.

The first miracle of all

The other big question about the Annunciation is usually forgotten, which is a pity because it is rather more interesting for us as we live our lives.

Mary had to be aware of the nature of the decision she was taking – of what the question meant and what her answer would mean – or her Yes would have been nothing but passive acquiescence ('God asks, so I'll do it') or the toss of a mental coin. On the other hand, if she had been fully aware of her responsibility for the future history of billions of human beings for evermore, she would surely have been crushed by that knowledge and could not have made a decision. The size of the decision had to be moderated without altering its nature; or else Mary's power to decide had to be strengthened (without biasing it) so that the fate of the human race could be truly and freely decided. Whichever way round it was, that was the miracle.

You know how hard it is to rescue a spider from the bath without squashing it, and you are only ten million times bigger than the spider. Multiply that ten million by infinity, and you will see how much of a miracle was needed at the Annunciation.

Oddly enough, some people will find this story familiar if they think about it, because this is a kind of miracle that does still happen, though not to everyone and perhaps not (except to saints) more than once or twice in a lifetime. The characteristic vice of our age is the vice of prudence, an endless 'What if?' We have mortgages, career plans, responsibilities of all kinds, so that we cannot live for today like the lilies of the field.

Anxiety about the consequences so often stops us from doing something, or even from doing anything at all. And yet – just sometimes – all this is held at bay by God. A question is posed, 'This is huge: will you do it or not?', and one finds oneself stood on a high mountain ridge separating two different futures. God intervenes: not to swing the decision one way or the other or hide the view, but to preserve one from vertigo. Take care not to give too literal a sense to the word, but God makes the whole question *uninteresting*, so uninteresting that we are able to cope with it. This is a way for God to turn 'divine power and human weakness' into 'divine weakness and human power' for just a moment – the Infinite giving power to the Finite.

I said it doesn't happen often, nor to everyone, but perhaps I am wrong. It is hard to tell because it isn't something people talk to each other about. In any case, Mary's being able to answer Gabriel at all is the first miracle of the Annunciation.

'Could' and 'could'

There is one final thing to be said about 'Could she have said No?', and it is this. There are two meanings of 'could'. When we looked at God's omnipotence we saw that there are things that God can't do because they are impossible, like making four-sided triangles, and there are things that God can't do because he could not do them without being false to his own nature. Think of something like persecuting the innocent and promoting the wicked. You might say that God can't do these things *and still be God*.

I am like God. I have the power to do things which, if I did them, would make me not be me. Sometimes it is the recognition of this fact that stops me doing them. Lying would make me a liar, stealing would make me a thief, and that (not the fear of detection or punishment) is what stops me doing these things. On the other hand, I do not always obey this law of my own being. That is what being a sinner means. There are things that I can't do *and still be me*, but nevertheless I do sometimes do them. Then the way to wholeness is for me to be made *me* again by my Maker, in Absolution.

The fall of Eve and Adam was their taking on power before they were ready to distinguish between 'have the power to do this' and 'can do this and still be me'. The Virgin Mary alone was conceived without that original fall. So the answer to the 'Could she have said No?' question may be that on the one hand she had the power to say No, which makes her decision a true decision, but that (knowing what she knew) she could not say No without un-Marying herself. Which, not being fallen, she would not do.

Perhaps this is what the Immaculate Conception was for.

The trouble with virginity

Virginity is an embarrassment. Anything to do with sex is embarrassing because there is too much reality in it, but this applies especially to virginity. Virginity is an embarrassment partly because of the way things are today, and partly because we don't understand what it is.

In our 'in church' mode, we despise the world for its distorted values where the body is concerned. In our 'outside church' mode, we often accept them. Where sex is concerned, that means believing, deep down, that sexual activity is the right *and the duty* of every human being. It follows that virginity is an unnatural state which needs an excuse: extreme youth, or ugliness, or psychological abnormality. If you are a virgin and don't want to be one, we pity your misfortune. If you are a virgin and say that is what you want to be, you are mistaken and we pity your delusion. All in all, a virgin is either a loser or a freak. As you might imagine, this is not a terribly good basis for contemplating the Virgin Mary.

The root of our confusion about virginity is our own misunderstanding of what virginity is, of what chastity is: indeed, of the role of the body in the wholeness of the person.

The forgotten fact at the bottom of it all is this: *Christians do not have bodies.* A body isn't something I *have.* I don't have a body; I *am* a body. I don't have a soul; I *am* a soul. I am both: at once and together and inseparably.

Chastity is misunderstood and misrepresented as being a matter of *not* doing something. It isn't: it is something positive in its own right. It is an assertion of the wholeness of self, of body and soul as one. It is unchastity that is not doing something, because unchastity consists in *not* being whole but demoting the body so that it is not *me* any more but only an object, a thing I possess and do what I like with without affecting *me*.

If you do mistakenly think of chastity as a 'not doing', with no particular rationale except for, 'You mustn't,' you may be able to avoid losing a battle tomorrow but you will probably lose the war. It is like refraining from stealing because there is a commandment against it, as opposed to living the love of neighbour so fully that stealing from him becomes impossible. It is like (if you are a Jew) abstaining from pork merely because it is forbidden, as opposed to abstaining from it out of love for the Lawgiver and his laws.

When I dedicate the whole of my being, in chastity, to another person, it is called monogamy. It is a living and positive thing: it leads to self-fulfilment, not self-frustration. Virginity is simply the name we give to chastity when I offer the undivided wholeness of my being not to another person but to God. The honour of virginity is not the abstention from bodily acts but the glory of being whole combined with the generosity of offering that wholeness. This is the reason why the imagery of marriage is also the imagery of religious vows, and the reason why the ceremony of taking those vows is so often accompanied by readings from that dazzling oriental love poem, the Song of Songs.

The trouble with miracles

The first chapter of the First Book of the Maccabees draws a picture of some Jews who have found the right formula for life in a multicultural society. They build themselves a gymnasium 'just like the Greeks'. They disguise their circumcision to avoid upsetting people. They don't ask indiscreet questions about where the meat they are eating has come from, in case it came from a pagan sacrifice.

It is possible for a Christian to be a direct spiritual heir of those sensible Jews. It is even quite attractive. You might call such a person a 'compatible Christian'. Compatible Christians live in a multicultural society – which is to say, one whose culture consists in not having a culture. They arrange their lives 'just like the Greeks', and they disguise their baptism to avoid upsetting people – or even, since they have internalised the multicultural values, to avoid upsetting themselves.

I think most of us doze ourselves into compatibility now and again. It is so comfortable to be compatible, and so safe.

Here is how 'compatible Christianity' deals with miracles. Everyone agrees that miracles can't happen, so I don't believe in them either. This might be tricky for me, because Christians do believe in them, but the 'I/we' distinction comes to my rescue. I can still confidently say that 'we believe in miracles', meaning that 'we Christians' believe in them, without having to believe in them myself. 'We believe' is not a statement of belief, only a mark of identity.

This all works rather well until someone takes the Bible and points to a page and asks me, 'Do you believe in this miracle or do you not?'

I can handle the Old Testament all right. It all happened in the olden days, after all, so probably most of the reports are wrong. People weren't as clever then as we are now and they didn't know as well as we do what is possible and what isn't. Besides, over the centuries, word of mouth can so easily amplify the simplest occurrence until it becomes a full-blown miracle. The flooding of the Black Sea by the Mediterranean in about 5500 BC gets handed down through the generations until it gets written down as Noah's Flood. Basically, the nice thing about the Old Testament where miracles are concerned is that it is all far away and a bit mythical, and no one will expect me to have opinions about a myth.

The New Testament is trickier because its writers intended it to be history and not myth. After making due allowance for human fallibility, it ought to show us more or less what a camera would show if we could send one back in a time machine. Fortunately for 'compatibility', most of the New Testament miracles are healing ones – the blind see, the lame walk, the mad become sane. Healing miracles happen inside people, not outside where we can all see laws being broken, and with a bit of handwaving we can write them off as psychosomatic one way or another. As for the other miracles – Lazarus could have been in a deep coma all along; the five thousand could have started as quite a small crowd and got more numerous in the telling . . . and so on.

Two really awkward miracles resist these comfortable compromises. They are the Virgin Birth and the Resurrection, and, awkwardly for 'compatibility', both of them occur in the Creed and neither of them can easily be explained away. Of course, people have tried – particularly biblical scholars, for whom explaining away is something of an occupational hazard.

With the Incarnation and the Resurrection we come up hard against the limits of compatibility. There is no way out. If I say I believe in God's power, then I have to believe in it. If I do not, then I shouldn't be wasting my time standing up in church on a Sunday, lying about what I believe.

As far as the actual *possibility* of the Virgin Birth is concerned, yes, God is omnipotent so God could have done it – that is the brutal truth and there is no getting away from it. It seems peculiar, in any case, for me to permit God to send signals down the synapses of a blind man so that he sees or a paralytic so that he walks, or to cure one woman of a years-long haemorrhage, and yet *not* to permit him to intervene in another person's body in a slightly different way. Both are interventions in the physical order of things, so either both kinds of miracles are possible and believable or neither is.

There is another, more refreshing way of looking at the miracle of the Incarnation. We know that God doesn't perform senseless miracles, so let's look at how the miracle of divine intervention makes sense in the conception and birth of Jesus.

How God works

This is the kind of theology I don't find myself doing for myself, but I do admire the result when it is done. It is an appreciation of the internal resonance of salvation history taken as drama, 'theo-drama' in Balthasar's phrase.

There is a definite pattern to God's interventions in salvation history. They have so often come through women, and often in the birth of extraordinary men.

Isaac is born, through God's power, of Sarah long after she is past the age of childbearing. Rachel, the infertile, gives birth to Joseph, and Hannah gives birth to Samuel, who is consecrated to God before his birth. In the New Testament, the pattern is repeated: the infertile Elizabeth gives birth to the greatest of the men of God: John.

Following God's established pattern, he intervenes not with overwhelming power but in the tiniest way possible, at the moment when, through the wonderful moment of conception (the passage from non-life to life), the smallest act can have the greatest effect.

Into this pattern the birth of Jesus, to a woman who is even more unable to have children than Sarah, Rachel, Hannah or Elizabeth because she has never even slept with a man, fits beautifully. Given that miracles can happen at all, the beauty of this one shows how right and true it is. And in Mary's fertility, Israel itself, which has been sterile for four or five hundred years after the last of the prophets fell silent, conceives and bears the greatest fruit of all.

The power of the Spirit

A whole section of the Creed is going to be dedicated to the Holy Spirit, so the mention of the Spirit here is a kind of advance appearance. Its immediate function is to exclude definitively the idea of 'Joseph as father of Jesus', which is one of the ways of evading the truth of Jesus as God *as well as* man. But it does good work in other ways as well. For one thing, it is appropriate. The Holy Spirit is the life-giver, so at the Incarnation the Spirit is the right divine Person to be the giver of organic life.

There is another reason why it is good to be reminded of the role of the Spirit as the agent in the incarnation of God the Son. It helps with our understanding of the Spirit. The Spirit is the fully non-human Person of the Trinity and so tends to fade into odd corners when we are being anthropomorphic about God (which we usually are). It is easy to fall into the trap of the Spirit as a 'junior member' of the Trinity if the main thing we remember about the Spirit (apart from doves and flames) is old arguments over whether the Spirit proceeds from the Father and the Son or from the Father only.

Scripture already offers protection against falling into that trap: it helps, for instance, to remember that in the second verse of the entire Bible the Spirit is mentioned, by name, floating over the waters at the start of the Creation. Now the Creed offers another protection. If you think of the Spirit as being junior, proceeding from the Son as well as the Father, then you will have to think of the Son as more junior still, becoming incarnate by the power of the Spirit. And that adds up to a contradiction.

The relationship between the members of the Trinity is one of equals, and making it into a hierarchy just does not work.

18

And became man

Et homo factus est

'Which is more important, Christmas or Easter?'

This is the kind of question that annoying people ask. They want to show you they are cleverer than anyone else: but it is easy to see through them. The obvious answer is Christmas, so you can instantly deduce that they want to tell you that the right answer is Easter.

Christmas is certainly obvious. At Christmas we visit our friends, have parties and give each other presents. At Easter all we do is wonder why we have a four-day weekend at a time when the weather isn't good enough to enjoy it yet. The ordinary people vote for Christmas, so the enlightened answer must be that Easter is the most important feast. That, at least, is what the annoying people are trying to say.

Yet we have the best possible evidence on the side of Christmas: the liturgy and the Creed. Regularly in church, everyone stands up and recites the summary of our faith. Once and once only during this recitation, we bow (or even kneel) as a mark of respect for the greatness of the event we are naming. When is it? Not the death of Jesus, but his birth. Not the Crucifixion, but the Incarnation. Not Easter, but Christmas.

Practice is wiser than high-minded theory, and the liturgy has got it exactly right.

Yes, of course it is true that Jesus died for us, and yes, of course it is true that death is a big thing for us human beings, so having someone die for us adds up to a very big thing indeed. But still death, although big, is not unusual. It happens to everyone.*

---

* 'It is given to most of us to die at one time or another in our lives.' Alan Bennett, *Forty Years On* (1969).

On the other hand, that the Infinite Power that made the galaxies should be shut up in a human body – *that* is unique. If we didn't have reliable evidence for it, it would be incredible. It still is: look how many people refuse to believe in it. Its generosity transforms the cosmos. It turns the universe from a collection of atoms just like any other collection of atoms into the marvellous 'kind of place where such a thing could happen'. That is why, when we meet the aliens, we will rush to tell them what God has done here on earth: it changes everything everywhere, not just here.

The Annunciation may have turned the power-relationship between infinite Creator and finite creature upside down, but the Incarnation completely smashes it: the Creator *becomes* a creature.

There are so many hidden miracles involved. Mary, by rights, ought to have been reduced to ashes, like Semele, by the presence of God, and it was a miracle that she was not. How much more, then, should the body of Jesus have been vaporised at the very first instant that God came to dwell in it. For how can finite and infinite co-exist in the same body?

The Transfiguration is a glimpse of what must really have been going on the whole time. The miracle was not that the Transfiguration happened when it did but that there was ever any moment in the life of Jesus when it wasn't happening.

For these reasons it is not at all surprising to find that many people, at many times, have considered the Incarnation to be well worth disbelieving. They have thought it an impossibility, or a contradiction, or – coming back again to that abiding sense that so many people have of the dignity of deity – it is Just Not Right: if God does this, God is truly well out of order.

And so they need to get round the unacceptable doctrine that makes us bow in church every Sunday. There are two ways of getting round the scandal of God becoming man. One is to say that Jesus is God, not man, and the other is to say that Jesus is man, not God.

This is literally what 'heresy' means: αἵρεσις, 'hairesis', a picking and choosing. Each of the two ways out is a heresy because each one picks and chooses, holding on to one half of the whole truth – which is that Jesus is *both* God *and* man.

The trouble with heresy – with picking and choosing – is that the consequence is an unbalanced faith, and building on an unbalanced foundation will sooner or later lead to disaster.

Jesus as God only

Let's make Jesus a purely heavenly being, either God himself or a spirit sent from God, something like the Angel Raphael who went for a walk with Tobias in the Book of Tobit.* We then avoid the God-plus-man embarrassment, and this is why many people through history have tried taking this view.

Unfortunately, this sets off another problem, and a worse one.

Raphael is a good parallel. In the book of Tobit, Raphael has no biography. He pops into the story from nowhere when he is needed and pops out again when his job is done. He pops in as a young man and pops out as the same young man. He was never younger in the story, never born, and so when we find out that he has been an angel all along, one of the seven angels who stand in the presence of the glory of God, we don't feel in the least bit cheated. We don't expect eternal spiritual beings to have life stories like us.

The Gospels are a different kind of literature altogether. In them, Jesus has a complete human life. He is conceived and is born, is a baby and then a boy and then a man, and finally he suffers and he dies. He does all the things that Raphael does not.

If Jesus is nothing but God or an emanation from God or a messenger from God, then this entire human biography is not true. God (or God's phantom) has gone far beyond the job of enlightening us and progressed well into the realm of deceit. The babyhood is all a pretence, the childhood is a pretence, and everything else is a pretence too, all the way through the 'life history' of something that is not really human but has been made to look human: of a fake. So, in the end, the Gospels are a record not of real life but of a pantomime. A God who lies to us like this is not a God we can trust.

* Tobit 5–12.

There is another consequence too, which goes beyond the truthfulness and trustworthiness of our God. If Jesus is just God pretending to be a man, or a non-human spirit sent to enlighten us, then *no man has ever risen from the dead*. Where, then, is our own hope of resurrection?

Jesus as man only

So let's lean the other way instead, and escape from the distasteful 'both God and man' by saying that Jesus is not really God, only a man: a good man, naturally, but just a man like other men, and because he was good, they killed him.

The trouble this time is that 'Jesus is only a man' runs up against what the Gospels tell us. It means that when he told us he was God he was either mad or lying. It was a pretty silly kind of a lie, because it got him killed.

Or, alternatively, the evangelists and Apostles were lying to puff up their master's importance, and that was a pretty silly thing to do too, because it mostly got them killed as well.

'Jesus was a good man' is the line that modern pagans like to take when they want to feel tolerant. They don't exactly deny Jesus, only the fact about him that makes him who he is. As 'compatible Christians', it is very tempting for us to do the same. Both sides can then sing together, in bogus harmony. The pagans feel tolerant and we feel grateful to be tolerated. Nobody rocks the boat.

But some boats need rocking, and the event we are talking about rocked the universe. It is important not to slide into denying that Jesus is God, because that really does contradict the historical evidence.

Unfortunately, that last sentence needs to be qualified. For some people, contradicting the historical evidence is their profession. There are human motives for this. It is human nature to love knowing things that other people don't know: that the Bible is a secret code, that ancient gods were really ancient astronauts, why Elvis killed President Kennedy and how the moon landings were faked. It appeals to the gnosticism in all of us – the love of secret inner knowledge. Books that tell you 'what nobody else knows' sell in their millions. So when anybody stands up and says that the Gospels are untrue, or are fakes, or that the evangelists had a secret agenda, or that they didn't understand what their own words meant (poor fellows, they were only ignorant foreigners, after all), he does not get killed the way most of the Apostles did. He receives fame, television appearances, professorships and money.

The best thing to do about this is to ignore it all and read the Gospels without distraction, as if they were written by people who knew what they were saying and wanted to say it.

But if you do get distracted, C. S. Lewis provides an effective antidote. A professor of English literature himself, he maintained that if you think that the Gospels are a literary construct then you should judge them as literature. If you do this with the Gospels, he says, you end up with a clear choice. Either you believe in a sincere narrative written in mostly not very good Greek, by people who aren't writers but can't let that fact stop them writing because what they had to say *had to be said* and only they can say it. Or you believe that 'some unknown writer in the second century . . . suddenly anticipated the whole technique of modern, novelistic, realistic narrative'* – which is clearly incredible.

My own favourite argument for the authenticity of the Gospels is the way they contradict one another. Contradiction is exactly what you would expect when people are really doing their best to report their experiences rather than artfully design-ing a foundation document for a new religion. If you live in a family, or you have anyone you share a past with, you will know exactly what I mean. Part of being together is regularly bringing the past back to life by telling one another stories about it. When you do this, you are just as regularly surprised at how quickly people's memories diverge. For instance, I may be sure that one thing happened before the other, while you are equally sure that it was the other way round. Only one of us can be right, but neither of us is lying.

---

* C. S. Lewis, 'Modern Theology and Biblical Criticism', collected in *Christian Reflections*.

If we ever got round to writing a Gospel of Us, we wouldn't hold committee meetings to vote on what must have happened: we would each of us, humbly, have to tell our own story, and never mind the contradictions.

Jesus as God and man

Let us accept the challenge of what the Gospels and the Creed tell us about Jesus instead of dodging it. Let's believe it, and try to understand it.

Yes, it is outrageous that the same person should be God and man at once. It challenges our ideas about what it is to be human and what it is to be God. It gives both anthropology (the study of man) and theology (the study of being) tricky new data to handle, but that is what sciences are for: to receive new data and understand them.

Anthropology and theology sound like specialised subjects, but they aren't. Every one of us practises them the whole time. Any human being, in order to function at all, has to have an implicit anthropological theory, a theory of other people. Babies don't have one, and acquiring a 'theory of people' is recognised as an important stage in child development. Every human being, to function at all, has to have an implicit theological theory, a theory of Being and of our own relation to it – at the very least, some sort of sense of what an answer to 'What am I?' might be.

These theories grow out of what we know, what we experience, and what the Gospels tell us. Contemplating the fact that Jesus Christ is true God and true man is a refreshing way of getting our own ideas sorted out and disentangled. Here are some examples.

He was made baby

> *The cattle are lowing, the baby awakes*
> *But little Lord Jesus, no crying he makes.*

Christmas carols paint beautiful pictures but they are not intended to be theological treatises. Some carols do alert us to great truths, but 'Away in a Manger' is not one of them. Quite innocently, it sneaks in a little bit of sentimental heresy.

It shouldn't spoil our enjoyment of this carol to remember that Jesus is 'like us in *all things* except sin'. It would be lovely to have an unbothersome baby and get some sleep at night – but whether you are a calm, laid-back baby or a fussy, fractious one is purely a matter of temperament, not sin.*

Jesus is like us in all things except sin, and that means that in all things except sin, Jesus was like us. When we have food poisoning, or a rotten cold, or spots, and we grumble to him about it, he knows exactly what we are talking about because he has been through them himself. God the Son did not become man and then avoid the undignified aspects of being an animal. That would have been cheating: if he had done that, he would only have been pretending to be one of us.

He was made boy

The thing that Jesus was, when he was a child, was – a child. Nothing more, because anything else would have been a fake. When he was twelve, he was a twelve-year-old child. Being a twelve-year-old child is not a sin, and being God does not mean avoiding being twelve.

People who ignore the childishness of childhood and read the story of the Finding in the Temple end up obliged to believe that evading his parents' supervision and giving them days of agony and anxiety was in some way The Right Thing For Jesus To Do. They have to believe that filling one's parents' hearts with terror is perfectly all right if one is a growing young super-being with a job ahead of one. They have to take 'I must be about my Father's business' as a full, authoritative statement – something like the glow of superhumanity penetrating through the thin costume of a human body and putting his mere mortal mother and father

---

* St Augustine claims to have been an attention-seeking sinner even when he was a baby, but St Augustine trained as an orator and does sometimes get carried away by his own rhetoric.

firmly in their place. A film-maker would undoubtedly mark this moment with an other-worldly light shining out of the magic child's eyes: the moment when the parent birds realise that they have been nurturing not a bird like themselves, but a cuckoo from beyond outer space.

I have described these people as ignoring the childishness of the child Jesus, but perhaps I am being unfair. Perhaps they have never been children themselves: it can happen. Perhaps they were never twelve. As it happens, I was, so for their sake here is a story of what being twelve is like.

When I was twelve, I didn't express my twelveishness by sitting at the feet of wise men and astonishing them with my own wisdom, but I did express it by defusing a terrorist bomb. I did this without considering any of the following questions, every one of which I would have answered entirely correctly if you had asked me at the time:

1. How likely is it that the IRA would choose to plant a bomb in an open field in the middle of the English countryside, half a mile from a Catholic school?
2. Do you really believe that bombs tick the way they do in films, and do you believe that whatever ticks is a bomb?
3. If you come across a bomb, do you go towards it or away from it?
4. If you come across a bomb, do you go up to it and fiddle with it or do you go and tell someone who will know what to do?
5. What do you think the farmer will say when you have broken his electric fence machine and all his cows have wandered off?

That is the thing about being twelve. Each of the strands of one's mind, separately addressed, is fully capable of giving an adult answer to an adult question. If asked, Jesus would have had all the right answers.

1. Ought you to tell your parents where you are going? YES.
2. Should you drive them to panic and distraction by utterly disappearing from sight? NO.

A twelve-year-old has the answers and the answers are right, but unfortunately the strands of good sense don't stick together yet, and each of them goes its own way. Jesus in the Temple is at that age and at that stage. Being God-and-man does not exempt him from the process of growing up.

When you see this, Mary's preservation of the remark 'I must be about my Father's business' makes sense. The whole story is not the magic super-child putting its parents in their place. It is simply – and if you have been a mother, or have had one, you will know this – 'one of the sweet things that children say', to be preserved, cherished, repeated and retold.

What God did not know

There is more to be said about what Jesus was up to in the Temple, because, apart from the business of forgetting his parents' existence, it was exactly the right thing for him to have done. It was research.

This has to do with the nature of knowledge. God is omniscient just as God is omnipotent, but just as 'omnipotence' doesn't mean being able to do absolutely *anything*, so 'being omniscient' does not mean knowing absolutely *everything*. This is not impiety; it is logic. It boils down to the fact that there are different kinds of knowledge. The philosopher Thomas Nagel wrote a paper charmingly entitled 'What Is It Like to Be a Bat?'* in which he pointed out that however many 'bat facts' we accumulate – about bat anatomy, bat physiology, bat behaviour or whatever – this does not mean that we know what it is like to *be* a bat. We can see batness from the outside, but not from the inside. Perhaps one day we will be able to simulate on our computers every nerve cell in the body of a bat, every neuron in a bat's brain. We will be able to apply bat-stimuli to our computer model and observe bat-responses. But still – even then – we will have no notion of how to answer the question, 'What is it like to be a bat?'

* Reprinted in *Mortal Questions* (1979).

This is not merely a human limitation. It is a logical impossibility to know what it is like to be something. Because the impossibility is a logical one, it is not only impossible for us but also for God. God, as Creator, cannot know what it is like to be a man. He cannot know what strawberries taste like even though he can (if he wishes) put strawberries together atom by atom, and (if he really wants to) put together taste buds atom by atom as well. God cannot know, without experiencing it, what exactly people feel or think. This, then, is one of the reasons for the Incarnation. In order to move us and enlighten us in a commensurate way rather than a thunder-and-lightning, overwhelming way, it is necessary to know what it means to be us, and that can only be done by actually *being* one of us.

This theme of 'learning by being incarnate' pervades the Gospel rather like ants in a lawn: at first you don't see them, but once you have spotted one ant, you have got your eye in and you start to notice them everywhere you look.

Time and again, for example, I begin to see Jesus talking to us in the way you and I would talk to a six-year-old. When we do that, we know exactly what the truth is that we want to convey in answer to the child's questions, but the tricky thing is seeing the world through a six-year-old's eyes and imagining hearing our words with a six-year-old's ears. It is hard, but we have to do it so that we can take the truth and put it into exactly the terms that will make sense in the hearer's mind. Listen to what happens in the Gospel and you will hear Jesus picking his way carefully through the same kind of task, taking the concepts he knows his hearers have and using them to convey the divine truths that only he can tell them. This is why it made sense for him to be interested, from when he was a child, in what the wisest men of God thought and how they thought it.

He was made man

One final miracle will complete the story. It is the first one that Jesus performed.

By the time of the wedding at Cana Jesus is fully aware of his identity as God and as man, and he has consequently worked out what his vocation is. He is ready to embark on his mission, and like any dedicated young man, he is impatient to start it now, right away. Also like any young man, what 'right away' really means is 'tomorrow'. If you have gone swimming from the beach you will know the feeling. It is that moment of hesitation before you plunge in and get wet all over. In one sense, you know you are going to do it, and that you want to do it, but you also know you don't want to do it just yet. You do anything to put off the definitive moment, paddling out on your toes, on your tiptoes, on your toenails. It is a human way to behave.

And so here is the wedding and here is Jesus, standing on tiptoe watching the wave coming in. He is on the point of plunging into the future he knows he is here for. Not that he can foresee what that future will be, or foresee his crucifixion, because that would be prescience of a non-human kind, and therefore cheating; but he knows it must be a plunge into complete dedication, an absolute surrender to 'whatever happens'. It must be complete *non*-autonomy, being wholly carried along by the wave that is approaching.

So what does he do at that moment? He is God, but he is human. He stands higher and ever higher, on toes that barely touch the sandy bottom by now. He wriggles, he fidgets, he looks embarrassed. When the steward comes to them with his problem, he hisses under his breath, 'Not *now*, Mum.'

And Mary? Does she talk to him, kindly, supportively, or even reproachfully? She does not. She listens to him the way a good mother does – which is to say, not at all. She does not argue or try to persuade. With the dispassionate love of a really good mother, she pushes her son out into the water the way a mother penguin pushes its chick off the cliff.

Without discussion, without asking permission, she turns to the servants and says, 'Do whatever he tells you.'

II.c

Rescue

Crucifixus etiam pro nobis sub Pontio Pilato;
passus et sepultus est,
et resurrexit tertia die,
secundum scripturas.

For our sake he was crucified under Pontius Pilate,
he suffered death and was buried,
and rose again on the third day
in accordance with the Scriptures.

The parable of the signpost

In the search for truth and understanding, there are many things to help us. There are books and stories, teaching and prophecy, theories and doctrine, and, of course, there are people. But really, the truth is beyond any of these. From that fact there arise two errors which can distract us from our search.

The first distraction is when we treat a guide to the truth as if it were the truth itself, final and unalterable. There are many examples in the physical sciences: to take an elegantly pithy one, scientists use the name 'atom', which means 'unsplittable', for an entity that other scientists then go and split. In theology, the clearest example is when people rip a saying out of its scriptural context and insist that it is word-for-word literally true, when all the saying is trying to do is *point us* to the truth.

The second distraction comes from trying to avoid the first one. We learn the lesson that everything we encounter on our journey to the truth is not the final truth, but we learn it too well. If we were children we would go on saying 'Are we nearly there yet?' over and over forever, but as adults we are too wise for that. We either despair of knowing anything and give up trying or decide that since no one can ever know the truth anyway, we can make the truth be whatever we want it to be. Both options are fatal.

Einstein said that the way to get to grips with a problem is to make a picture of it. So here is a picture.

Signposts to the truth

The picture is so simple that a child could have drawn it. A green hill, a blue sky behind, and on the hill there is a white signpost with black letters painted on it. The letters say LONDON 83½ MILES. And that is all.

The morals to be drawn from the picture are straightforward.

The signpost is not London. An idolater will treat the signpost as if it were London itself. He will give it all the attributes he ascribes to London (wicked metropolitan desirability, perhaps). A fundamentalist will admit no fact that is not written on this particular signpost and will spend his life measuring the exact direction it is pointing in, to the nearest tenth of a degree; forgetting that wood warps with time and roads do not go straight forever. What both the idolater and the fundamentalist have forgotten is that the first thing any signpost says, even without any words being painted on it, is WHAT YOU ARE LOOKING FOR IS NOT HERE. They also forget that journeys are meant to be made, not measured.

The signpost is not London. A seeker for certainty will discover that it isn't, and despair. If there is no packaged, pinned-down truth, he thinks, then there is no such thing as truth at all. He forgets that although the signpost says NOT HERE, which is a negative thing, it also does something positive: it indicates where the place it is pointing to is.

The thing is, *the signpost is not a failure.* It starts by asserting that the destination is worthwhile (who has ever seen a signpost saying TO NOWHERE IN PARTICULAR?) and that the destination exists and is reachable. It continues by saying that the destination is somewhere in particular, and by pointing in the direction of that 'somewhere' it tells one which way to go.

Further aspects of the signpost will come up in the next chapter, which looks at the Greek and Semitic approaches to wisdom. This is important because, as Christians, we are simultaneously Semites and Greeks. But let's finish with a mathematical example. It doesn't need to be understood in order to follow the main argument, but it may at least prove entertaining.

A mathematical analogy

Here is a simple sum.

$$1 - \tfrac{1}{3} + \tfrac{1}{5} - \tfrac{1}{7} + \tfrac{1}{9} - \tfrac{1}{11} + \tfrac{1}{13} - \tfrac{1}{15} + \tfrac{1}{17} - \ldots \ (\textit{and so on})$$

The parable of the signpost

This is not a difficult sum if you have a calculator or are good at fractions, but there is one snag: the sum goes on for ever. There is no moment when you can stop and say, 'I have arrived,' because wherever you stop, there are more steps ahead of you.

The relevance to signposts is that this sum-going-on-for-ever is not a failure but a success. You may never actually arrive at the answer, but the further you go through the sum, the closer you get to it. And so it is with signposts.

Never quite getting there can be a frustration, especially in theology, where our subject is so important: our own nature and our relationship with Being Itself. But it is not a failure and we should never be discouraged. And when we get to heaven, perhaps our understanding will also reach its final destination.*

---

* For the benefit of any mathematical reader, the answer you would have got if you really had gone on for ever is exactly $\pi/4$.

19

He was crucified

We are almost exactly half way through the story, and a steady rhythm has become established. The Creed goes past and the words come along, one by one or in groups, and there is always something to say about them. It may be more, it may be less, it may be deep or not so deep, but always there is something.

Until now.

The Crucifixion is something one can say nothing whatever about.

This is unexpected. We have coped with so many big things. There has been everything, and the creation of everything, and our relationship with the creator of everything (or rather, his with us), and the start of the whole story of salvation. For every phrase that we stand up and say, there has been something good to think about and reflect on.

But the Crucifixion is different. To be precise, it isn't that nothing can be said about the Crucifixion: you can always open your mouth and say *something*. It is that we know, deep down, that the act of saying anything at all about the Crucifixion is somehow not right. What can be said doesn't need to be; and what needs to be said can't be said in words.

If the Crucifixion is something not to be talked about, perhaps it is time to fall back and regroup and approach it from a different direction. What is it about the Crucifixion that makes talking about it not the right thing to do? If we try talking about *that*, perhaps we will get somewhere. So here is an attempt.

Crucifixion means death. It is a death of a particularly slow and unpleasant kind, but that is not as important as the fact that it is death at all. Intellectually speaking, death ought not to be anything problematic, since, after all, everyone we know either

150

has died or will die: it is the one great universal fact. All the same, there is the same sense about death that there is about the Crucifixion: talking about it is not the right thing to be doing with it.

Death is not docile. Death does not fall into the same category as all the other things that we see or experience, things that can be talked about without any difficulty.

As anyone who has encountered it will know, death is not actually sad or terrifying or any of the other things one might conventionally say it is. Or rather, it might or might not be any of those things, but they do not penetrate to the depth of it. Any given death may be sad or not sad, but what death always is is *big*.

Death is so big that everything else is tiny in comparison. Death is our contact with infinity. In the face of the infinite, all things are infinitesimal, just as an astronomer looking at the biggest mountain in the world would see it as being only a trillionth of a trillionth of a light year in height.

By the bigness of death, the landscape, which a moment ago was so full of things that seemed important to us, is cleared and simplified. At the same time there is a sense that this new scale of values is the real one and it is our old preoccupations that were unreal. As we go through the decontamination rituals from this contact with the infinite – funerals, mourning – we are not only returning 'to normality' but back from contact with true reality to a slightly unreal 'normal' life.

This fact has a profound effect in terms of what can be said about death. All big experiences are in some sense unsayable, just as God is unnameable and unnumberable. To say *anything* about something is to tame it just a little and take one step (a tiny one) towards pinning it down. And death is the great untameable and unpindownable.

Practical examples of how death is 'something about which nothing can be said' can be found in the way death is talked about by people whose job involves it. Medical students are famous for this. ('The first three minutes of life are the most dangerous,' says the poster in the hospital. 'Yes,' adds the student, 'and the last three minutes can be pretty tricky too.') Soldiers with experience of combat find the world divided into two halves: the people they can't talk to about it because it will mean nothing to them, and the ones they don't need to talk to about it because they have been there too.

Thus it is not surprising to expect the Crucifixion, in its character of death, to be untalkable-about as well.

This untameability and unpindownability tell us something not just about death but also about ourselves and all our attempts to tame the infinite and put it in a box. You might think, 'The bigger something is, the less boxable,' and at first sight there is indeed nothing less puttable in a box than the universe, with all its galaxies, stars and supernovae. In reality, however, it is easy for me to separate myself from all that and put a box-lid between us. All I have to do is go out on a starry night and not look up. Strictly speaking, it is *myself* I have put into a box, rather than the Infinite, but the separation is just as effective.

What goes for the cosmos goes for anything at all that savours of the Creator. Whatever is big, whatever is transcendent, whatever is overwhelming, I can keep it at arm's length by saying things about it. The things I say may be true things and even wise things, but the key point is that they work just like the box-lid. They maintain the separation between me and whatever I am talking about. It makes for a nice, safe, comfortable life. Being *in* reality is a challenge, but talking *about* it is easier. I remain comfortable, I remain untouched: I remain the dispassionate observer.

As a method of separation and self-protection, it all works. By words, I am able to keep myself separate from the whole Creation and from each individual created thing: separate and safe. There is only one thing I cannot keep myself from and separate from, and that is death. However tiny the box I make to keep myself inside and everything outside, however soundproofed I make it, one thing is always in there with me, on the same side of the lid as me: it is death.

As long as 'saying things about something' implies labelling, docketing, classifying, pinning down and boxing up – so long will talking about the Crucifixion seem indecent, inappropriate, absurd.

Talking about things is an act of the mind; but boxing up and pinning down are not the only mental acts. It is time to look again at what *loving with the mind* means.

Semite and Greek

The religions of God all have a common root in Abraham. The story of Abraham is a story of the gift of fertility to a sterile marriage and the gift of unsettledness to a man who is settled, old and rich. It is a call by God to man, not a visionary-on-a-mountain discovery of God by a special man. The call by God to Abraham is more than a single event. It is the start of a relationship, a WHO-to-WHO relationship, which is destined to last forever, and beyond forever.

This relationship has its ups and downs, as anything involving human beings always will. It has its mistakes and its rough moments, but it weathers them, and out of it all, understanding grows. The Jews come to see that what they are in a relationship with is not a god, but God. In the end, they are presented with the logical extension of this truth, which is that what God is in a relationship with is not just the Jewish people but the whole of humanity.

This understanding did not come by intellection, ratiocination or philosophy. The Jews acted as lovers, not thinkers. Like all lovers, they had no time to theorise about what they were doing because they were too busy doing it. When I love you and am with you, I want to live it, not analyse it; when I am missing you, I don't need to read a book to tell me what wishing you were here is like. I know what it is like because I am living the experience. The Jews were too busy being *in* the relationship to want to think *about* the relationship or stand on one side and inspect it as if it were some kind of laboratory specimen.

I am going to call this understanding-through-living 'the Semitic way' rather than 'the Jewish way'. This is because, although the Jews started it, the later children of Abraham had the same way of going about things. 'Semitic' is reasonable because both the Jews and the Arabs are Semites speaking Semitic languages, and both Judaism and Islam preserve this particular mode of understanding in its purest form. God in the Old Testament warns intending thinkers, 'My thoughts are not your thoughts.' God in the Koran demands obedience, not subtle argument.

The Semitic path to wisdom in the first millennium BC was unprecedented and revolutionary. But it was not the only path, or the only revolution. For as long as the Hebrews had been researching reality by living it, another people in another corner of the Eastern Mediterranean had been doing the exact opposite. They had been researching reality by studying it: by reasoning about it. These people were the Greeks.

The Greeks came as waves of wandering tribes into the settled glory of the ancient Near East, but compared to all the barbarian invaders of civilised lands throughout history, the Greeks were unusual. They neither burned everything they came across, like the Mongols or the Danes, nor let themselves be taken over by it, like the Goths or the Normans or the Ottomans. The Greeks looked at the ancient cultures they met, and the fruits of their thousands of years of learning, and instead of being awed, they asked, 'Why?'

For example: the Babylonians, and the Egyptians after them, had recorded the fact that eclipses recur in a cycle a little over eighteen years long ('the Saros cycle'). The Greeks did not just meekly swallow this. Instead they asked, 'Why?', and carried on asking it until they had measured the Earth, the Moon and the Sun and the distances between them.

Or again: the land of Egypt was inundated yearly and buried under thick, fertile mud, which made agriculture both possible because of the fertility the Nile mud brought and at the same time impossible because all the landmarks had been buried and nobody knew where the field boundaries were. The Egyptians accordingly became expert surveyors and geometers. The Greeks, seeing this, asked 'Why?', and went on asking it until they knew *why* geometry worked and not just *that* it did.

The Greeks needed to know about everything. They needed to know why music works and why some chords are beautiful while others are ugly; they needed to know how the weather works, and why, and why some places are healthy to live in and others unhealthy. They needed to know what makes good plays good and bad plays bad, and good political constitutions good and bad ones bad.

The psalmist, as a Semite, is sometimes aware of his uprightness, sometimes of his sinfulness, and he sings of both. Aristotle, as a Greek, wants to know what makes right right and wrong wrong.

The Greek enterprise was unprecedented and it was glorious. It still is, because we are still ancient Greeks even now. When we debate, or when we do science, it is as Greeks that we do it. So when we treat the truths of our religion as something that ought to make sense, we are looking at it in a Greek way. We are doing a Greek thing.

The odd thing about the Greek adventure is that religion was the one thing the Greeks never really managed to be Greeks about. This is because they had one thing missing: as pagans, they did not have God. They looked for the truth hidden behind their local cults, and behind the smoke they found nothing. The Greeks could think about anything, but when they tried to think about *everything*, their thinking ended up being based on nothing, because for all their attention to Being-as-known, they had no access to Being-as-experienced. And it shows. The Greeks evolved some elevating philosophies and some marvellous theories of the cosmos but, looking back on them from our own vantage point, it all still seems to end up being about nothing. It feels like a huge electric machine which is perfect in every detail and yet useless because nobody has yet plugged it in.

So the situation at the turn of the eras was this. On the Semitic side there was Being without much in the way of reasoning. On the Greek side there was pure reasoning without, as yet, anything for that reasoning to be *about*.

Something had to happen. It did, and we are the result.

Coming together

As Christians, we are Semites, like all the other children of Abraham; but as Christians we are also Greeks in the tradition of Plato and Aristotle. We are both of them at once, but that does not mean a kind of blending or merging like mixing red and white paint to make pink. Our Semitic selves and our Greek selves live side by side in us and we are equally both of them at once.

To make a change from mathematical and physical analogies, here is a biological one.

We all know that plants make food from light (to be precise, they make sugars out of carbon dioxide, water and light in a process called photosynthesis). That is half the story: the more visible half. The other half is deeper, and interesting. The only organisms that are *truly* capable of making food out of light are certain bacteria, and in particular certain 'cyanobacteria' – blue-green bacteria that live in the ocean.

As you look out of the window on to the kitchen garden, you may feel that this new story does not quite fit what you can see: rows of green cabbages waiting to be eaten. The solution to the puzzle is why I am telling this story at all. Inside every cell of every green leaf of every cabbage – and of every green plant on earth – there is a tiny pocket ocean with a few of those bacteria in it. We call them chloroplasts. Their colour gives the leaf its colour, and the food they make feeds the plant so that it can grow, and it feeds us.

There have been some mutual adjustments over the couple of billion years this has been going on. By now, the bacteria would be lost if you were to release them into a real ocean, and die; but then the plant without the bacteria would be lost as well, and turn white and die too, from lack of food.

The point of this tale is that the collaboration between plants and bacteria is not a matter of the two things merging into one. Neither can live without the other, but they still keep their separate identities.*

---

* For instance, the chloroplasts reproduce by splitting in half, the way bacteria do, while the host plant, like all really evolved organisms, reproduces by sex.

The parallel with 'Semitic' and 'Greek' cultures is as follows. A 'pure-Semitic' culture is limited in what it can do, because its truths are absolute truths and so its encounters with other cultures can only result in absolute victory or absolute defeat and destruction: think of the story of Elijah against the priests of Baal.* A 'pure-Greek' culture is limited in another way. Being made of pure reason, it will end up with 'reason for reason's sake' – ultimately, reason without any reality to reason *about*. It is equally doomed in the long term. Just as with plants and their chloroplasts, only the combination of the two cultures has a future.

Leaving biology behind and returning to an older metaphor: right and left are opposites, but it is good to have both because with a right eye and a left eye you see straight and don't bump into things. Conversely, indeed, when we find ourselves off balance, it is probably because we have been seeing more with one eye than the other.

Semitic and Greek seem too opposite to exist in the same culture or even the same mind, and it required force to bring them together. Just as the Incarnation united God and man in one being, so its consequences forced Semitic and Greek together to a point of union. It happened like this: Jesus himself, the living culmination of the Semitic relationship, gave his disciples the command, 'Go, and teach all nations'. At that time, the Jews were an island in a Greek-speaking world, and the 'all nations' to which the preachers were being sent had a Greek culture.

I do not mean that the Greek-speaking population of the eastern Mediterranean were all practising philosophers. Of course they were not: but when people did make the effort to think clearly, they would naturally find themselves doing it along established philosophical lines. Something of the apparatus and vocabulary was ambient among them – in the air rather as a kind of degraded psychological thinking is in the air for us. If I disagree with you, I am 'in denial' about the truth; if I resent something you have done to me, I haven't 'processed the experience' appropriately yet.

* 1 Kings 18:22–40.

To 'go and teach all nations' always requires you to speak their language, and that does not mean knowing the dictionary words for hat, horse and halibut, but understanding the way the language thinks. Only then can you re-present the truth in terms of the other nation's way of thinking – just as, when light casts the shadow of an object onto a surface, the shadow has to adapt itself to the contours of that surface.

St Paul is our best witness, as he describes how the Jews and Greeks think differently: the Jews demanding signs (events and actions with a meaning) while the Greeks demand wisdom and will argue all day to get it. Paul, in communicating the nature of Being to a world that thought in Greek terms, had to find a *Greek* way of conveying a *Semitic* truth. This was the real moment of hybridisation, and a tricky one. The task seems as impossible as injecting an alga into every cell of a leaf: reason tends to pin down and it is in the nature of Truth not to be pinned down. In his letters, you can watch Paul getting to grips with this. You can see him struggling to pick the right Greek words for what he wants to say, or even inventing terminology as he goes.

In a sense, the whole enterprise is doomed because the Infinite is unpindownable, but only in a sense in which 'doomed' does not imply 'futile'.

Doomed but not futile

This tale of Semite and Greek brings us back to why saying anything about the Crucifixion sounds so wrong. The whole business of 'saying something about' belongs to the Greek side of the experience: it belongs to understanding, with inevitably a certain amount of pinning down and boxing in. It neglects the other side, the Semitic side, which in the case of the Crucifixion (indeed, of death generally) is not only important but indispensable.

The Crucifixion really needs to be *encountered* more than it needs to be talked about. The best that can be said about words is that they can get one into a position in which that encounter is possible. Once positioned, the encounter itself has virtually no need of words. After the encounter, we might be like the soldiers who communicate the burden of their shared experience by saying nothing about it: their silence is communication, because they know they are being silent about the same thing.

Encounter requires experience, and experience comes from life rather than from reading and study, so that for a book like the present one to recommend encounter amounts more or less to saying, 'Close this book, and live instead.' It sounds paradoxical, but something like that *has* to be said, because the inappropriateness of talking about the Crucifixion at all, which I complained about at the beginning of this chapter, comes directly from treating a solid reality in a one-eyed way, by 'Greek' reason alone.

I cannot give instructions, but I can at least offer inspiration. For me, the greatest inspiration is the work of Julian of Norwich. Here is her story.

In the small hours of Friday 13 May 1373, a thirty-and-a-half-year-old woman called Julian lay at death's door. More than half paralysed, she was propped up so that in her last moments she could gaze upon the crucifix which was being held up before her.

And Jesus bled.

From four in the morning to after nine, Julian was given a series of fifteen visions, or 'showings', centred around the Passion of Christ, its sadness and its overwhelming joy and heavenly glory.

As soon as the showings finished, her sickness came back.

> Then came a Religious person to me and asked how I fared. I said I had raved today. And he laughed loud and heartily. And I said, *the Cross that stood before my face, I thought it bled fast.* And with this word the man I spoke to became all sober, and marvelled.*

Julian was, above all, a sensible woman, and she didn't believe in magical apparitions. This is normal among true mystics: they are suspicious of anything they are shown until they have made absolutely certain of who it really is that is showing it. Still, on hearing the holy man's words, Julian was ashamed that at one instant she

---

* Julian of Norwich, *Revelations of Divine Love*, chapter 66.

could have so eagerly listened to the Lord and, at the next, have so quickly dismissed the whole experience. She spent the next twenty years of her life making up for that error.

From 'a simple creature, unlettered', Julian became a woman well and deeply read in contemporary theology and spirituality, and a sound practical theologian in her own right – practical, not building theory upon theory but taking the whole of lived experience and making sense of it, setting it in context and learning what it has to tell us about the things of heaven.

Julian's *Revelations of Divine Love* was finished in 1393. It is the greatest work of spirituality ever written in English. I shan't say more, because just as too much reasoning can be a way of avoiding living, so too much reading about a book can be a substitute for actually reading it and encountering the author soul to soul. But even before you read her, Julian is worth knowing about, not only for the direct value of her work but also because of the example she sets. Her encounter with the Crucifixion was more direct than ours is likely to be – but we need to have an encounter of some kind too, and the first step is to find a way of lowering the defences that reason puts up, even for a short time, to behave as experiencing Semites rather than purely as analysing Greeks.

The signposts

Literally, signposts point the way to places. Metaphorically, they point the way to reality and truth. Having established the distinction between Semitic and Greek, it is worth seeing how the two cultures approach signposts. We need both, so it is important to be able to distinguish between them.

The Semitic approach to signposts is seen in the Old Testament. For the Semites, *events* are the signposts. The Old Testament narrates the whole of history as a love-letter from the one unnameable LORD to man. Each event is a word or a sentence in that love-letter, whether it is a birth or a death or a battle, or a young man cheating his brother of his inheritance.

Accordingly, the Old Testament conserves these signposts above all else. Even when the words written on the signpost have faded or peeled away, the signpost itself must be preserved as it is, and not repainted. Future generations have to be able to have a direct encounter with that very signpost and thus with the original event itself: with that particular phrase in the long love-letter of the LORD. It would be tempting for scholars to erect a new, shiny, metal signpost in place of the crumbling wooden one, with an inscription deduced by the combined labour of the experts and enamelled onto the metal for permanence. It would be the obvious thing to do, really, but for the most part it is not done.

There are words, even sentences, of the Bible that now mean nothing, either from errors in transcription over the centuries or just because the original meanings of the Hebrew words have been forgotten. These stand as a permanent puzzle or problem to be argued about afresh by each new generation – because each such argument will be a fresh encounter with the original reality. That is better than having a substitute forged by a consensus of later scholars, however wise or holy those men may have been.

From a certain perspective, this 'holding on to the past' is absurd, just as following the ritual and dietary laws of Moses is absurd: but it is a kind of absurdity familiar to people who know what it is to be in love.

That is the message of the signposts to us Christians as Semites. For us Christians as Greeks, signposts are important not so much for what they are as for what they do. A signpost indicates where one's destination is, just as a map does; and indeed, if we have a good map, we have less need of the signpost.

Because the use of a signpost is now in what it *does* rather than what it *is*, it is reasonable for a new generation of surveyors to come along with more accurate instruments and take the old signpost down and put up a new and better one. The chemist John Dalton, laying the foundations of the atomic theory in 1808, made the formula for water HO. We make it H_2O, a simple Greek-style revision. As Greeks, we don't read Dalton any more: we read the latest revision of the latest edition of the latest chemistry textbooks. On the other hand, as Semites we still read Isaiah.

There are many advantages to the Greek approach. It lets you learn about life without having to experience it all first and then spend nineteen and three-quarter years thinking it through, the way Julian did.* It also lets you put distant things on the map in terms of coordinates you already know. You can even put your new-style signposts in rational places – such as at the top of a hill with a good view – rather than in the arbitrary locations which the LORD seems so fond of choosing.

Being Greek is a help, but it has its risks. As will be seen in the next chapter, an explication, a 'mapping' of the Crucifixion in terms of debt (debt incurred, debt repaid) will only make sense as long as our concept of debt makes sense, and the same thing goes for a map laid out according to the concept of justice. A signpost placed on the top of a hill called Debt Repaid will mean nothing if brambles grow up and choke the hill so that you can't see out. A signpost on a slope called Justice will point nowhere at all after a landslide has come and dumped it into a neighbouring swamp.

The ever-changing landscape is a problem when we try to read the devotional or explanatory works of the past. If what used to be a fine open road is now tangled with briars or infested with leeches, the words that once pointed so far and so clearly can easily end up pointing to nothing. The most inspiring expressions of prayer and devotion can end up not meaning anything that now seems to us to be acceptable. The choice seems to be between abandoning them, which is sad, or treating them as 'just one of those things we Christians like to say' – in other words, as meaningless noise.

And yet we today still have the same questions about the Crucifixion that everyone has always had: why, and what for?

The next two words of the Creed are going to give us the answer.

---

* With charming precision, Julian insists on that exact number.

20

For our sake

When it comes to translation, the shortest words are often the hardest ones to deal with. This is because the long intellectual words usually have one exact meaning, while the short ones pack a lot into a small space. Here is a good example. What does the Creed mean by 'for us'?

It is possible simply to fall back on authority and believe verbally that God the Son was crucified 'for us', without ever stopping to think what 'for us' might mean. The excuse would be that it isn't our job to know these things. The clever people who wrote the Creed (we'd say) knew what they meant, and all we need to do is parrot their words without thinking what we are saying.

This cop-out is forbidden by the commandment to love the Lord our God with all our mind. I am not saying that it is necessary to be a theologian to be saved: indeed, one of the wonderful things about Christianity is that this is not the case. We don't all have the temperament or the capacity to theorise in that kind of way, and a good thing too. It is quite all right for a simple soul to answer 'What does "for us" mean?' with 'I don't exactly know' – of such is the kingdom of heaven. But for anyone, simple or not, to answer 'What does "for us" mean?' with 'Nothing really,' or 'I can't be bothered to think about it' – that is another matter entirely. It is an evasion and a scandal.

I am not demanding (and I am not saying that God is demanding) a carefully worked-out theological justification for everything. But since the commandment to love with the mind tells us that thinking about God makes sense, it is important to get some idea at least of what sort of sense the phrase 'for us' might make.

There is a basic problem with thinking about abstract things, which is that one can only think about them in terms of concepts

163

one already has, and those concepts are not fixed: they change as time goes on. Or rather, the names of the concepts change their meaning. What is the Pole Star today will not be above the North Pole in a thousand years' time. In the seventeenth century, 'longitude zero' meant the island of Ferro,* and '20° East' meant Paris; today, zero means Greenwich and 20° East means Kraków.

When there is an explication of Jesus dying on the cross 'for us' in terms of justice, and *justice itself* subsequently shifts its meaning, all our coordinates go wrong and all the insights that the idea of justice gave us become inaccessible to us, unless we know about the change. Even if we do know about the change, what used to be a limpid flash of understanding, when 'justice' meant rightness, becomes an arid exercise now that 'justice' means something else and we have to calculate backwards to locate its original meaning.

Again, when there was a reality about debt and a rightness in dealing with it, the Passion as a repayment of the debt incurred through the Fall made sense. Now the meaning of 'debt' has changed, the explication in terms of debt is not accessible to us any more.

This is, of course, why Jesus talks so much about things rather than concepts – about vines and towers and lost coins – because things never change. To read St Paul you have to be a bit of a theologian, but to read the Gospel you only need to be human.

Justice

The first concept that has been twisted by time is justice.

The word 'justice' used to mean both rightness and putting things right. It used to mean taking a broken situation and finding the best thing to do to make it not broken any more – not to make it unbroken (not even God can make things not have happened) but to make it *no longer* broken.

---

* The westernmost of the Canary Islands. Measuring from Ferro (El Hierro) was practical because it meant that every longitude in the Old World was a longitude *east*.

Justice is intrinsically between persons, and as a living thing it is applied to people by a person: Solomon hears the case of the two women who are claiming the same child, and Solomon works out a solution.*

But time moves on. Institutions take over from people and justice gives way to law: rather as (as I think Ronald Knox once said) every religion has a tendency to subside into an ethical code. Next, the law ossifies into a machine. 'Ministries of Justice', such as every banana republic has, are ministries not of justice but of tuning the machinery of the law to serve the interests of the powerful. As a final absurdity, because nobody wants to claim to be *against* justice, '[something] Justice' is a rallying cry for every campaigning group, rather like 'rights'. A satirist has suggested that drug dealers could easily defend their right to sell pills to schoolchildren if they only did it under the banner of Chemical Justice.

What it all adds up to is this: any response to salvation history – from the Fall to the Redemption – that sees it in terms of justice and the value of justice can only work as long as we remember what that 'justice' is. And if all we ever hear is the changed meaning of the word, the oppressive institutional meaning, we forget what justice is and can't imagine anyone loving it. Any explication of the Atonement in terms of 'justice', however enlightening it once was, will now fall flat. To rescue it from seeming perverse and grotesque, it needs a whole bunch of explanatory footnotes, and the footnotes strangle it so that the whole thing decays into dry legalism. It might, with labour, be understood with the head, but never with the heart.

Debt

The same thing that happened to justice has happened to debt: debt has also had the meaning drained out of it.

Debt is between people. Debt is when I owe you something. Debt establishes a relationship between us in that I am your debtor

* 1 Kings 3:16–28.

until I can pay the debt back. The debt may arise because you have given me something, or because I have wronged you in some way, but the result is the same in either case. There are even debts that it is almost impossible to imagine paying back – as when you save me from drowning, for example. Paradoxically, there is in that case a sense of obligation working in the inverse direction, because, having saved my life, you find yourself feeling a certain duty of care towards me thereafter.

The sin of Adam places mankind in debt to God in this stronger, life-saving sense: and, indeed, there is about God's subsequent relationship with us a certain air of the creditor's paradoxical debt to the debtor.

An understanding of salvation history in terms of that debt can make sense. So can the notion of a debt so great that man cannot pay it but only God can, which is why God becomes man. There are still difficulties for many of us in terms of the currency in which that debt was repaid (we are squeamish about crucifixions), but still this kind of outlook could potentially be fruitful and a sure foundation for understanding.

Unfortunately, all this can only make sense if debt makes sense: and it doesn't any more. If, with the passing of time, 'debt' has come to mean 'money' and nothing else, its true meaning has been lost and cannot easily be recovered. Along with this loss of meaning comes its correlate, which is that 'debt' in this new sense is usually owed to organisations (that is, to subhumans) and not to human beings. Such debt has no basis in reality but can be conjured into and out of existence at the stroke of a pen. When the creditors then buy and sell the debts among themselves, they are effectively buying and selling the debtors, which is even more inhuman.

To take 'debt' in *this* debased sense and attempt to apply it to the heat and torment and flies of a certain April afternoon in first-century Palestine is obscene and absurd.

And thus, again, the beautiful, the enlightening explications of the Redemption in terms of a debt become undecodable, unsayable, unthinkable – to our loss.

At-*one*ment

There is another possible explication of the Atonement which doesn't seem to have been poisoned in the way that justice and debt have. Indeed, this way of looking at it has been staring us in the face for a long time, because the very word 'atonement', properly spelt and pronounced, gives us the key.

Mankind is in a state of brokenness. Everyone knows this. Even the pagans know it, and make myths about it; but we as Christians can see it in a clearer way. We can see it more clearly because as children of Abraham we are in a WHO-to-WHO relationship with Being Itself, and our brokenness can be seen as a brokenness in that relationship.

This is good, because as human beings we live in a tissue of relationships. Relationships flare and they fade, and they break; but they can also be healed. So if we look deeply into our own lives and their past breakings and healings, this gives us a privileged viewpoint from which we may be able to understand the breaking-of-a-relationship that is the Fall and the healing-of-a-relationship that is the Redemption. This is not a technical construct such as one might build when talking in terms of justice or of debt. It is a picture, and one that we all know, even as children. It is not the high theology of the experts, but at least it is good low theology, and it may help.

Let's imagine a story and start it with two things: an established relationship and the sin that breaks it. To save inventing names for the characters, I will call them 'you' and 'me'. As for the sin, I will not choose anything passionate, like murder, or clever, like burglary, because those sins have some courage or ingenuity about them, and for my story I need a sin without any redeeming feature.

So let us say you have a possession you cherish: a beautiful antique chess set. One day, when I am your guest, I snaffle one of the pieces: let's say a bishop. It is what I do next that gives the sin in the story its full nastiness. I do not take the stolen bishop to possess it or sell it, which would at least have respected the object's value. I just throw the chess piece into the mud by the side of the road, where no one will ever find it.

There is nothing noble about this sin. It is small and creepy, and all the details make it smaller and creepier still: see how careful I have been to pretend it isn't really stealing by throwing the thing away, and to pretend it isn't really stealing *much* by taking only one small object (but in truth, ruining the whole set by doing so). This is a sin prompted by a little slimy devil, not by a grand fiery one. It is the kind of sin to have restless nights about – not so much because of the sin itself as because of thinking, 'How could I be the sort of person who could do such a spiteful thing?' All these characteristics make it perfect for the present example.

Before I committed this sin against you, you and I were at one. Now we are not. That is objectively true. It is true whether I tell you what I have done or whether I don't. It is true whether you know what I have done or whether you don't. In every case, the outcome is the same: if we still appear to be at one after what has happened, it is a lie; if we don't, it is a tragedy. Either way, we who were once at one have ended up at odds.

The question is then: how can we be at one again?

A scriptwriter or storyteller has many choices here, but they all have to respect the same basic principles. First, notice that we can never go back to how we were, only forward. Not even God can make a thing un-happen. Next, the simple solutions aren't solutions. Cash won't make everything all right again: that is obvious. A more subtle calculation in terms of debt might see me digging the piece out of the ditch, or haunting antique shops and auctions until I find a new set, buy it and ruin my own set by removing a piece from it in order to restore yours. All sorts of good plots for a story are possible: but they all fail. Repaying the debt like this can't work. Even if the balance of payments between us, counted in terms of chess pieces, is zero, that does not mean that we are back to where we once were.

Once our being at one, our at-oneness, has been broken, it cannot be mended by going back. It can only be mended by going

forward to a new at-oneness. It is a matter of psychological observation that the new at-oneness, if it is achieved, will be closer,
more 'at one' than the old: 'It heals stronger at the break.' But
that is not what is important here. What I think is important is
that, for the at-oneness to be restored, *both of us* have do something about it.

We need a word for this, and that brings us back to
atonement.

Most of the high grand words used in ethics and theology
come from suitably high grand origins, from Latin or Greek.
Atonement is different. It started life not in grandeur but in unpre-
tentious English simplicity. When you are not 'at one', you need to
be made 'at one'; to be at-oned, and the act of at-oneing is naturally at-onement.

'Atonement' soon acquired the elevated manners of its grand
neighbours, and by pronouncing its middle syllable 'tone' we
discreetly gloss over its humble origins. What I now propose is a
stripping back of that genteel polish. Humble origins are nothing
to be ashamed of, and an important piece of meaning became
obscured when we polished the word.

To make things clearer, I will spell the stripped-back word
'at-*one*ment' with a hyphen, and pronounce its middle syllable as
'one' rather than 'tone'. At-onement is the act of causing to be 'at
one' once more. That is what has happened between God and
fallen man.

'Atonement' (the way we use the word nowadays) is a kind of
being sorry, only more so. I have done something bad, so now I
make up for it; I atone for it. This atonement is really only about
me: all you need to do is stand and watch.

At-*one*ment, unlike atonement, is not just about me. It is something you and I both have to do. Both of us have been at odds – I
with you and you with me – so now we both have to come together.
We both have to become at one. We both have to *at-one*.

You may well object that you are the injured party here. You
never did anything wrong from beginning to end in the breaking
of our relationship, so why should you have to do anything to
mend it? Tough. That is what love is.

In love, I 'in-you' myself and you 'in-me' yourself.* When I suffer, you suffer, so we both share in the suffering of sin even if I committed the sin and you did not. (If you find this a hard doctrine, then think back to what you felt when you last heard of a bad thing done by someone you really loved. You felt more than just the distant pity of a spectator.)

You might also accept the principle of at-oneing, but object that you have done your share by forgiving me and that the rest of the process is up to me. That is not quite accurate. Forgiving is indeed necessary (for your good as much as mine), but it isn't an act of at-onement in itself: all it does is make the at-onement possible.

What you need to do to at-one us to each other will vary from case to case. Discovering it requires discernment, it sometimes requires subtlety; it always requires love. The important point remains: at-oneing or at-onement is something that you and I both have to do.

As with people, so with God. To the extent that God and man are not at one, *both* God *and* man have to act so as to bring back the at-oneness. And they have to find the right way to do it.

To me, at-oneing is the key to what Jesus did. If we start instead from 'atonement', the high, grand version with 'tone', then we start with the idea that someone has to make up for what happened: since, at the Fall, man sinned against God, now man has to make up for it to God somehow. From there, a relentless and inhuman logic takes over. We, as mere human beings, could not make up for the Fall (it was too big), so God the Son has to become man to do it on our behalf.†

This is not the most helpful of explanations because we are none of us very good at seeing how someone can atone on behalf of someone else, or even how anyone at all can atone by suffering. At best, we can get our heads round it rather than our hearts. This kind of 'high theology' passes us by or even becomes a bit of an embarrassment. Or worse: when heretics read this as Jesus 'the

---

* 'S'io m'intuassi, come tu t'inmii'. Dante, *Paradiso*, IX.81.
† 'On our behalf' is indeed one possible translation of *pro nobis*.

good God' somehow placating Jehovah 'the bad God', the whole thing becomes toxic.

On the other hand, at-*one*ing is something that *by its very nature* has to be done by both sides. It follows that an act by God is exactly what is needed here: an at-oneing act by man alone is intrinsically not enough. God has to at-one just as much as man does. And although we can never hope to think according to the Father's logic, and so can never hope to see exactly why the incarnation of God the Son was the necessary way to go, we can at least see that *something* had to be done by God, and not only by man, for us to be once more at one.

Why crucifixion?

As St Paul complains, the cross is a stumbling block both for Jews who seek signs and for Greeks who seek understanding. It follows that, as Christians, being a bit of both, we stumble twice over. I want to make an attempt at a different angle, which might make us stumble a little less: one that follows the theme of at-onement rather than atonement.

I begin with purely human at-onement, to set up the pattern.

I have a friend I will call Catherine. When she was a little girl at school, all the other girls ignored her because she was English and therefore different from them. So she fell into the habit of stealing little things to give them to other girls, hoping to become visible to them. It is a common enough thing at a certain age, and, as is common, the teacher caught Catherine and there were tears and understanding and pity and forgiveness.

Catherine was forgiven, but she was not yet *at one*.

A day or two later, the teacher announced that she had found some money in her pocket, and would someone please go to the sweet shop and get some sweets with it for the class? She chose a girl to go: she chose Catherine.

This action was the at-onement. It was right: so right that Catherine still remembers it seventy years later. The core of the rightness of what the teacher did was that the teacher, the creditor, the one who was not the sinner, handed over control to the sinner *without conditions*, resolving to let whatever was going to happen as a result happen.

In the problem of you and me and the chess pieces, the same kind of resolution might bring our own process of at-oneing to completion. For instance, you could tell me that you have to go out tomorrow evening and have no one to look after the dog, so could I come in and dog-sit for you? Just like Catherine's teacher, you at-one by renouncing control and letting whatever is going to happen happen. To clarify the point: if you left me alone in the house when you went out *but took care to turn your security cameras on*, then you would be retaining control and the whole at-onement would be nullified. More than that: you would your-self be poisoning our relationship by establishing distrust at the core of it. Love and self-protection cannot mix.

If this is, as I think, a universal pattern where at-onement is concerned, it sheds light on the Crucifixion from a different direction. It gives us a new possible angle from which the whole thing might make sense to us: a new angle that might help when other angles seem unhelpful.

To clear the ground before starting: *it is not the case* that in the manger in Bethlehem there lay a going-to-be-crucified baby. *It is not the case* that John in the Jordan baptised the going-to-be-crucified Son of God. To ascribe 'future crucifixion' like this would amount to denying the existence of free will in human affairs and to reduce Judas, Caiaphas, Peter and Pilate to the status of puppets.

'God the Son became incarnate and accepted crucifixion' misses the point slightly but significantly. It would be more enlightening and more accurate to say, 'God the Son became incarnate and accepted whatever would happen as a consequence of his incarnation, up to and including crucifixion.' Just as in at-oneing yourself to me after the incident of the chess piece you give up control over the situation, just as in at-oneing herself to Catherine her teacher gave up control over what Catherine would do with the money, so in God's at-oneing himself to us, God gives up control. He says, 'Let whatever happens, happen.'

At its core, perfect love is like writing a blank cheque. You fill in the date and the name and you sign it, but you leave the amount blank. If you are lucky, the payee will fill in an amount that is right and reasonable; if you are less lucky, he will fill in an amount that covers everything you possess. Your act of love was the same either way. What makes it an act of love is not the particular outcome, but the fact that you have given control over the outcome to the other person.

The key to the At-onement is that the omnipotent God embraces contingency: he puts himself, like us, on the receiving end of 'what happens'. As we live contingent lives, so too will God. As human beings, we *have* to accept whatever the outcome of the world's events turns out to be, and so too, while incarnate, will God. As incarnate God, the Son accepts the whole course of his life on earth, whatever it turns out to be. And in this way he makes himself at one with us.

Seeing it this way also protects us from some mistaken views of the Father's role in all this. The silly picture we can so easily get of a Father sending his Son off to suffer and die – which sounds more like a cruel father than a loving one – is no longer there. The Father does not cruelly send his Son on earth to be crucified, but generously sends his Son to be one of us without setting any limit on what the consequences might be.

I am not claiming, with this story of at-onement, that this is how it was. Rather, I am offering another signpost to point towards what happened. Like the signposts of justice and of debt, the signpost of at-onement is not the whole truth but points towards the truth. If justice and debt have been devalued in our eyes so that their signposts are of no use to us, the signpost of at-onement may help.

21

Under Pontius Pilate

Sub Pontio Pilato

God is that which cannot be pinned down. So Dionysius says, and he is right. But God's action in the world *can* be pinned down, and very much needs to be. That is what Pontius Pilate is doing for us here in the Creed.

The Incarnation is an in-meating. That has to imply an in-whereing and an in-whenning, and Pontius Pilate supplies both the time and the place. What the actual time and place are is not as important as the fact that the Passion *has* a where and *has* a when, because stories that lose their where and their when blossom into a mass of legend which starts by decorating them but ends by obliterating them. Alexander the Great (356–323 BC) forms a fine example. Alexander, king of Macedon, led the Greek armies into Asia and had conquered the Persian Empire by the time he was twenty-six.

Alexander is a legend and his exploits are unparalleled in human history. But being a legend makes one a magnet for myth, and before long the mythical 'Alexander' came to obscure the historical one. 'Alexander' was the son of an exiled Egyptian pharaoh; he travelled to the ends of the earth and encountered Amazons and giants and men without heads. Every traditional tale of marvels attached itself to him until the man himself all but disappeared. The *Alexander Romance* was one of the most popular books of the Middle Ages.

Jesus Christ is greater than Alexander and so even more of a myth magnet: you only have to look at the surviving fragments of the apocryphal Gospels to see how he attracts the myths. From the very start, the factuality of who Jesus was and what he did, and where and when, had to be guarded and protected from the myth-makers. The Creed plays its part by tying Jesus to a specific historical time and place and person.

There are good reasons for using a Roman official to do the pinning down. Rome was the legitimate local authority and the Crucifixion was a legal act. It was carried out by the duly constituted authorities as a result of due process of law. Crucifixions today are carried out by mobs and rabbles, and crucifixion has not been part of any country's legal system since Japan abolished it in 1873, but in the first century AD what happened to Jesus was not abnormal at all. It was how the world worked. One can't understand the real outrageousness of the Crucifixion without first understanding how normal it was.

Pilate provides a definite time and place. He was prefect of Judaea from AD 26 to 36. It was an exceptionally difficult posting. Rome in general tried to rule its provinces as lightly as it could, partly out of principle and partly because it consumed less Roman administrative effort that way. (It has been estimated that the civil service of the whole Empire was smaller than a single city's administration is nowadays.) For the Romans, the ideal province was one that yielded as much in terms of taxation as it was capable of providing, was stable and was not subject to internal sedition. In return, the province was protected against exploitation and oppression (in theory if not always in practice), and against invasion and external threats.

The trouble with Judaea was that it was a hard place to run. The simplest action – the mere carrying of imperial standards within the boundaries of the city of Jerusalem – might cause such offence as to threaten stability. The Jews were unreadable. A large gathering of people might be an innocent pilgrimage or festival (so that it would be fatal to interfere with it) or it might be a prelude to insurrection (so that it would be fatal not to).

And in addition to the balancing act that came with the territory, there was always the risk of intrigue further afield. Pilate's eventual downfall came as a result of the Samaritans ('whose blood Pilate had mingled with that of their sacrifices'*) complaining of harsh treatment to Lucius Vitellius, the governor of Syria, who in turn reported the matter to Rome, where the Emperor

---

* Luke 13:1 (JB).

Tiberius summoned Pilate to answer the charges. Tiberius died while Pilate was on his way to Rome, and Pilate, as one reference book puts it, 'thereafter disappears from authentic history'. The myth machine got to work, and various traditions have him committing suicide, or being eaten alive by worms, or, on the contrary, being respected for being in his heart a Christian: in the Coptic Church he and his wife are honoured as saints.

It is a salutary spiritual exercise to look at the surface of other people's acts and try to imagine what different inner realities can manifest themselves in the same set of outwardly visible actions. Peter betrays, repents and has new life; Judas betrays, repents and is overwhelmed by despair. In such an exercise, we know so little about Pilate that he can stand for anything: from blinkered officialdom unable to look beyond itself to an ordinary man doing the best he could in the face of threatened riot and massacre. It is a good and humbling exercise to put oneself in his shoes and ask oneself, 'Would I have done anything different?'

In pursuit of this exercise I should like to defend Pilate against one unfair charge. In the Passion narrative of St John, Jesus says he has come to bear witness to the truth, and Pilate replies, 'What is truth?'

Francis Bacon interprets it:

> What is *Truth;* said jesting *Pilate;* And would not stay for an Answer.*

This is not justified by what John has actually said, and Bacon is interpreting it the way he does because of the point he is trying to use it to make. Here is an opposite interpretation:

At the time of his meeting with Jesus, Pilate has spent years in a region where 'what the truth is' is not an amusement for leisurely speculation and where matters of religion are at least as important as 'how we can get enough to eat': sometimes more so. He has had to hear about or even listen to any number of mountebanks stirring up trouble and claiming to possess the truth. Now

---

* Francis Bacon, 'On Truth', in *Essays* (1625).

he has come face to face with a man who has nothing to mark him outwardly as someone special, but who nevertheless has more reality about him than anyone else he has ever met.

On meeting someone who carries this authority with him – and who can make the most amazing claims (such as that about king-ship) in such a matter-of-fact way that he is clearly stating and not boasting – nothing could be more natural than to ask him for the answer to the question everybody needs a proper answer to:

'What *is* truth?'

22

He suffered death

It is the heretics who shape our creeds. When we take the trouble to stand up in public and say that something is true, we do so because its truth needs to be asserted. We know that there are people who don't believe it, or won't, or can't.

Some heresies are actively malicious: they twist the truth intentionally. Others are more well-intentioned: they try to adapt the truth so that it fits with what we can understand or what we think is correct behaviour on God's part.

The motives are opposites, but both kinds of heresy do harm. The truth is the truth, and when the truth is difficult, it is usually difficult for a reason. To evade the difficulty is to miss the point.

It was clearly not right that Jesus Christ, God and the Son of the living God, should suffer on the cross. More than that: according to any normal person's notion of what is decent divine behaviour, no really good and loving Father would ever have permitted such a thing. Still less would he have sent his Son into the world for that very purpose. Any reasonable person knows better than that.

Someone, therefore, who penetrates beyond the comfort of hearing holy and familiar words and actually starts to listen to what they mean is going to find difficulties in what these words tell him. In particular, someone who, out of a sense of what is decent and right and good, is unable to believe that 'Jesus Christ, Son of the living God, sent by his loving Father, suffered on the cross' has to get out of it somehow. Here are the main ways of escape:

1. God the Father **is not loving** at all. This is the dualist's way out, taking the theme of 'the good god and the bad god' and identifying the bad god with the Jehovah of the Old Testament

and the good god with the God preached by Jesus in the New. A good God would not have sent the Son to suffer, but 'God the Father' is not good.

2. Jesus Christ **is not the Son of God**, but just another holy man. Then the problem disappears, because we all know that bad things happen to good people sometimes.

3. Jesus Christ **did not suffer** on the cross but took it all in his stride. He treated all human evils – toothache, colds and crucifixion – with the same Buddha-like detachment. There was nothing passionate about the Passion.

4. **Jesus Christ** did not suffer on the cross. Some early heresies let Jesus do all the good things – the travelling, the preaching, the hearing – and then when the suffering starts Jesus is taken up into heaven and his place taken by an angel.

One can see the motives for each of these ways out, and they are not dishonourable ones. The heretics may be wrong in reinterpreting what the Creed says, but they are right to have difficulties with what it is telling us. If we don't feel those difficulties ourselves, then we may not be engaging completely with the truths we say we believe.

Going through the solutions to the problem one by one:

1. The 'good god and bad god' dualism isn't available to us because we have just proclaimed our belief in one God, the maker of all things visible and invisible.

2. 'Jesus as simply man' is not available as a way out because we have proclaimed Jesus as God.

3. 'Not really suffering' means that Jesus pretended to be one of us but never was. If a man is nailed, he suffers; if Jesus, nailed, did not suffer, then it follows that Jesus was not a man. All the time he was on earth, he never was one of us. It was all just a performance. No man has ever entered heaven. This way of escape does not work, because we believe in a God who is good and does not lie.

4. 'The part of Jesus Christ was played by an angelic actor' replaces a lifelong lie by a short-term lie that covers just one

particular episode. But it is still a lie. It shows us a God who is at our side until the going gets rough, and turns the Passion into a grotesque pantomime. So that escape, too, is excluded.

One can see the reasons why people would want to make an intolerable story tolerable and an indecent story decent. We are bound to feel the same need, but we must not give in to it, because truth is more important than decency. If anything needs to be adjusted, it is not the truth of what happened at the Crucifixion, but our notions of what is decent or tolerable. The Son's life on earth was dedicated to taking on humanity and going through with it. That could not mean going through with it *as long as it was tolerable* (when the fun stops, stop), but going through with it *all the way*. Only thus could the humanity be lived in truth; and if the price of that truth included suffering, then suffering was part of the price that had to be paid.

There is another, more distant perspective which may help. It involves revisiting the parable of the scissors. At the heart of the trouble we have with 'Jesus suffered' is the idea of a *good* God who allows his Son to *suffer*. Surely a contradiction, we say. In reality it is as much of a contradiction as the closing blades of the scissors are a collision. That is: the closing blades are not quite a collision, and the not-quiteness means that the scissors do what they are meant to do, which is cut. In the same way, the juxtaposition of goodness with suffering is not quite a contradiction, and the not-quiteness sharpens our ideas and gives them clarity.

23

And was buried

In reciting the Creed in church, we bow for the Incarnation (or kneel, at Christmas), and for the Passion we stand up again and square our shoulders. A visiting anthropologist, watching, would know from this that here is a religion with a very particular perspective on being, life and death.

If we were to continue to suit the action to the word, then at the mention of Christ's burial, something new and more extreme would happen. We would gather up our belongings and leave the church, because it is all over. Jesus is dead. He will be dead for ever and ever.

We, looking back on it all, know that something more happened, but the disciples, living through it, did not. It is worth reflecting on this because to go, '. . . was buried, [*quick breath*], and rose again,' as if it were just a smooth matter-of-fact progression through the events, means skating over the real shock of what happened. The Resurrection doesn't mean much if you make it just the next item in a list.

Inevitably, given who we are and the time we are in, every step of Holy Week, from Palm Sunday to the burial, is seen by us in the sharp light of the Resurrection. That light shines backwards in time and illuminates everything. It illuminates it brightly, *but it illuminates it from the wrong side*. Now and then, as a spiritual exercise, it is worth putting our blinkers on and narrowing our field of vision until we are in the disciples' time, not our own, and seeing what they saw at a time when the events of Easter were unimaginable.

I suppose an adventurous priest, realising the impracticality of emptying the church completely and then bringing everyone back in again, might approximate to the experience by trying a minute's silence after the word 'buried', just to see what the spiritual effect would be. (I would not like to be in that congregation myself: the great thing about the Mass as a background to prayer is that it is exactly the same every time.)

The close proximity of the burial with the Resurrection in the Creed and the effect that has on us is part of a wider fallacy which applies to all biography and all but the best-written history. You might call it the biographer's fallacy. If the subject of a biography falls off a bridge onto the trees below on page 100 of a 400-page biography, we don't take it especially seriously. Conceivably, he lay in a coma for weeks and everyone despaired of him, but even if the book says that, the reader can't help holding on to the thought, 'Never mind, it all comes out right in the end.'

To take another example, suppose that the subject of the biography is someone we know as a great literary personage. He gives up his job in, say, the summer of 1881 to become a writer, and struggles in poverty and obscurity until the autumn of 1883, when someone produces a play of his and he becomes famous. It would require heroic powers of empathy to avoid muttering, as the story approaches Christmas 1882 and the cold sets in and even the rats start to shiver, 'Don't worry, old chap: only another ten months to go.'

This is why it is a good spiritual exercise to try experiencing the pause after 'buried' as if it had its true length. You can try to think yourself out of 'The next thing is coming along in a minute' and into 'This state of affairs is final, definitive, permanent.' If the exercise is successful, making yourself one with the disciples in this way will reveal the Resurrection at its true value.

In times of trouble and stress, it can also be heartening to try the same spiritual exercise in reverse. In my own life, if I am stuck in a difficult situation – one I could not endure if it was going to go on for ever – it will put new strength into me if I am able to remember that I am in the same position as the subject of that biography. At Christmas 1882 he was not in a countdown to success, but in a 'forever' of failure. And yet something happened.

Or, to put it in a more concrete way: in my own biography, I am always reading the last page so far, and I never know what God is going to write on the next one.

24

And rose again

The Resurrection is everything.

The Resurrection is *evidence*. It is by its light shining backwards in time that we have come to know the truth of the theological statements we have been committing ourselves to all through the Creed. To take one example, we know and proclaim Jesus as the Son of God not because of Peter's flash of inspiration (flashes are dazzling but not always true), but through the light of the Resurrection.

The Resurrection is *the way things are from now on*. Its light shines forwards as well as backwards. God the Son at-oned himself to us at the Incarnation and committed himself to whatever might happen as a result, even up to crucifixion and death. But at-oneing cannot be undone and it works both ways. If the Son handcuffed himself to us, we are handcuffed to him. The bond that dragged him through the length and depth of the human experience will drag us one day into heaven.

The Resurrection *disqualifies Christians from being normal people* like the pagans. We know something they do not, and it is not a decorative add-on but the hinge of everything. It would be lovely to be 'compatible Christians', just like normal people but that little bit nicer, but it isn't possible. To be a Christian is to believe in the Resurrection. Not to believe in the Resurrection (as the pagans don't) is to be not a Christian. No comfortable half-way state is possible.

The Resurrection *makes Christianity disprovable*. That is to say, it makes Christianity a science. The defining characteristic of a science is not truth, but disprovability. To be scientific means to make statements that could be disproved. Take the law of gravity, for example. If I were to turn my glass of water upside down and the water didn't fall out, that would prove that the law of gravity is wrong. It would not be flawed, but exploded. No amount of authority could restore it, and we would all have to begin again at the beginning.

What makes gravity scientific is not our observation that the water always falls out of the glass but the fact that if it ever didn't, we would have to stop believing in gravity. In the same way, if we ever had solid historical proof that Jesus not only died and was buried, as the Creed says, but also *stayed* dead and *stayed* buried, then the Resurrection would be false and the whole of Christianity would be exploded. It would not just lose its foundation; it would become actively false. If we still found a way of believing in the existence of a personal God at all (which is unlikely), it would not be a loving God but a malicious God who delights in shams and deceits: not our Father, but the Father of lies.

This is why it is so tempting for ordinary Christians living in the world to repress a full-blooded belief in the Resurrection. As long as we neither quite believe nor quite disbelieve, we can feel unchallenged and safe. Our faith can never be shaken because there is nothing in it to shake.

There is no question about it: relying on belief in the Resurrection can make one nervous. It is a belief that depends on a particular historical fact and, as a scientific belief, is disprovable just as the law of gravity is disprovable. Now to put all one's trust in, to put one's very identity at the mercy of, a historical event which could conceivably be untrue is, frankly, terrifying. It is far, far safer to live in compromise and calm. It is far safer to make 'he rose again' not an act of commitment to a truth but just a cultural badge with no real-world meaning. Blessed are they who do not believe in anything very much, for they can never be disillusioned.

There is one more motive that people can have for not wanting to put their trust in the Resurrection. It comes back to that devilish idea that religion ought to be a pure and spiritual thing that floats far above the imperfect realm of matter. We had trouble with this some pages ago, when we embarrassingly proclaimed our belief in a God who made himself meat. We knocked that 'pure spiritual religion' on the head then, but here it is again, creeping back to life and once more whispering in our ears. 'We are talking of high and heavenly things,' it is saying, 'so how could it possibly be decent or dignified to have such exalted matters depend on specific earthly historical facts?' Surely putting one's beliefs in the hands of archaeologists like this shows disrespect for the omnipotent spiritual Power? Far better, the little devil whispers, to leave belief in the Resurrection to one side.

The Apostle Thomas faced a devil a little like this one and defeated it. We cannot know now whether he was tempted by it himself or whether he was inspired to crush it for the sake of others who might be tempted in future. Either way, it was crushed by his action, and a good thing too. The story behind the story in the Gospels would go something like this:

Thomas believed from the start that Jesus Christ had risen from the dead. What he wanted to be made incontrovertibly clear was whether (a) Jesus had risen and returned to heaven where he belonged, from where he could look down benignantly upon us while we, looking up, felt suitably spiritual about him; or (b) Jesus had risen from the tomb and was here on earth, still both body and soul, walking about with us. On this depended whether Christianity was to be a pure and spiritual religion (destined to fade away eventually in a glow of generalised uplift) or a religion such as there had never been, embracing matter and affirming it: meaty, messy and involved.

Was it 'He is safely back in heaven, where he belongs,' or was it 'He has gone before you into Galilee'? We know which answer Thomas got.

Where the Resurrection comes from

Scripture nowhere narrates Christ actually rising from the dead. Instead, it narrates a collection of episodes illustrating people who discover that Jesus is alive. To his *rising* there are no witnesses; to his *being risen* there are many.

The witnesses do not completely agree, and their stories narrate the discovery from different points of view. They are not always entirely coherent, and that is exactly as it should be. Anybody's past is a collection of jigsaw-puzzle pieces. Mine is and yours is. The pieces begin to change shape as soon as they have been cut, and they never fit together perfectly after that.

If you have ever had anything important to you happen in the past, a really big thing, something so big that it changed everything, then if you think back to it you will almost certainly find parts of your own narrative that don't fit together: two things that can't both be true. That is normal. It is human. What is instructive is your reaction when you think back and notice the discrepancy. You do not conclude that the memories you have are of something that never happened after all. You merely note that you have two memories that don't fit together, and you carry on believing.

What applies to one person applies to two or more. If you have a brother or sister with whom you share memories and keep them alive, it can easily happen that you find yourselves remembering something important that was said in a conversation, but disagreeing totally about which of you said it. That does not mean that the thing was not said or the conversation did not happen: quite the opposite. Indeed, criminal investigators say that if two witnesses give exactly the same description of an incident, that means that they are probably both lying.

(As it happens, that key phrase, 'loving the Lord your God with all your mind', is a good example of exactly this. In Matthew and Mark, Jesus says those words; in Luke it is not Jesus, but the lawyer he is talking to.* That inconsistency is a guarantee of authenticity. It shows that 'who said which words' was utterly unimportant to the evangelists. They were not trying to use the words to make a point: the only motive that they had for reporting this conversation was that the conversation had taken place.)

---

* Matthew 22:37; Mark 12:30; Luke 10:27.

What the Resurrection is

The raw fact that Jesus is risen being established, there follows, in the history of the Church, a time of reflection and coming to understand exactly what it was that had happened and what it all meant. That, too, is perfectly normal human behaviour. First you establish the fact of an event, and then you sit down to try and make sense of it. In this case there was a lot to make sense of. An incarnate God had never happened before, so we did not know the rules. Was this nothing more than an 'a good man raised by God' story of a specially spectacular kind? If it was more than that, then who and what was Jesus? And what was it that happened, exactly? Did God raise Jesus, or did Jesus raise himself?

Doctrine evolves in theology just as it does in the other sciences. Given the events, the theory of them is worked out, just as in the physical sciences; given some phenomena, the theory of those phenomena is worked out. This takes time and skill. It takes experts who are willing to follow lines of thought all the way and see whether they lead in the right direction or not. (I knew a monk at Downside who would raise his eyes patiently to heaven like a cheap pious painting, saying holily that he supposed that theologians were also God's creatures. But that was only his fun: they really do have their uses.)

You don't need to be a specialist to appreciate the development of doctrine. In the very early Christian hymns quoted by St Paul, Jesus empties himself and comes down from heaven and suffers, and as a reward, God raises him higher than the angels. That is the simplest story, the least theory-laden one. It is the easiest to teach and to believe; and, of course, it is poetic, a hymn not a tract. All it says is that Jesus is more than human. Until one starts constructing the theories behind it, there is nothing wrong with it. Once one *does* start constructing theories, it turns out that what the hymn says is not quite adequate.

A physical analogy is found in the history of gravity. Aristotle's theory was that anything, when not constrained, tends to go to its natural place, and that for earthy things like you and me the natural place is down, not up, while for fiery things like flames the natural place is up, not down. It was a theory of *place* rather than *force*, and it worked up to a point. But in the seventeenth-century scientific revolution the theory was found not to lead anywhere useful: it was true in a sense but not true enough, and the theory of universal gravitation took its place. This is exactly parallel to how doctrine develops.

By the time the creeds came to be written, the divinity of Christ was established doctrine and, in step with that, it was possible, and right, to say that Jesus *had risen* from the dead rather than *being raised* from the dead.

The old hymn is not really wrong, which is why we still recite it. Given that Jesus is God, it follows that 'God raised him' and 'he raised himself' are so nearly synonymous that any hairs that are still left over can safely be left to be split by the seminarians.

This is what the development of doctrine is. It does not mean changing our minds but unfolding them, thinking more deeply about what we already know. It is not one doctrine turning into something else but an embryonic doctrine unfolding into its adult form. The tadpole loses its tail and becomes a frog.

This is the moment to bring out a nice little bit of grammatical pedantry. It may amuse some and edify others. If for you it does neither of these things, pass it by.

Until the Resurrection, the last thing Jesus Christ actively did in the Creed was descend from heaven. After that, it is all passive: it is done to him. He *was* in-meated. He *was* made man. He *was* crucified, he *was* subjected to suffering, he *was* buried. Only now at the Resurrection do we once more have an active verb: he *rose again*.

This grammar brings out the passivity that God the Son took on when he took on our flesh. It emphasises how, in emptying himself to be us, he emptied himself of agency and became as powerless as we are. This was what he had to do if he was to at-one himself with us.

Coming back or going forward

There are precedents in the Bible for people dying and coming back to life as a result of the power of God. It happened to the son of the woman of Sidon in Elijah's time, it happened to Jairus' daughter and of course to Lazarus. In each case, it can be truly said that they came *back* to life. That is, the life they came back to was the life they had died out of, with the same frailties and infirmities, and the same end: death. It has been said that Lazarus has to be pitied because having died once already, he was going to have to die all over again.

One obvious difference in the case of the Resurrection was that Jesus did it by his own power, while all the other people were raised from the dead by someone else. But that is not the most important difference for him or for us.

Jesus did not come *back* to life, to this life that ends in death. He came *forward* to life: to risen life, eternal life. He did not undo his death as the deaths of Lazarus and the others were undone. At the Resurrection, history went forwards, not backwards.

Faced with the Crucifixion and the Passion, God did not undo them. It seems to be a general rule that God cannot make things not have happened. In particular, God cannot make human actions un-happen because that would make us puppets, not agents – 'run the program again and again till it gives the right answer'. So God's action in the world can only ever be by way of going forwards. The Passion has not *not* happened, and the marks of the nails are still on the body of the man who sits on the throne of the universe.

This is a lesson for us. In our own lives, when something terrible happens, such as a serious accident or a bereavement, we wish above all that it hadn't happened. We would give anything for it not to have happened. We might even, in our extremity, pray to God for it not to have happened. That is logically and theologically impossible, but there is never anything wrong or immoral in praying for impossible things, even logically impossible ones. It may be the only way we know of saying what we need to say. Petitionary prayer is not commands or magic wishes: it is a way of telling God as clearly as we can what we mean.

Whatever the terrible event may have been, if you look back on it (perhaps years afterwards), you will almost certainly see the resurrective power of God working in your own life. It will have worked as it always works: by doing, not undoing. It is not that the heat, the pain, the smells of the Crucifixion have no longer happened. They *have* still happened, but something has been made out of even them.

I don't advise ever telling anyone this. It isn't something you can put to someone who is in that kind of extreme situation: only God would be able to say it, and even he usually refrains. Even long afterwards, looking back, it takes a moment of great tact and intimacy to share with *anyone* a sense of the truth of the doctrine. But it is true all the same. That is the salutary thing about contemplating the death and resurrection of Jesus: even after we have thought of them so many times, there is still something more they can tell us.

25

In accordance with the Scriptures

Secundum Scripturas

Drama works best when it works like life. Conversely, one way of understanding life is to look at it the way one would a drama, using the mental tools one uses when watching a film or a play.

This is especially the case when the life in question is not one single human life but the life of the whole human race as it goes through the drama of salvation. The Swiss theologian Hans Urs von Balthasar devoted five volumes of his theological master-work to what he called *Theodramatik*,* theo-drama, God-drama. I mention this to demonstrate that looking at the history of salvation in this way is not necessarily either disrespectful or inappropriate.

One of the key elements of drama is surprise, and the Resurrection is about the biggest surprise there could possibly be.

In drama (and, indeed, in story generally) there are two kinds of surprise. A surprise can be inorganic or it can be organic. An *inorganic* surprise is when the playwright realises the play has been going on too long and decides to bring it to an end *right now*, without much reference to what has been going on before. In ancient Greece, a god might turn up to resolve the situation; in more modern times, an unexpected legacy could be one way of doing it. The point is that this kind of surprise is extrinsic to the drama up to that point and to the characters as they have been unfolding. (Of course, sometimes this kind of arbitrary surprise is what people actually want. The classic office-boy type of thriller is full of inorganic surprises: every chapter or two you get a new gang or a new weapon or a sudden ambush for no reason other than to keep the pages turning.)

---

* *Theodramatik* (*Theo-Drama* in English) was published in five volumes between 1973 and 1983.

An *organic* surprise is one that is intrinsic to the story and fits the characters and the world they inhabit. An organic surprise is harder to achieve, but it is more satisfying to watch or read because the surprise is a natural part of the story. A way of recognising an organic surprise is that, although it is a surprise when it arrives, when you come to think about it afterwards, it turns out to have been inevitable all along. If you like, it is a surprise from the front but not from the back. When you look back on the story it makes much more sense with the 'surprise' than it would have without it. The surprise was there from the beginning, one might say, and the 'moment of surprise' in the drama is just the moment when it is revealed to us.

The film *Fight Club* is one that I like to cite when I try to make this point. *Fight Club* is a film one grows out of, and it is best watched in a cinema full of people who haven't grown out of it yet; but it does make a good, clear example. The surprise at the beginning of the last reel of the film is that one of the protagonists turns out to be a figment of the other protagonist's imagination. What confirms this as an organic surprise is that if you see the film a second time it is not boring at all, even though you know what is going to happen. What you get on the second viewing is the clunk of things falling into place. All manner of anomalies that seemed like mistakes the first time round (odd bits of dialogue, unfinished situations, and even one spectacular bit of miscasting) turn out, once one knows the whole, to be not only *not* mistakes but actually pointers to and prefigurings of that big surprise. Indeed, the film has been telling us all along what is going to happen, and we never noticed.

The Jews had a film of their own. It was the Law and the Prophets and the chronicles and the love songs and fairy stories that make up the Old Testament, accompanied by all the commentary and exegesis that went with them. The Jews watched their film over and over again until they knew practically every frame of it by heart; but it was missing the last reel. It always stopped *just before* the big surprise, and so however deeply they came to understand it, it was an understanding of something incomplete: a story interrupted before the end. The Jews argued over what the surprise might be, and even over whether there was a surprise to be argued about.

The Incarnation came, and then the definitive surprise: the Resurrection. God, as dramatist, cannot act arbitrarily or inartistically, so the surprise of the Resurrection is an organic one. The walk to Emmaus is like the second viewing of the film: the viewing after you know that there is a surprise and even what the surprise is. You have watched it all through and seen anomalies and infelicities and the parts that don't seem to be there for any reason. You have been given hints and heard prophecies. Now that the surprise is known, you go through the film again as you walk to Emmaus with a stranger. Just as with *Fight Club*, you see the mistakes are not mistakes after all: they are pointers to what was going to come and has now happened.

This shift of perspective gives a new meaning to everything that came before it. To give just one example, even a great poem-series such as the Songs of the Suffering Servant in Isaiah, well worthy to be included in anthologies of high points of world literature along with the *Iliad* or the *Agamemnon*, is transformed. From being a poignant reflection on the human condition, it becomes a song about someone we now know and about what happened to that someone. It fits so well that it will never again be possible to think of it purely in isolation.

The walk to Emmaus teaches the disciples at length how the whole of history has been working in theo-dramatic terms. The understanding gained on that walk is the justification for the huge part the Old Testament has ended up playing in Christian liturgy. And if you look at it, the walk itself works theo-dramatically because, most appropriately, it is only at the end of the walk, after they have come to recognise what their history has been leading up to, that the disciples are capable of recognising that the man who has been walking with them and telling them about it is Jesus.

Theo-drama is a powerful tool and, like any powerful tool, it should be used only with the appropriate safety equipment. You wouldn't use a chainsaw without its guards. Balthasar himself spends the first volume of his five in justifying the whole idea of theo-drama before he embarks on applying it.

I say all this because one can easily be put off by the kind of swollen-headed biblical commentator who sounds as if he is intent on explaining why everything in the Bible was invented by the authors and never really happened: not explaining or expounding it but trying to explain it away. It seems to be a hazard of that particular profession.

But we are perfectly good critics ourselves, of both fiction and the shape life takes. We all have the ability to see the rightness in a story that works right, and we can see it equally well in fiction, life and history. Our salvation may be an immeasurably higher thing than any book, film or play, but that is no reason not to relate to it with our dramatic faculties as well as all the other tools of the mind.

This is what the phrase 'according to the Scriptures' is all about. It is fitted grammatically to the Resurrection because the Resurrection is the hinge of the whole apparatus, but it applies to the whole of the story of our salvation.

'The third day'

Most people know that 'the third day' is because the Romans did not count days the way we do. They include the beginning and end of the period in the count, so that the day after tomorrow is 'the third day': 1, today; 2, tomorrow; 3, the day after tomorrow. The modern Latin languages still do this, which is why it is impossible to say 'fifteen days' in French: *quinze jours* means 'a fortnight'.

That much is straightforward; but some of the thematic links in the Old Testament are a little unsettling. For instance, the time spent by Jesus in the tomb finds a parallel in the Book of Jonah, where the prophet (whom Jesus himself recognises as a forerunner*) is in the belly of the fish for three days and three nights.†
The Fathers of the Church love this parallel, but strictly literally it isn't a parallel at all because Jesus' three days last only 36 hours and Jonah's add up to 72.

---

* Matthew 12:39–40.
† Jonah 1:17.

The answer has to be that while some of the pattern-finding in Scripture that takes place after the Resurrection is strictly literal, overall it is a much richer business than that. The Jews saw the written Scriptures as a generations-long conversation (and sometimes quarrel) with the Lord, and a conversation is a conversation, not a computer program or a legal argument.

In a good conversation, you propose themes that may be taken up at once or that may surface again later when the time is perfect for them. Conversation is partly an exchange of information but also (I am tempted to say *mostly*) about jointly constructing a work of interplay of words and ideas. It is, indeed, music, but made out of words and ideas instead of sounds. You might compare the art of conversation to chamber music, or to improvisational jazz.

I think we can see salvation history in this way too.

Now, when you make a conversation, you do not always take up the themes in the exact way in which they were laid down: it would be a singularly literal and boring conversation if you did. And when you make music, you most definitely do not repeat the same notes in the same key on the same instrument time and time again. Half the point of music is to take a theme and present it a way that is transformed but somehow still itself. What happens in music is so much deeper than ordinary language that language can't be used to explain it: still less, to explain it away. As George Steiner says, 'Asked to explain a difficult *étude*, Schumann sat down at the piano and played it again.'*

So I would say that the 'third day' of the Creed and the 'three days and nights' of Jonah are not to be related to one another literally (raising silly questions about arithmetic) but related *musically*, the way that the parts of a work of music are related.

Indeed, were I properly educated, and single-minded, and Swiss, I would follow Balthasar's example and write a study of *Theomusik*, of salvation history considered as music rather than

* George Steiner, *Real Presences* (1989), chapter I section 4.

as drama. But apart from my lack of qualifications for the task, another point has just struck me. The five-volume study of *Theomusik*, of theo-music, if it is to fit its subject matter, should not be written, but sung.

II.d

Fulfilment

Et ascendit in cælum,
sedet ad dexteram Patris.
Et iterum venturus est cum gloria,
iudicare vivos et mortuos,
cuius regni non erit finis.

He ascended into heaven
and is seated at the right hand of the Father.
He will come again in glory
to judge the living and the dead
and his kingdom will have no end.

26

He ascended into heaven

Et ascendit in cælum

Continuing the theme of salvation history as theo-drama (but in a far less learned way than Balthasar), one can't help feeling that the Ascension is too theatrical for modern tastes – even a little bit vulgar. High truths ought to be revealed in a high way and to enlightened persons (or so the devil responsible for this feeling whispers): not flaunted on a hillside and presented in crude physical terms so that anybody standing on the right hill on the right day will see it, enlightened or not.

There is a lot to be said about snobbery as a road to apostasy (it is a surer way than persecution), but this is not the place for saying it. What I want to do here is examine what happened at the Ascension, and how it happened, in purely dramatic terms. Let us try to put ourselves, as much as we can, into the shoes of 'God the dramatist'.

Literally, 'drama' means 'an action' or 'a thing done', and one can define drama as an art that conveys its meaning not only by means of words, like a poem or speech or tract, but by means of actions and events.

There are two things to be aware of before one can really set about imagining what it is like to be God the dramatist. They make the dramatist more powerful than a human one, but they also make him less free. One of them concerns reality; the other, truth.

Where reality is concerned, human drama is made of fiction and pretence. Nothing that happens on the stage of a theatre really happens. The murder victim gets up off the ground as soon as the curtain comes down and is ready to play the same part again tomorrow. As we file out of the theatre at the end of the performance, stunned by an evening of drama and suspense, the only correct answer to 'What happened?' is 'Nothing.' Because nothing really has.

In God's drama, all the people are real. They are real in themselves, and real in the part they play in the drama as a whole. All the events are real: when the curtain comes down at the end of time, everything that has happened has still really happened.

This is quite a limitation for the divine dramatist, because people act for their own reasons and they can't be forced to do something *only* because the plot at a given moment demands it. A human dramatist is playing with unreal characters and can make them do what he wants: God can't.

The other difference between human drama and theo-drama concerns truth. Of course, we love truth and we seek it; but as human beings our participation in the truth is partial and incomplete. I, the playwright, can't see it all and I, the playwright, am able to select a still smaller piece of truth to act as the 'truth' of my play. In creating anything, there has to be selection, or the creation will be a sprawl, not art.

In theo-drama, what the dramatist knows is everything (God *is* Truth) and what he needs to convey to us is everything – or everything we are capable of receiving. The human dramatist can pick and choose his material, but God the Dramatist cannot.

The Redemption as drama

If you had to write the Redemption, how would you go about it?

The core of the drama of the Redemption is the Son uniting himself to us and by that union rescuing us. He embraces the powerlessness of fallen man and, going through that life of powerlessness, brings it and us into a reality of liberty and power.

It is obvious from the beginning that this drama requires incarnation: in-meating. If God does not become incarnate then he does not embrace our powerlessness.

The rest of the story almost writes itself. Human beings are born, so Jesus is born; they grow up, so Jesus grows up. All the way through, the drama goes the way the drama has to go. The arc of Jesus' life is the arc of a man's life, because Jesus is a man..

This holds up to and including the Crucifixion and the death of Jesus. Given the twin constraints of truth and reality, the dramatist has not really had any choice up to that point. It goes further than that: even the Resurrection, which seems so exceptional, is the only thing that could have happened.

It is worth pausing for a moment to notice something of the dramatist's style in all this. He is always subtle and never overwhelming. The actual moment of Jesus' birth is a quiet, ordinary birth like any other, hidden away in a nice, warm, dry, comfortable stable away from the crowds. The actual moment of the Resurrection is hidden away in a rocky tomb with a great stone in front of it. When angels appear, they never steer the plot; they never even command: they announce and suggest and ask, and their first words to us are always, 'Do not be afraid.' A woman rescuing a spider from the bath is not as delicate with the spider as God is with us.

And then, after the risen Jesus has walked and talked with his disciples and explained to them things he could not have explained to them before, the dramatist's final task arrives. The central character in the drama is still on stage, and he needs to be got off in a way that is faithful to both the reality and the truth of the divine drama.

The exit is necessary. Theologically and philosophically, the place for a risen body that can no longer die is not on the changeable, mortal Earth, but beyond it. Dramatically and psychologically, the need for an exit is urgent because our Saviour's presence must be temporary. Oxygen is life-saving, but a patient kept on oxygen too long forgets how to breathe. Plaster holds broken bones together, but a limb kept too long in plaster atrophies and becomes useless. A teacher who teaches you everything and answers your every question makes you unable to think for yourself.

The theo-drama of the risen Lord being on earth has a purpose; but that purpose could only be completely fulfilled if the Lord's time on earth came to an end.

How to write the final scene

In stage terms, we are looking for an exit and a curtain. For once, the divine dramatist finds himself completely free.

He has not been free up to now. There were intrinsic reasons why the Incarnation should happen, and if it was to happen then it had to happen the way it did. The same applies to the Crucifixion and the Resurrection. Things had to happen in a particular way so as to be in accord with the essential nature of what was going on. But with the Ascension there are no such considerations. It is a simple stage exit.

The dramatist can accordingly turn his fullest attention to the audience and what will work best for them. The audience are the disciples, and through them, the rest of the human race.

This is a moment when it is worth putting the book down for a bit and trying to work out an answer for yourself. The great principle of drama is 'Show, don't tell.' So making Jesus tell his disciples he will be in heaven tomorrow and then the next day making him not turn up for breakfast will not work in any dramatic sense. Being a failure dramatically, it will fail to teach what it has to teach.

You can try various solutions. I suppose you could have Jesus dissolve into blinding light in a kind of super-Transfiguration, but I can't see any advantage that that might have over the Ascension apart from being different.

Having thought through all sorts of alternatives, you will, I think, come back to a literal ascension as being best and truest in dramatic terms. It is simple. Everyone will understand it. Everyone knows heaven is not above us (heaven doesn't have a *where*), but 'up' is conventionally the heavenly direction. Going up has a precedent, because Jesus is not the first prophet who departed upwards. Elijah went before him. That is the 'theo-musical' resonance and, like good music, it takes up the theme in a new form, showing that Jesus was more than a prophet. Elijah *was carried up*, Jesus *rose* by his own power.

Jesus rises a little way and a cloud takes him from their sight. The cloud is the curtain that brings this act to a close. The drama on earth is over, in what was (after all) the simplest and clearest way.

Let's finish by listening to what the angels have to say. In the New Testament they have mostly been telling people not to be afraid, and quite right too, because they are the messengers of the Infinite, and anyone who is not awed flat by the presence of the Infinite is a fool.

But look: since the Resurrection, the angels have changed their tune. They no longer say, 'Don't be afraid.' They say, 'Don't look here; look somewhere else.' Don't look into the tomb for Jesus, because that is only where the dead are. Don't look into the sky for Jesus, because the sky is only a symbol.

A new theme has come into the music: *Stop looking in the wrong place.*

27

And is seated at the right hand of the Father

Sedet ad dexteram Patris

The story of the Creed now leaves the Earth behind and sticks to the risen and ascended Son of God. It leaves behind this speck of dust flowing in the immensity – or, if you prefer it that way, the sump at the bottom of the universe – or even Julian's 'little thing, the quantity of an hazel-nut' which 'might suddenly have fallen to naught, for littleness'. It leaves our tiny Earth behind and the almost-as-tiny universe. It moves to heaven, which is outside space and time.

There, three thrones are set. At the right hand of God the Father, who thought of it all and made it all and loves it all, God the Son sits enthroned, through whom the first-making was done (as Julian puts it), and by whom the again-making.

Thrones are not for just sitting on. Thrones are for reigning from, and so Jesus reigns. God did not make a mechanical universe to be wound up like a clockwork mouse, set running and thereafter ignored. He rules over it, he reigns over it, and by virtue of this it has order and life. Reigning is a continuing activity which is bound up with the flow of time, and as such it is the province of the Son.

A man is on the throne of the universe.

God the Son

I tried life drawing once. It is harder than it looks. Sometimes when we were in difficulties our teacher would tell us to stop trying to draw the model and draw everything that was not the model instead. For instance, if she had her hand on her hip, we would draw not her body but the empty triangle between upper arm, forearm and torso. This worked in the most marvellous way. When we drew 'not the model' and gave it a determinate shape, the model herself acquired shape and proportion, free from the errors we usually made. Artists call this 'drawing the negative space'. It is a good technique, and it works for doctrine too. Sometimes looking at what is not the truth gives a clearer and more proportionate sense of what the truth is. What the heretics do not believe shows us more clearly what our own beliefs are.

Arianism as a heresy is older than the Nicene Creed. It holds that Jesus Christ is not God at all. Heretics are divided over what this Jesus-who-is-not-God is. Some of them say he is just a good man, others a creature (presumably superhuman) specially created and sent to us by God.*

Looking through the actual observable events the Creed has narrated, from the Nativity onwards, every one of them can be taken in an Arian sense if you try. A man was born miraculously, but it doesn't need to have been God: even Islam has the Virgin Birth. A man was crucified: but that happens every day, and we don't say that every man who is crucified is God. A man died: but that happens every day as well. The Resurrection? God can raise a man if he wants. Even the Ascension can be just God taking a man up to heaven in the same way he took Elijah.

The moment in the Creed when it becomes really impossible to Arianise is now, when we say that 'he sits at the right hand of the Father'. A mere man cannot reign in heaven; nor can a specially created super-being. Jesus could not be at the Father's right hand if he were not God.

It is worth spending some time on the attractiveness of Arianism. It dates from around AD 300: from the adolescence rather than the childhood of Christianity. It is a heresy in the literal sense of the word, a *hairesis*, a 'picking and choosing' of doctrines. It believes in the oneness of God, as we do, but insists

---

* 'Arianism', strictly speaking, means the latter, but I will lump all the related heresies together under the heading 'Jesus is man, not God' and call it Arianism. It is incorrect, it is thoroughly unscholarly, but it makes the story easier to tell.

on it so strongly that it finds itself rejecting the Persons of the Trinity.

Gregory of Nyssa (335–395) found this a hot topic when he visited Byzantium:

> If you ask the money-changer to change your money, he philosophizes on the born and the unborn. If you ask the baker for some bread, he answers 'The Father is greater, and the Son is lesser'. If you ask, 'Is my bathwater ready?', the answer is 'The Son was created out of nothing.'*

Doctrine and ideology were as popular a sport in fourth-century Byzantium as in seventeenth-century England or twenty-first-century America. Then, as now, they were fun for those who enjoy that kind of thing and, as a bonus (then as now), they were a magnificent way of putting other people in the wrong.

An enlightening part of Gregory's account is that it is the money-changer, the baker, the bath attendant who arianise. These are the people most likely to have come into the city from outside, so in their origins they will have been more affected by superstition and residual paganism than people like Gregory (indeed, 'pagan' means literally 'what goes on in the villages').

It seems to be a general rule, among different people and in different times, that a recent history of paganism makes Arianism more likely. When the invading Vandals were converted from paganism, they first became Arians and only later and after much struggle did orthodoxy prevail.

This makes sense. When monotheism has liberated people from believing in many gods, the last thing they want to do is slip back to having many gods again. Therefore they reject with enthusiasm anything that might dilute or compromise their new beliefs.

The very first Christians felt little temptation to arianise because many of them were Jews and thus congenital monotheists. Having been secure with one God from the start, they did not

---

* *Oratio de deitate Filii et Spiritus Sancti* (PG46:557B); but I found it quoted in Mary Stewart's excellent 1973 novel *The Hollow Hills*.

see the Trinity as a form of backsliding into polytheism but as a going forward into deeper understanding. It was when very recent pagans came across our Trinitarian 'monotheism plus' that they took fright and threw the Trinity away for fear of sliding back into the grip of the pantheons they had only just escaped.

The principle of negative space applies here. Arianism stimulated the Church to get her theory sharp and clear: by drawing the shape of not-Arianism they drew a better shape of orthodoxy. We may barely tolerate theologians sometimes, or we may give a little holy smile and say that they are also God's creatures, but when you are building a whole life on the truth it is essential to get the truth exactly right. If Jesus is not God then everything crumbles. The whole of the Gospels are a pantomime and the whole of salvation history is a delusion and a fake.

The truth is that Jesus the Son is God. That is why we can say 'he is seated at the right hand of the Father'.

At-oned with the King

The Son oned himself to us in his birth and life and death and we stay oned to him in his resurrection and ascension. It does not stop with his enthronement. Because the Son reigns, we too are kings.

As a matter of Catholic ritual every baptised man and woman has been anointed as priest, as prophet and as king. Like every sacrament, this is not purely symbolic: it does something real. The anointing confers a privilege, but also a duty.

I am writing this book because that is my way of being a prophet, and when you communicate the things of God to others, that is yours. You are a good prophet if you do it to the right people, at the right time, in the right place; less so if you don't. We are all bound to get it wrong sometimes, but that mustn't stop us doing it: if a thing is worth doing, it is worth doing badly.

As priests, we bring man closer to God not out in public, as the ministerial priesthood does, but in the quiet corners of life. You may be doing it already without even knowing it. I shall say no more about it here.

As kings, we rule. You and I have responsibility for the good order and wise government of whatever it is that we have been set over, whether it be a room or a realm.

Theologians (who are also God's creatures) have done a lot of work on the priesthood of the laity, but none that I am aware of on our kingship; though this may just be me being ignorant. If it hasn't been done, it needs to be.

On the other hand, life is possible without theologians. Perhaps working out the kingship of the laity is actually part of our job as kings. In that case, here are a few simple points on which our thoughts might hang:

1. Each of us has a kingdom, a realm whose ordering is our responsibility. It may be big or it may be small, and many of us have more than one.
2. A king does not tyrannise, but rules his kingdom for its benefit and good order. ('Ruler = king or queen' and 'ruler = tool for measuring and making edges straight' are actually the same word, and for good reason.)
3. The king exists for the kingdom, not the kingdom for the king. The king is the servant of all because he rules all, and to rule is to serve.
4. A king does not grumble like a servant, or scheme like a court eunuch. Instead, he acts.
5. A king does not say that things ought to happen, but makes them happen.
6. Renunciation is the exercise of kingship over one's self. Thus St Thérèse of Lisieux teaches us that even with no visible kingdom, one can still be a king.
7. Kingship over the natural world means caring for it. Kings exercise dominion, not domination.

Some of this may ring a bell; some may not; some of it you may disagree with profoundly. In each of those cases, you and I are both right: I because I have made you consider your kingship seriously, and you because you are considering it.

28

He will come again in glory

Et iterum venturus est cum gloria

Self-oppression is the best oppression. It is cheap and effective, and it works. It works as well for groups of people as it does for individuals and, best of all, it is self-sustaining. A properly bullied person stays bullied for life, saying every day, 'There is something wrong with me, which is why they picked on me.' The bully may have gone away long ago, but every day the face in the mirror carries on his work.

A properly oppressed section of society splits into two. The larger part devotes itself to keeping its head down and seeming as normal as it can, keeping out of trouble by living according to the values of its enemies. After a few generations, this becomes second nature and the values of oppressor and oppressed become indistinguishable.

The smaller part does the opposite. It erects its difference into freakishness. It only feels truly itself when it is actively being different from everyone else, a standing reproach to everybody, rubbing people's faces in it and frightening the horses in the streets. This, too, becomes second nature: 'If people don't think there is something wrong with us, we must try harder.'

All this applies to any identifiable minority, and there are many examples, but what matters here is the role of Christians in an anti-Christian society. In England, they are following in the footsteps of the Catholics, who have been living in an anti-Catholic society for some five hundred years.

The choice for the oppressed seems to be between submersion and fanaticism, neither of which is very appetising, but there is a third choice as well. It is to be free.

Because you *are* free. The only thing holding you down has been you: that is what self-oppression is. If you want to stand up straight, and do, nobody will stop you. On the contrary, anyone worth anything will look at you with respect because, deep down, truth is always respected.

For many people, the false choice offered by self-oppression has an effect on how they approach the Creed. Naturally, they recite it firmly and truly while they are in church, and they believe it too, but they are not fanatics. When they step out of the church door, the statements they made with such sincerity begin to blur and fade. It is not cynical submersionism, just a natural adaptation to the different context they find themselves in. We are all of us adaptable.

It is easy to push aside what the Creed has been saying because it belongs to the other world or to the distant past, but the Second Coming breaks this pattern. It does not belong to the other world but to this one, and it does not happen in the past to people we can assume to be more ignorant than us. It lies in the future, and it is going to happen to people who are at least as clever and enlightened as us, if not more so.

Submersion won't work; fanaticism is out of the question. This is all to the good. It leaves freedom as the only choice: freedom to believe, to believe with our minds.

The trouble with the Second Coming

There is no denying that the idea of the Second Coming is troublesome. People who pay too much attention to it come across as a little odd, from the unkempt man carrying his THE END OF THE WORLD IS NIGH placard through the streets, to Sir Isaac Newton, poisoned with mercury from his alchemical experiments, making elaborate and futile calculations about the prophecies in the Book of Daniel.

This was already a problem in Jesus' time. When he was preaching the end of the world, he was pestered by people asking him, 'When?', 'When?', although the 'when' of the Second Coming is the least important part of it.

It must have felt like when you throw a biscuit on the floor and your dog doesn't notice. You point to the biscuit . . . and the dog comes and sniffs at your finger. Jesus points to the end of the world and, instead of looking in the direction he is pointing, people come to him and ask, 'When?' Like your dog, they are looking in the wrong place.

Jesus does answer their questions all the same. His answer is clear and authoritative. 'I don't know,' he says. There are things the Father knows and the Son does not, and this is one of them.*

The intriguing thing is that Jesus was one of us. He knew enough of human nature to know that something like this was going to happen if he talked about the end – and yet he talked about the end all the same. That shows that what he had to say was important enough to need saying no matter what the risks.

So why preach about it? What is the end of the world *for*? Why is it so important to preach it despite the risks of misunderstanding? One answer could be that, in the Gospels, the end of the world is something we need to be ready for because we do not know when it is coming. But that is not all that persuasive because the same thing is true of death, and nobody needs to be ready twice over.

Nevertheless, I think that the gift of death is still some sort of key to this prophecy and this doctrine.

There are probably about as many ways of thinking about the Second Coming as there are people thinking about it, so what I propose has no particular authority. If it helps to shed light on it from a different angle, that will be good.

The gift of shape

The angle I want to offer takes up the theme of 'theo-music' once more.

My life has a shape. It has a beginning and an end, and everything between the beginning and the end, every event, every time of life, gets at least part of its meaning from where it lies on that trajectory.

* Mark 13:32.

Music has a shape too. Music by its nature stretches across time, and its parts do not show their full meaning and significance until you have heard the whole. When you have sat listening through three-quarters of a piece of music, you have not yet really heard any of it. Only when you have heard the whole can you perceive the whole. Then you will also perceive the true meaning of its parts as parts of that whole.

The end of a piece of music is not to be mourned. It needed both a beginning and an end to give it its shape. The end is not a termination but a completion.

As with music, so with life. In the Passion according to John, Our Lord's final word is not 'It is over,' but 'It has been completed'. Nobody cries because a symphony has ended: a piece of music that went on for ever would not really be music.

As with life, then, so with the life of the world. The Second Coming does for the life of the world as a whole what death does for our lives as individuals. It gives it a shape. Thanks to the Second Coming, the life of mankind as a whole has not only a beginning but also a conclusion.

In the mythology behind *The Lord of the Rings*,* J. R. R. Tolkien describes death as 'the Gift of Man'. With the Second Coming, the Gift of Man is mirrored in the Gift of Mankind.

Our place in the drama

If theo-music can be a guide to the rightness and goodness of the Second Coming, theo-drama provides a hint as to why too much inquisitiveness on the when and the how of it is so good at driving people off the rails. As characters in the drama of history, it is not appropriate for us to know how and when the drama is to end,

---

* The best-selling Catholic novel in history. '*The Lord of the Rings* is of course a fundamentally religious and Catholic work; unconsciously so at first, but consciously in the revision . . . the religious element is absorbed into the story and the symbolism.' J. R. R. Tolkien, letter to Robert Murray SJ, 2 December 1953, reprinted in *The Letters of J. R. R. Tolkien* (1981).

and that is why we go so wrong when we try. A play in which, at the end of the fourth act, everyone on stage knew what was going to happen at the end of the fifth act would not be a good play. Nor would one in which the characters spent their whole time wondering which act they were in.

The Second Coming will be a surprise: Jesus has told us so. So was the long-expected First Coming, and the when and the how of it were a surprise to everybody. Remember the nature of dramatic surprise: *before* it happens, looking forwards in time, the surprise is surprising; *after* it happens, looking backwards in time, the surprise turns out to have been inevitable. To us, the Incarnation makes perfect sense because we are looking back at it from the road to Emmaus, while the Second Coming makes no sense at all because we are looking forward at it and it seems nothing but a swirl of prophecies and wild imagery. But think for a moment exactly how much sense the Incarnation made in the first century BC. Nobody could have predicted when the salvation of the world would happen, still less how; some people were even sure it would not happen at all.

Like any dramatic surprise, the Second Coming will not shatter our story but fulfil it, and bring out its true and proper meaning. Once we know the whole, we will say to one another, 'This is the best way, it could not have been otherwise.'

'Not with a whimper but a bang'

Curiously, although the doctrine of the Second Coming of the Son is such a specifically Christian one that belief in it can be quite challenging, the idea of *an* end of the world flourishes much more widely, sometimes in peculiar ways. This provides the opportunity for an unusual kind of evangelism, one that does not offer answers but simply gets people thinking towards the right questions.

Here is a game I played with some clever people a few years ago. It works better when played with friends, and I thoroughly recommend it.

The game begins with a postulate: the astronomers who watch the orbits of distant objects in the solar system have discovered one that will strike the Earth on Sunday 10 April 2033 at 9.23 in the morning, Greenwich time. The observations have been made and refined. The calculations have been checked and repeated. The prediction is certain. The asteroid is bigger than the one whose impact on a spring day sixty-six million years ago wiped out the dinosaurs. This time, *all* life will end.

That is the scenario. The game consists in asking everyone: what are the consequences of this?

A criminologist could be inspired to wonder about the effects on the convergence of penalties. By the autumn of 2032, a burglar would risk a life sentence, while a murderer would be certain of receiving no more than six months.

An educationalist would wonder whether to stop educating the young because education is for fitting them for careers, and there won't be any careers. Or should they be educated all the more, because learning is a good in itself?

An economist might possibly think about inflation. The only value of money is what you are going to do with it, so when there is no time left to do anything, there will be no value in money. By the end of March 2033 you could offer a street-sweeper or a train-driver a million pounds to do his work, but why would he bother to do the work even if you did pay him that?

On the other hand, someone who had thought properly about what work was* would say that the value of the work you do lies in the work that is done, not in the money people offer you to do it. A swept street is good because a clean street is good, and a driven train is good in that it takes people to where they want to be. Not every street-sweeper and train-driver will think like that, but pride in one's work is more widespread than most economists imagine. So the trains may still run.

A friend of mine who was a consultant in public health medicine admitted that she rather looked forward to being able to encourage people to improve their quality of life by smoking and drinking more.

---

* For instance, Pope John Paul II, whose encyclical *Laborem exercens* so few people took the trouble to understand.

Even liturgy faces interesting questions. Sunday 10 April 2033 is Palm Sunday, so a fine devotional exercise is to compose special liturgies for 'the Lent without an Easter' – or should it be called 'the Lent before the universal resurrection'? We are about to hand back the world to him who made it and confided it to our care. At 'the Last Mass', do we thank, or apologise?

I bounced this idea off some of my friends, and the response was humbling. The most unexpected people thought about it both deeply and well. A friend from salsa class with few ideas (one would have said) beyond girls and dancing was full of questions and arguments, as if after a lifetime of not being fed, his soul had at last found something to get its teeth into. He wanted to rush off and ask all his friends the same question and see what they had to say.

Another friend's response was rather moving. She was in the early years of the kind of life we all officially envy: married, two incomes, a steady upward path mapped out both financially and professionally. She went very quiet when I told her about the end of the world. Then she said, 'If this was real, I would leave the job and the London flat and everything, and move to the country with the children to be poorer, free and happy.'

I nearly asked her, 'Why don't you?', but even with good friends there are places one does not go.

All in all, it was with high hopes that I went to a dinner that I knew was going to be attended by a group of clever people who had climbed high in their various professions. I imagined all those brilliant minds catching fire. I imagined myself as the editor of a book on the theme, with sparkling contributions from experts in every field . . .

I told the clever people the story just as I had told it to my friends, and I asked them the same question. But the people round the table were all dead. Perhaps the long path they had trodden to their various eminent positions had squeezed the humanity out of them. Not one of them had an idea worth writing about. One spoke up and said that anarchy would inevitably take hold as time ran out. I was expecting him to go on to say that he would help to organise people to maintain law and order, but no, he told us he would stock up on ammunition and retire behind high walls and stay there until the end came. That would, of course, amount to life imprisonment. He deserved it.

Leaving aside that disastrous dinner with the already dead, I can thoroughly recommend the end of the world. It enlightens and liberates because, by giving time a shape, it gives it a meaning. It can bring health and proportion to the minds of people who are still alive, and liberation with it. And it might liberate you as well.

29

To *judge the living and the dead*

Iudicare vivos et mortuos

The Last Judgement is a godsend to painters. It offers them a composition that spreads splendidly in a vertical as well as in a horizontal direction. At the top there is the Father in heaven, reigning. Jesus is in the middle, judging, and below them there are the dead rising from their tombs, and also sinners being consigned to hell. All over the picture there is room for body after body after body in every possible state: anxious, relieved, joyful; doubtful, terrified, despairing; clothed or naked. Above it all, angels float in limpid air, and at the very bottom, devils stir up the fires with pitchforks.

The Last Judgement is a godsend to people who disapprove of other people. They can exercise their disapproval in full right-eousness, contemplating with equanimity the future eternal damnation of their enemies: always dispassionate, of course, and never gloating. Rising from their contemplations, they take care to inform their enemies of their fate: not in anger or cursing but with bland, innocent faces because, after all, they are only making a simple statement of fact.

The Last Judgement has been an inspiration to composers. The ancient hymn *Dies Iræ*, 'The Day of Wrath', reflects on the coming dissolution of everything. Overwhelmed by it all, it expresses our fear at the coming judgement and pleads for God's mercy. Mozart's *Requiem* has a magnificent setting of it, and Rachmaninov uses the plainchant melody several times in his works. When I looked it up, the list of musicians who have used it one way or another was endless.

I have a quite specific reason for taking the *Dies Iræ* as a point of entry to consideration of the Last Judgement. The Liturgy of the Hours prescribes this hymn for the last week of the Church's year: that is, the week in late November between the celebration of Jesus Christ the King of the Universe and the beginning of Advent. Advent looks forward not only to Christmas but also to the Second Coming, so this is the perfect time for a hymn about the end of the world.

The Universalis website,* which I created, gives the Liturgy of the Hours for every day of every year. Accordingly it displays the *Dies Iræ* at this time. But one November a few years ago I received an email from an indignant reader of the site, reproaching me for putting such a miserable hymn on to the page. 'It is not at all conducive to prayer,' he said.

He really had much more to disapprove of if he had put his mind to it. After all, the unsettlingness of the *Dies Iræ* is simply a logical product of a religion whose founder stated explicitly that he had come to bring a sword into the world, not peace, to divide fathers from sons and alienate brothers from sisters. That founder said he longed to see the world in flames. He told gloating stories of the torments in store for rich men, even respectable ones who were good citizens and paid their taxes. He promised eternal punishment to people who did not do as he told them, and recommended self-mutilation as a way to escape an eternity of being burned in fire or eaten by worms.

None of this is, according to my correspondent, truly Christian. A true God is a loving God who hugs you and tells you how good you are really and it's all all right. The idea that there might be more to God than cuddliness, that God might also be a God of justice, and that justice might be not only good and true but also terrifying, simply does not enter this man's head. He is almost certainly one of the people who take care to say at the beginning of Mass, 'I have sinned (but not greatly).' In any case, he is a symptom of a tendency that is always present to some extent in religion: a tendency to think that our God is above all a God of niceness.

But God is not nice: God is just.

* universalis.com.

The love of justice

Despite all the ways people find of twisting it, justice is something we all believe in and all need. The very fact that we complain about its abuses shows how much we respect it, because it is not possible to abuse a bad thing or a valueless one. Indignation at abuse is an indicator of the value of the thing abused, and cynicism about 'Ministries of Justice' is really a blanket thrown over the fire of indignation to stop it blazing up and consuming the world.

A sense of right and wrong is universal. When people know that someone's behaviour is 'well out of order', they say so. Their judgement is usually right, and it is apprehended directly, not theorised into existence by lawyers. To pick up on the spectrum described in an earlier chapter, it is Semitic rather than Greek.

A child needs right and wrong more than it needs almost anything else. A child has an innate sense that right and wrong exist,* and it needs to see that they are present in the world it lives in. It is heartbreaking to watch when children do something deliberately wrong in the hope that their parents will see it and tell them off. Without right and wrong, children have no compass with which to navigate through life. 'If you do not tell me I am well out of order, it can only be because the whole world is.'

The psalmist rejoices in justice. He glories in the fact that the Jews have the Lord's laws, statutes and decrees and that none of the nations do. In his day-to-day life he longs for justice. He is forever asking the Lord to come and judge his case. He has no doubt that he is in the right: all he wants is a proper hearing, and just judgement.

That is one side of the question, but the psalmist sees the other side as well: 'If you judged us,' he says to the Lord, 'who would survive?'† When it is a question of a shifted fence or a stolen cow, he may think that he is more in the right than his enemies; but

---

* Teaching the child what *is* right and what *is* wrong amounts to developing this innate sense and giving it something to feed on.
† Psalm 129(130):3.

when it comes to absolute value, he is certain that he is in the wrong. He is so certain of this that he makes the speech for the prosecution himself before God has a chance to say anything, because he wants to make sure that the right verdict is reached. He knows he is in the wrong, and says so. He is able to say he is in the wrong because he sees past his own guilt to the abundance of God's mercy. The sooner he gets judged, it seems to him, the better it will be. Without sin, there can be no forgiveness.

The Church's view of justice builds on the psalmist's. The main change from the world of the Psalms is that the Church has learnt how God's mercy is delivered. It is not handed out distantly from on high. It comes through the judge jumping down to become one with the accused and to go through life as his brother – through life, and also through death.

We all do want to be judged. Imagine that an action of yours has caused someone else to suffer greatly. Clearly, your action has to be dealt with: if nothing else, you need to come to terms with it yourself. So – was the action culpable or innocent?

- If your action was innocent, then there is no problem. Regret will suffice.
- If your action was culpable, then there is no problem. You have repented, you are contrite, and God in his mercy will forgive you.

If you don't know which of the two it is, you can do neither of these things. Your past festers. Your action causes you continuing pain. Indeed, it can overshadow the rest of your life: I have seen it happen. The guilt of the *perhaps* guilty is agonising. If it were real, it could be cured; if it were unreal, it would not need curing; but if it is neither real or unreal, then there is nothing that can be done.

You need the just and all-knowing Judge to tell you with absolute authority that you are innocent; or with absolute authority tell you you are not, and then with infinite mercy wipe you clean.

It is not at all certain that the Father is capable of doing this. The Father does not know what it is like to be us because he has not been one of us. The Son has. And, indeed, the Creed specifies that it is the Son who is going to be doing the judging. It all fits.

To take the idea further for a moment: we are used to talking about the Incarnation as leading to the salvation of mankind. But perhaps the Incarnation was also important in its own right, because it alone would allow us to be finally judged by a God who is a man like us.

Is the Last Judgement just?

My good correspondent disapproves of the *Dies Iræ*, and presumably of the Last Judgement, and possibly therefore of God: who does God think he is, judging us and consigning us to eternal punishment? Before discarding this man entirely, let's try to get to the root of the trouble, because we all share it to some extent. It comes, I think, from looking at things with the wrong eye.

Jesus is a Semite, and he is talking to Semites. The Semitic relationship with God, with Being, is an intensely personal one, a matter of passionate direct encounter rather than cold Greek logic. The language is suited to the culture: Hebrew, the language of the Old Testament, is direct and concrete in expression. Hebrew does not do abstractions. In Old Testament language, it is not possible (for example) to express concern about the increasing prevalence of violent crime in rural districts. But one can fear the sword in the wilderness.

The terrible images of the end of the world and of eternity in Jesus' preaching are the way to express these realities in Semitic terms, and they only work for those with a Semitic mind and culture. This is not only a matter of the concrete directness of the language; it also depends on the listener already being in an intimate (if turbulent) relationship with a being of infinite power, rightness and love.

If that is not your culture, then you need to adjust your perspective accordingly. That is what we need to do because, as Christians, although we are Semites we are also Greeks. Semitic language taken literally as if it were Greek turns out a mess, and its message is obscured by irrelevancies. Could the Garden of Eden have been paradise, Voltaire asks,* if Adam and Eve had no shampoo or nail scissors? For a more pernicious example, take James Ussher, the seventeenth-century Protestant Archbishop of Armagh, who added up all the lifetimes of the patriarchs and deduced that the world must have been created in 4004 BC. This kind of 'reading Semitic as if it were Greek' might be thought to be simply comic, but it is harmful because certain kinds of people take the exercise, and the answer, seriously. They like believing nonsense if it is holy nonsense.

To make proper sense of the Last Judgement, and stop disapproving of God, it is necessary to do a double transposition. First, to get behind the surface of the Semitic imagery to understand what the imagery is really saying; second, to translate that truth into terms we hybrid Semite–Greeks can understand. This is not a question of watering down or explaining away, but of seeing from a second direction in order to see the solid whole. It is hard, but it is not as impossible as it might seem.

Everyone is different, but pressing the sore spot is usually a good first step to finding out what is hurting. Here is a possible catalogue of what the Last Judgement looks like if taken literally and without any reference to our existing relationship with God:

- We are **judged** on what we have done.
- The judgement is **black and white**: you are good or you are bad.
- **Sentence** is passed on the bad.
- The punishment is **infinite** and eternal.

In each line I have emphasised the words in which the difficulty lies.

In his beautiful and wise book *Resurrection Is Now*, Dom Aelred Watkin says that a sure road to disbelieving the truth is to disbelieve the terms in which it is presented, without looking

---

* In his poem *Le Mondain* (1736), quoted in Nancy Mitford, *Voltaire in Love* (1957).

behind them to see what they are trying to say.* So what follows now is an exercise in 'looking behind the terms'. The viewpoint it presents is not new. You won't see it in paintings and you won't see it in the *Dies Iræ*, but it does have respectable antecedents throughout theological history, and deeper, pre-Christian roots in the philosophy of Aristotle. It does not replace the paintings and the hymns. On the contrary, it gives them their proper value because now we will be seeing and hearing them say what they mean and not what they don't.

The tipping scales

The idea of judgement after death did not come into the world with Christianity. It can already be found in Plato, and even Plato did not invent it: he refers to it as if it were an established myth. He probably heard it from the Egyptians, and they in turn may have learnt it from Zoroastrianism, which means that by the time of Christ it was already more than a thousand years old.

The origins of the idea are pre-Christian, and the idea in the form in which it is bred into our culture – our 'default setting', if you like – is not Christian at all. Some of the trouble we have with the Last Judgement is precisely because we are applying pagan imagery to the understanding of the Christian doctrine. The more we forget to think about Christianity, the more 'default pagan' we become culturally, which explains why we find the problem of judgement so acute.

This long-established pre-Christian picture of judgement might be called the tipping-scales theory. The souls of the Egyptians after they are dead are weighed in the scales of the gods. If the scales tip one way, the soul goes one way; if the scales tip the other way, it goes the other.

As time goes on, this comes to be seen more literally as a drawing-up of accounts, of debits and credits. The tipping-scales theory becomes a bank-manager theory. It works like this:

* Dom Aelred Watkin, *Resurrection Is Now* (1997).

Take a human soul. Take all the good that the soul has done and put it in one pan of the scales. Take all the evil and put it in the other. Hold the scales up and see which way they tip. 'Where they tip, there you go.' You go one way if the evil outweighs the good, the other way if the good outweighs the evil.

This is an enjoyable theory. It appeals to the accountant in all of us. It is capable of accurate codification as a kind of moral calorie-counting. It is a great guide to life because it lets you be just good enough without the risk of being too good. Simply calibrate how many halfpennies given to beggars weigh the same as, for instance, one back-stabbing or a single lie; and remember to keep your accounts up to date and check your balance regularly. At some times and in some societies it has been done like this – and not with good results.

Living according to the tipping-scales theory is cold and calculating. More important than that, the theory itself is inherently wrong. It works in terms of black and white with no shade of grey in between. On the boundary between bliss and damnation, at the limit, at the edge, the tiniest of differences will make not just a big but an *infinite* difference to the outcome. Physicists call this a 'discontinuity'. Half a feather floating down onto one pan or the other can make the difference between the verdict that you are good or that you are bad – utterly, completely and for ever. That is quite clearly not right. It goes against the sense of justice we all have. If God behaves like this, then God is well out of order.

In religions in which the will of God is everything and human reason is nothing, this objection has no force because the mere fact of God deciding something makes it right: if it seems wrong to us, then so much the worse for our misaligned sense of right and wrong. That sounds harsh, but it can turn out more tender in practice. I am impressed, for instance, by John Buchan's description of his own Calvinism.* It displays a belief in the inflexibility of God's judgement, but one that is balanced against a strong countervailing trust in God's mercy. John Buchan was a good and

---

* In John Buchan, *Memory Hold-the-Door* (published posthumously in 1940).

humble man and his doctrine does not seem to have done him harm, but all the same it is hard to see how arbitrary rules plus unanalysable mercy can be properly 'lovable-with-the-mind'. So let's carry on trying to find a way to love God with the mind, as we have been told to do.

Doing and becoming

It is time to put the tipping-scales theory to one side for a while, and with it the judgement that 'where the scales tip, there you go'.

Let's go back to the roots of action and to what it is that actions actually do.

Consider a free action. Psychologists are fond of showing us how our actions are constrained by our psychological state – in other words, by who we are at the time. We are less free than we think. All the same, every action is *to some extent* free, or it wouldn't count as an action at all. We are never purely clockwork. There is always at least some freedom.

One's nature constrains one's choices, but the mechanism works in the opposite direction as well. Each free choice I make changes me. Each instance of 'what I do' influences 'who I am' – possibly by a tiny amount, but it does. Aristotle in his *Ethics* was already pointing this out 2,500 years ago.

I remember once thinking about killing someone, though not for long and not getting as far as making really detailed plans. Although that fact itself is uninteresting (probably most of us have done it), what I find it interesting to observe, looking back, is the forces that were pushing me not to perform the act I was considering. Morals had no part in it: it did not matter that killing was wrong. Nor did squeamishness put me off, or the risk of getting caught. None of that. The really strong argument for not killing the man was that if I did, *I would become a killer*. What put me off the act was that it would change me, and change me irreversibly.

In practice, the real decisions we face in life are far less dramatic. Each of them is smaller and changes one less. But they do change one, and they change one cumulatively because there are so many of them. It all adds up: who you are affects the action, and the action affects who you are. (It is like Newton calculating the orbit of the Moon: the Moon's motion affects its position, and the Moon's position affects the way its motion changes over time.)

I have just said, 'It all adds up,' but this addition isn't the inhuman accountancy of the tipping-scales theory. The total at the end of it all is not when the Recording Angel tots up the columns in his book and compares them. The total of all my actions is me, myself. My life has been full of acts of becoming: now, at the end of it, *I am what I have become.*

'You are who you have become.' It sounds like a law of nature – and if you look round you, it is. Look at a young tree, blowing in the wind and leaning this way and that as the wind takes it. Look at the same tree years later, when it is old and rigid. Now it can no longer bend, but the shape it has acquired will show you which way it has been leaning throughout its life.

The analogy is not perfect, because of course a tree is entirely dependent on external circumstances: the tree does not blow itself. But I think the picture still helps.

Becoming and being

'You are who you have become.' This is not a judicial sentence but a diagnosis. At death (it says), there is an end of becoming, and you are who you are. As the unknown author of a second-century sermon puts it:

> We should repent of our sins while we are still on earth. When a potter is making a vessel and it becomes misshapen or breaks in his hands, he shapes it again; but once placed in the oven, it is beyond repair.*

If you have become someone who is leaning towards others in love, then that is what you will be. Love is an 'in-othering', a removal of all barriers, and the joy of heaven consists in holding

---

* The so-called 'Second epistle of Clement to the Corinthians', VIII:1–2.

nothing back, giving everything and receiving twice as much in return. When a positive number is multiplied by infinity it becomes infinitely positive, however tiny it may have been to start with. If you have become even slightly positive, you will be infinitely positive, infinitely open, and heaven for you will be infinite giving and receiving.

But if you are the opposite of this – if your whole being is ordered towards *you*, and other people exist only in so far as they can serve your ambitions and desires – if people are not people at all but objects to be used – then that is who you will be. You are what you have become. When a negative number is multiplied by infinity it becomes infinitely negative. Everything about heaven is the same as it was in the positive case: the removal of all barriers, and the unconditional in-othering. But it will be something you strenuously reject.

Except that it is impossible to reject reality. If other people now impinge on you as their true selves, they will inevitably do so as persons and not as objects, because persons and not objects is what they are. But you – you only want objects, not people. Hell is other people, says Sartre. Heaven is the same 'other people' that hell is. The difference between the two is down to who *you* are: who you have chosen to become.

The light of heaven is the light of other people's presence and the presence of God; but to the lost, the light of heaven *is* the fires of hell.

Becoming: an example

All this theory deserves an example.

I have a friend who made herself a slave to success. It killed her. But don't worry, this is not a sad story. It illustrates the saving action of God.

My friend was intelligent and well educated. She wore her learning lightly because it was a joy to her. Her conversation sparkled, and when it sparkled, to be with her was a delight.

But she had enslaved herself to success. It was a pernicious enslavement because, unlike achievement, 'success' can never be attained: for each hill you climb, there is a higher hill beyond it. You travel forever because it is impossible ever to arrive.

Whenever my friend achieved anything, her devil whispered to her, 'If you have done this thing then it can't have been anything special, can it?' Her head told her this was a lie, and she told me herself that it was; but still her heart believed it. Onwards and upwards she went in her career. As she rose, the air around her grew thinner and the people fewer. She went out nowhere in the evenings except where it was useful for her to be seen. She talked to no one unless there was a purpose to the conversation. At a reception she would always be glancing over your shoulder in case someone more important came into sight.

In the end, it killed her. I shan't go into the manner of her dying except to say that it was slow and it was medical. But it was a beautiful time all the same, because Jesus was with her: Jesus the vine-dresser.

'Cut is the branch that might have grown full straight,' says the Chorus at the end of *Doctor Faustus*. This particular branch had grown crooked. It was contorted, and its own tendrils had twisted back onto it and all but choked it. (Perhaps they would have choked it completely, in time, and perhaps that is why the merciful God had to have her die when she did.) The branch needed to be pruned to make it ready for eternity. 'You will be what you will have become.'

Through the days and weeks as my friend lay dying, the vine-dresser cut away a little here, a little there. He separated the inessential from the essential. He unwound the dead bits and freed the live ones. The operation was intricate; but the vine-dresser is skilled and his pruning-hook is sharp.

One day when I visited my friend in hospital, I took one look at her and said, 'You're back!' And because she *was* back, she knew exactly what I meant. The branch was free again. Its dead wood had been cut away and it was free to wave in the breeze and rejoice once more in the sunlight and grow leaves again. It was ready for heaven.

Yes, that branch could have grown straight from the beginning, all those many years ago, and no, it did not. That is sad. It grew distorted and had to be pruned back – and it was. The pruner cut away what was *not* the branch from what *was* the branch, and now it is flowering in the presence of Jesus who made it and saved it. In that story, regret has no place.

Healing and purgation

This example shows something of the nature of purgation. Purgation is like a surgical operation in which the 'not-me' is carefully cut away from the 'me', like the removal of a tumour or a wart. It can take place in this life, as here, or in the next: and that is what Purgatory is for.

The doctrine of Purgatory is easily half forgotten and when that happens, the half we still remember becomes strange and sour. Purgatory can end up as a place of punishment, a semi-hell, different in some way from hell but no one remembers how; or even as a place of probation as if the souls in it were retaking a failed exam. If those are the only available choices, then Purgatory really is best forgotten.

Orthodox theology assigns to Purgatory a different role, that of my friend's hospital stay in which the bad bits, the 'not-me' bits, are cut out, leaving a pure and unblemished 'me'. It is also where that newly free 'me' learns how to move again and live in reality and freedom. Dante explores this theology in the *Divine Comedy* with all his powers of intellect and imagination. It is one of a hundred reasons for reading the poem.

If you still have lingering affection for the tipping-balance theory of judgement, then it is time to leave it behind. There is no limit to the amount of surgery Jesus can do if he wants. A saint might need none at all; an international assassin might need almost everything removed to get to a 'me' whose eyes are not dead when you look into them.

Now an objection starts to appear. If there are no limits to what God is able to do in healing us, then that begins to sound like universal salvation for everyone, and Jesus takes great pains to preach the exact opposite. He tells us time after time that perdition is possible *for us*. He deploys all the horrors of fire and worms and anything else he can think of to make sure that we do not forget this fact. How can this be?

The consenting will

The story of the divine surgeon freeing the real 'me' from the tangle of 'not me' that envelops it is an encouraging one, but it omits one vital detail. Oddly enough, that detail is actually implied by the very image of a surgeon: *no surgical operation can be performed without the patient's consent.*

Everything we are told about God and his dealings with the soul tells us that he respects its freedom above all things, no matter what it chooses. If Mary had said No, Jesus would not have been born.

Having given us freedom, God cannot take it away. If at the moment of death the soul, however wicked its ways and however tiny its authentic 'me', turns towards God, the whole apparatus of surgery and rehabilitation is deployed to bring it to true and free being . . .

. . . but if not, not. God always gives us what we want.

This business of 'wanting' needs looking into further. It amounts to an act of the will, and the will is a puzzling and confusing thing. It is hard to talk about and hard to understand: perhaps nobody really does understand it. Will is not the same as action: I can will a thing and not do it; I can *not* will a thing but still do it. Another layer lies on top of this one because it is not only actions that are subject to the will: semi-paradoxically, *acts of will* are as well. It makes perfect sense both grammatically and psychologically to say, 'I want to want to do' something: I don't want to do it, but I wish I did want to. When St Augustine famously asked God for purity 'but not just yet', he was wanting to want to be pure, but not quite able to take that step.

The picture of 'character determines action; action determines character' is far more complicated once the will is added in. Perhaps one way to do it is to think of the will as a kind of muscle of the soul. It is always there; but if you never use it, it grows weak and lets you down at the moment you need it most.

Peter is the outstanding example of this. Peter thought he was able to stand side by side with Jesus and endure trial and persecution along with him. And he was absolutely right: if he had been formally stood up next to Jesus before the chief priests and before Pilate he would have boldly said, 'Where he goes, I go,' and he would have gone through with it, all the way to Golgotha. All that, Peter was ready and able to do. What Peter was not able to do was say the right thing when taken by surprise by a little servant girl.

Death is the ultimate startlement. At that moment, the choice a person makes is an utterly true reflection of who that person is. If there is any truth at all in bank balances, it is simply this: after a lifetime of selfishness and treating other people as objects, how likely is it that, taken by surprise without even a towel to cover you, you will turn your back on all that and suddenly embrace openness and the value of others?

Remember when you were learning to box. You were not learning it intellectually so that in the ring you could assess the situation, select the right moves and execute them. You were training your body how to react without thinking so that the right moves would execute themselves. That is what the training of the soul is like and why a good life is better than a bad one.

This is what lies behind the idea of repentance *in articulo mortis*, repentance at the moment of death. People pray for the grace of perseverance with precisely this idea in mind. It is not a question of 'I am afraid that I may fall into bad habits in the future.' It is 'I am afraid that, if taken utterly by surprise, I will act without thinking and thus reveal my true nature – and my true nature might not choose God.' We are all of us grand and noble and firm and courageous and magnanimous when we rehearse our role in this or that imagined scenario, but when we are startled, our real self has no time to put on that costume and we end up behaving in a small and mean way. Small and mean but, unfortunately, true.

At the moment when it counts, you will be what you have become because you have spent your whole life becoming it.

The soul can choose. It can choose the true me-ness of love and so choose God. Or it can choose to reject all that and embrace the false me-ness which, paradoxically, often manifests itself as idolatrous worship at the altar of ME. 'Don't you know who I am?' asks the Great Man insisting on his right to recognition.

And God replies, 'No, I do not know you.'

It is absolutely necessary, if God is the giver of freedom, that it should be possible for people to reject healing and turn their back on the true 'me' and hold on to their 'not-me' vices instead. If God did not allow this, then we would be toys, not people.

It is because of giving people what they truly want that in Dante's *Inferno* the words PRIMAL LOVE MADE ME are carved above the entrance to Hell.* If anyone does truly want the self and nothing but the self, they receive what they want. Spiritual coercion is impossible, just as love potions are impossible. And if what they want burns and eats them alive, that is a consequence of their choice of self, not a punishment.

I knew two monks who spent thirty years happily pursuing a long-running argument about the population of hell. We are required to believe that hell exists, but not that there is anyone in it. Father Illtyd liked to say that the mercy of God is limitless, and that God must find a way – like the pruning-hook in my friend's case – to strip back the not-self from even the darkest soul and end up with something (however tiny) that is real. But Father Mark would reply that God has given us free will and that if that freedom does not include the freedom to reject God, then that freedom is a sham: so if a soul wants to be lost, it can be. To which Illtyd's next response would be, *can* a being consciously, clearly and unambiguously will its own harm, or is it always pursuing *some* good – feebly, disproportionately, distortedly, mistakenly – and is not *every* good a reflection of the Good? But it is time to leave them. They both know the answer by now, and one day so will we.

And against all this elegant, rational thought, as convincing as it sounds, we still have to set Jesus' warnings of hell fire for errors that any sensible person would surely judge to be venial:

* *Inferno*, III.6.

not visiting the sick, for instance. There is no getting round what he said.

. . . to judge the living and the dead

The question of the way in which one is judged at death as opposed to the way in which one is judged at the Last Judgement has exercised some high theologians greatly. It is good that they should be thinking through it – it is important that they should – but for us ordinary people it seems a bit of a distraction. According to our own 'low theology', our task is to live and love. Instead of theorising, we ought to be getting on with it.

30

And his kingdom will have no end

Cuius regni non erit finis

We live in a temporary universe. One day there will be no more stars, and perhaps even no more matter. The Earth we live on is already half way through its nine-billion-year life.

What this part of the Creed is saying is simple, because simplicity here is all we need. The new world, the world after the Second Coming, has no end. Unlike our present, transient world, it is final and definitive. Moreover, God the Son still reigns over it, which is to say that he is the ordering principle of the permanent, definitive world just as he is of the transient, temporary one. It has no boundaries in time or in space.

A transient world followed by an everlasting world is the structure of time in all the religions of Abraham, although it is interesting to note that, historically speaking, the Jews came to this realisation quite late. It is as if they were so busy living their relationship with God that they never had time to turn aside from the present and speculate about a future state. A cheerful consequence of this is that one can refute the critics who say 'Religion is just pie in the sky' by pointing out that the Jews for most of their history were expected to be good without the incentive of any kind of future existence.

We live and we die, we are raised to a new kind of life, and that's that. The Creed has just added that our world, too, lives and dies, is raised to new being, and that is that. Beginning, transformation, completion: the religions of Abraham are linear.

It is different for the Hindus. They die and are not raised to anything, but are simply born again to die again, and so on for ever. Hinduism is circular, and Buddhism takes on the circularity in its own way. The Norse myths of long ago did for the world what Hinduism does for people: after the universal conflagration and the twilight of the gods, it all begins again. It is circularity on a cosmic scale.

This is not just religious stamp-collecting: 'My stamp is square and yours is round.' It has consequences. Jews, Christians and Muslims live once and for ever. They can say, 'This is THE life.' All a Hindu or Buddhist can say is 'This is A life' (and a truly enlightened Buddhist may not even want to say that).

For us, everything is once only. That is why everything we do is so important. When things happen in our lives or in this world, they stay in a state of 'having happened' for ever. God cannot make them un-happen, and they cannot re-happen themselves on the next turn of the cosmic wheel.

This influences our thinking and culture on a deep level. If we spend the only life we will ever live helping the poor and the sick, it will be because they too are in the only life they will ever live.

The world itself lives only once, which is why at the very beginning of the Book of Genesis we are told to reign over it and look after it.*

* Genesis 1:28.

III
LIFE

God the Spirit

Et in Spiritum Sanctum, Dominum et vivificantem:
qui ex Patre Filioque procedit.
Qui cum Patre et Filio simul adoratur et conglorificatur:
qui locutus est per prophetas.
Et unam, sanctam, catholicam et apostolicam Ecclesiam.
Confiteor unum baptisma in remissionem peccatorum.
Et exspecto resurrectionem mortuorum,
et vitam venturi sæculi.

I believe in the Holy Spirit, the Lord, the giver of life,
who proceeds from the Father and the Son,
who with the Father and the Son is adored and glorified,
who has spoken through the prophets.
I believe in one, holy, catholic and apostolic Church.
I confess one Baptism for the forgiveness of sins
and I look forward to the resurrection of the dead
and the life of the world to come.

31

I believe in the Holy Spirit, the Lord

Et in Spiritum Sanctum, Dominum

The Creed goes through the truths of our faith in the order in which the Apostles discovered them. The 'Father' section is what every Jew knew already. The 'Son' section takes us through the events of the Son's intervention on earth as far as the evening of the Ascension: it covers either what the Apostles had seen for themselves or what Jesus had told them about.

When Jesus left the Apostles to return to his Father, he promised not to leave them destitute: at the Son's request the Father would send them a helper. The Greek term in the Gospel is *paraclete*, which literally means 'someone called in to stand by one'. It is used, for example, to denote somebody who stands by you to support you in a court of law. Jesus did not say who or what that helper might be. The coming of the Paraclete was unimaginable, in the literal sense of being something one cannot make any kind of image or picture of. The only thing to do was to wait and pray.

On a certain Sunday morning in late May AD 33,* the day of the Feast of Weeks, Mary and the Apostles were together, watching and praying, and the Paraclete came: the Holy Spirit. They heard the coming of the Spirit in the sound of a rushing wind and they saw the effects of the arrival of the Spirit in the form of tongues of fire. But they did not see or hear the Spirit himself.

This is entirely characteristic of the Holy Spirit. The Spirit is wholly immaterial, wholly non-human, and known only by his

---

* Different scholars come up with different years. The year 33 is preferred by J. P. Meier in *A Marginal Jew* (1991–2009), which is quoted approvingly by Pope Benedict XVI in his book *Jesus of Nazareth: Holy Week* (2011). The arguments depend, for example, on the day of the week on which Passover falls.

effects: the manifestations of his presence and power. This is why the Spirit is so difficult to conceive of and so difficult to pray to. The Son became human for us, so the Son is easy. Admittedly, the Father is pure spirit, and non-human; but we are made in his image, so we have enough in common to be able to pray to him, argue with him and even complain to him. But the Spirit is wholly alien and unpicturable. All the 'pictures of the Spirit' in the history of art are pictures of *symbols of* the spirit: a dove, a tongue of flame.

Because the Spirit is so alien, it is possible to be puzzled about why the Spirit exists and what the Spirit is for. Really, the puzzle is why we have to have a Trinity at all. The Creed is going to get us there, but let's keep with the images for just a little longer.

Literally, in Latin, *spiritus* means 'breath', and especially the 'breath of life'.* (In biology, when we re*spire*, when we alternately in*spire* and ex-*spire*, when plants trans-*spire*, that is the same word.) This meaning connects the Spirit with life, and the idea of life is taking us towards the heart of what the Spirit is, as the next chapter will show.

The word 'breath' has other uses which also tell their part of the truth of the Spirit. When you look at breath, what do you see? Nothing: and that is what you see when you look at the Spirit. When you grab a handful of breath, what do you hold in your hand? Nothing: and that is what you get hold of when you try to get hold of the Spirit with your mind. The Spirit slips past our senses and past our attempts to grasp him. We can know him only by his effects.

There is one more fact about the word *spiritus*, which at first sounds like a mere accident in the history of words, but I think it

---

* The Germanic word for spirit is *Geist* – thus *Zeitgeist*, the spirit of the age, and *Himbeergeist*, raspberry brandy. The related English word is 'ghost', which has suffered from isolation rather as 'salvation' has, but in a different corner of the linguistic landscape. Small children have been known to be so frightened by ghosts that they hid behind their beds when saying 'In the name of . . . the Holy Ghost'. Eventually we gave up the battle and fell back on 'Spirit'.

also says something about the Holy Spirit. When the Romans were building an aqueduct and it had to cross a valley, they usually built a bridge for it, but now and then they ran pipes down one side of the valley and up the other. The architectural writer Vitruvius describes all this in detail, and at one point he says that care has to be taken in filling the pipeline once it has been built, 'or the *spiritus* will burst the pipes'.* This *spiritus* clearly means 'water pressure'.

This is a good image for the working of the Spirit: in many ways better than pigeons and flames. Imagine a steam engine or some kind of hydraulic machine. It may be vast and impressive; it may be intricate and ingenious; but, as constructed, it is dead. Only once it is given *spiritus* (in engineering terms, steam pressure or water pressure, whichever it is designed for) does it begin to move. It begins to come to life: thanks to the *spiritus*, it begins to be what it was made to be.

And so it is with us, because without the Spirit, we have everything *except* life.

---

* Plumbers call this phenomenon 'water hammer'. It bursts pipes and loosens joints, and more than once it has made a space rocket explode.

32

The giver of life

The key to understanding Christian doctrine is knowing which parts of it are Christian and which belong to the common heritage of mankind.

St Thomas Aquinas consistently follows this principle. In his work he repeatedly refers to pagan philosophers. For example, Aristotle concluded in his *Metaphysics* that there has to be a First Cause of everything,* something that causes rather than being caused and acts without being acted upon. To a Christian, that instantly says 'God'. Aquinas accordingly takes over Aristotle's argument and develops it to its logical conclusion.

The reason why Aristotle is important for Aquinas is that Aristotle is a pagan. If you are a Christian arguing from certain principles to a certain conclusion, then someone may object that you only invented those principles to give you the conclusion you wanted. Indeed, if you are an honest philosopher (as Aquinas is), you could make that objection against yourself. By looking outside Christianity and seeing that even pagans accept the principle you are relying on, that objection is defeated. (Aquinas similarly makes use of arguments from Avicenna, the greatest of the Muslim philosophers who built on Aristotle's work.)

To put the doctrine of the Trinity into context, we need to ask whether other thinkers and other religions have an idea of essential trinity-without-a-capital-T, essential threeness. And if they do, what have they made of the idea?

This is not a matter of trying to prove Christianity right.

---

* Logically first, rather than first in a temporal sequence. Aristotle believed in an infinitely old universe, which could not have a first moment of time.

Rather, it is a way of seeing where we stand. If trinity is widespread among human thinkers, then our distinctiveness lies in seeing that the trinity is a Trinity of persons. If trinity is not found elsewhere, then the very concept of trinity will be what makes Christianity unique.

Evidence from elsewhere

The basic subject matter of all religious philosophy is existence. This is understood in two ways: first, existence in the sense of absolute being (which is what we call God); and, second, the existence of things that might not have existed, such as the world and us. Going from the first kind of existence to the second is what we call the act of creation.

Pure **Being** is existence itself. This lies behind and beyond the actual things that happen to be. For this reason it lies beyond physical science, which can only ever deal with things that are. Even in the most advanced laboratory you will not find an 'ontometer', an instrument to tell you how existent something is.

Whether you look at the Indian philosophers or the Neoplatonists, pure Being is pure Being and that is all. Nothing can be said about it. It is timeless and does not change. It does not act (except perhaps in some incomprehensible kind of eternal self-contemplation). It cannot be reasoned about – it just is. It is itself, undivided and indivisible: the One.

For anything to happen and for anything to be created, something more is needed.

Act is the act of doing. In some mysterious way, Act divides the oneness of the One, since now we have the 'actor' and the 'acted upon', the 'doer' and the 'done to'. It divides Oneness in another way as well, because an act happens in time, and time is divided by it: 'the time before the act' and 'the time after the act'. Finally, if the Act is an act of creation, then there is 'the creator' and also 'the created'.

Dividing oneness sounds tricky, and it is. All philosophers, including Christians, have to find a way to navigate round the tension between the oneness of the One and the diversity implied by Act.

We have Being and we have Act, but there is one more principle to go. Most created things do not need it, but we do. Stars, planets, rocks and boulders obey the laws of their being, which are the fixed laws of physical science. A star shines because it cannot *not* shine: it has no choice. But there are creatures in the universe that are not entirely determined by physical laws. They can decide to do or not to do. That is, they are alive. I am one of these. So are you.

So **Life** is the third principle. A being that has been given Life has a choice. It is able to choose how to act, not always having to obey pre-defined laws. A clever (and perhaps useful) way of expressing the difference is to say that a being with life is a being capable of saying the word 'I' and meaning it. In a religion that has a personal relationship between creator and created, such a being is also able to say 'you' to its creator.

There are three principles: Being, Act and Life. And we have got to this threeness without considering Christian revelation at all. Every tradition that has thought deeply enough about the questions of being has to have come across it.

In the Hindu scriptures, the classic formulation of Brahman in the later Vedānta is *sat, cit, ānanda*: Being, Awareness, Bliss.

In Judaism in the last centuries BC (when the Jews had begun to learn from the Greeks how to philosophise), there are signs of the Wisdom of God and the Word of God, though they always seem to stop just short of being seen fully as persons since they cannot be allowed to detract from the oneness of the LORD.

In the Koran there are God, God's Command (*amr*) and the Spirit (*rūḥ*).* These are seeds that have not developed further in Islamic theology. If they ever did, it could not be as Persons in the Christian sense; but at the very least they would be modes of spirituality, convergent ways of approaching the One God.

---

* See especially the chapter entitled 'The Qur'ān and Christ' in R. C. Zaehner, *At Sundry Times* (1958).

That was a rapid and superficial summary. Deeper study confirms that while Hindus and Jews and Muslims are most definitely not Trinitarians in our sense – at no point is any of the 'threes' identified with God himself – a threeness of some kind is an intrinsic part of the 'being-and-creation' nexus.*

The conclusion is this: it is not the *threeness* of the Trinity that is distinctive about Christianity, because threeness is already implied as soon as you start talking about creation, whoever you are. What is distinctive is that the threeness is elevated into the threeness of the Persons of God. We are able to encounter God, WHO-to-WHO, person-to-Person, as Father, and also as Son, and also as Spirit.

The mind of the maker

There is another way of perceiving the threeness of the role of 'creator' without having to think about God at all.

God made me in his image; God is the Creator; therefore I am a creator too, even if a shadow-creator of shadow-creations. I am a sub-creator (this is J. R. R. Tolkien's term), and my act of creation is a shadow of what God as Creator is doing. So by looking at my own creative activity, I can learn something of God's.

Dorothy L. Sayers is the great exponent of this way of understanding the Creator by understanding oneself as a creator. Today she is remembered for her detective stories featuring Lord Peter Wimsey, but she also wrote ground-breaking religious plays and was a noted Dante scholar. In the early days of the Second World War there was an outburst of thinking about the future – 'Once this is over, what sort of world should we make?' – and Sayers' contribution was what she called 'a book on the Creative Mind'.

---

* Zaehner, in *Mysticism Sacred and Profane* (1957), cites, 'I saw that Lover, Love and Beloved are all one, for in the world of union all must be One' (attributed to Abū Yazīd); 'Union, He Who unites, and He Who is united' (Qushayrī); and even, from the Jewish side, 'The Master is the *Knowledge*, the *Knower* and the *Known*, since all three are one in Him' (Abraham Abulafia).

This book was *The Mind of the Maker* (1941), an exposition of Trinitarian theology in terms of artistic creation.

Any act of creation, Sayers says, involves three things:

The Idea is the overall idea of the piece: in *Hamlet*, this might be 'a young man coming to adulthood and discovering that the world is the opposite of what he expected, and so is his role in it'.

The Action is how the Idea manifests itself in terms of created characters and events. 'Hamlet meets his father's ghost', 'Hamlet has a mother and a wicked uncle', and so on. The act of creation takes the idea from a state of timeless perfection into an existence made of times and actions.

The Life is what happens when Hamlet comes alive and starts to think and act for himself. Once that has happened, there are things that Shakespeare can no longer make him do: not without Hamlet ceasing to be Hamlet.

Anyone can find threes in things, but Sayers' analysis is not just airy theory. Having established the doctrine, she examines its heresies, which she calls 'scalene Trinities', trinities in which one member is either over-dominant or diminished. Too much Act produces a thrill-a-minute narrative with no backbone, too much Idea can produce a play that is nothing more than a sermon preached through puppets, and so on. The scalene Trinities neatly parallel similar heresies in the history of Christianity. This must be the only book that consistently uses the Athanasian Creed as a method of literary criticism!

Sayers contends that for a healthy, living work to be created, the Idea and Action and Life all have to be present and in balance. In a play or a novel or a film, these are distinct faculties in the author. In the Christian universe, they are the distinct Persons of the Trinity.

Back to Christianity

If a trinitarian structure is inherent in any act of creation, it is not surprising that every religion with a sense of the Creation should at least have touched on it. What makes Christianity different is not that it finds a trinity, but what it does with it. It is the step that takes us from 'a trinity in the act of creation' to God as the Holy Trinity.

Wiser and more learned people will be able to trace the logic better, but I think the outline is straightforward. Christianity is a relationship religion. It is not *about* theorising, though theory is there thanks to the Greek strand in it; it is not *about* blind obedience, though obedience is there thanks to the Semitic strand. It is about a relationship that grows out of the Jewish relationship with the undifferentiated LORD. Every relationship is a WHO relationship, and as God-as-WHO reveals himself more and more, the oneness of God combines with the threeness inherent in the act of creation, so that the WHO of God as we relate to him reflects this: God is three WHOs, three Persons: not one. Looking back at **Being**, **Act**, **Life**, the Father corresponds to Being (omnipotent and eternal), the Son (through whom all things are made, and who operates in time) to Act, and the Spirit is the one who gives us Life.

With this understanding, the fact that the Holy Spirit should be alien and invisible and inaccessible and hard to reason about turns out to be natural (although we are still allowed to find it annoying). The Spirit is known through his works, and we cannot separate him from them as an isolated object of study.

The life-giver

All the foregoing is valuable and enlightening, but it is frustrating as well. Spirit means 'breath' or 'breeze' or 'wind', and those are invisible, ungrabbable things. You reach out and grab a handful of air. You bring your hand close to you and open it to see what you have caught, and . . . well, try the experiment for yourself and you will see exactly what a handful of air looks like.

If a Religious Knowledge exam were constructed the way modern examinations are constructed, with choices to be picked and boxes to be ticked, its Spirit section could have a 'fill in the blanks' question, saying:

The Holy Spirit is ⬚

The successful candidates would be the ones who wrote nothing in the box, because no answer is valid. The answer cannot be a specification because the Spirit cannot be specified. It cannot be a description because any description of the Spirit is beside the point.

Struggling to convey a sense of what the Spirit is, the best St Paul can do is to describe the Spirit's works, the Spirit's effects: you might say, the symptoms of the Spirit, the footprints of the Spirit.

The parable of the signposts gives the picture. Maps of the Spirit are impossible: the most that can be said is, 'If you want to be caught by the Spirit, try going this way.' So here are a few signposts, a few pictures of what cannot be seen in the handful of air you grab to see what it is:

- When you stop playing the notes and start playing the music – *that is the Spirit.*
- When the dance is not what the choreographer wrote but the dance is the dance – *that is the Spirit.*
- When the characters you write stop doing what you wrote and start doing what they do – *that is the Spirit.*
- When you stop saying your prayers and start praying – *that is the Spirit.*

The Spirit cannot be summoned or controlled, which is why Scripture describes the Spirit as the wind that blows wherever it wants to.

The Spirit as fire is such a fruitful image ('. . . and how I wish it were burning already') because although a pile of sticks cannot light itself, it can at least be made ready to be lit. A pile of dry sticks arranged to let the air through will catch fire from a spark, while a heap of damp leaves will not. Only a pianist who has practised and practised until the striking of each note is *not* a separate, consciously willed action will be able to stop playing the notes and start playing the music. And so it is with all the other images.

We have seen patterns in how God the Father behaves towards us, and the same patterns in the actions of God the Son. God the

Spirit is the same again. God never overwhelms. When he intervenes, he takes care to make the smallest intervention conceivable. He is in the still, small voice, not the whirlwind. He gives the tiniest spark that can set dry wood on fire, the tiniest seed that will take root in the fertile soul and make it fruitful.

The flame and the seed are God's job, the flammability and fertility are ours. They are passivities, you might say, but it is an active passivity we are talking about: a lot more than just sitting there waiting for something to happen. You might want lightning to strike and fill you with its power, but you must at least climb to the top of a hill, to where the lightning will come.

Conscious and unconscious

Being so ungraspable, the Spirit is hard to 'love with the mind'. But some of the hardness comes from our misunderstanding what the mind is. If by 'the mind' you mean a conscious, rational, logic machine that clicks, ticks and dockets its way from indubitable axioms to unchallengeable conclusions – in short, an Enlightenment mind – then yes, the Spirit is indeed elusive. But if you say that the mind is a conscious, rational, logical machine and nothing else, you are wrong. The mind is *not* a machine. Even the mathematical mind is not a machine. Even mathematicians (though they may sometimes deny it) see a theorem as true first of all and then, afterwards, look for ways to prove it: direct perception of the truth comes before reason.

The thin thread of conscious thought is like a torch beam in a dark cavern illuminating just one spot at a time, leaving the rest in obscurity. But conscious thought is not the only way we think. It is not even the most important way. In the 'all your mind' with which we are to love the Lord our God, there is a conscious and an unconscious part. The 'unconscious' does not mean the irrational or the stupid. It is a mind that makes sense just as the conscious mind makes sense: it just makes sense by different methods.

The unconscious mind is 'me' just as the conscious mind is 'me', but it never (as maths teachers always demand) 'shows its working' or explains how it does what it does. It simply presents its answer to a question I may not have realised I was asking, and it presents it not with detailed reasons but with absolute certainty. In all this it bears a certain resemblance to the way the Spirit acts. At the very least, it provides an example of an activity that is real but cannot be seen or grasped.

To pin down the abstraction, I will give one example of the kind of thing I mean. The activity it describes is trivial, but then the activity itself is not the point of the story. It is the moral of the story that counts.

From time to time, I attempt *The Times* crossword, with greater or lesser success. On one such occasion I was confronted with a clue that obviously demanded an anagram of 'A CORNISHMAN'. Now, that makes eleven letters, and in principle there are about ten million ways of arranging eleven letters in order – far beyond any rational systematic search. I stared at the clue for a while and gave up. I put down the newspaper and went out and lived my life. It was quite some time later that I passed by the crossword again and gave it a glance. In that second, my unconscious mind, without warning and without being asked, said two things to me. The first was the word ANACHRONISM, and the second was absolute certainty. The certainty was such that my hand started writing the letters into the squares before I had time to stop it. My hand wrote, and my thoughts trotted behind it, trying in vain to catch up. They caught up only when the whole word had been written, and fitted the space, and was seen to be correct. The whole thing was a humiliating and embarrassing success.

The most unsettling thing about all this was that the unconscious mind had done it all by itself without being asked and without telling me what it was doing. All that was left was for me to hear and obey. That was not the worst of it, either. The unconscious had done something I had never asked it to do, and done it without telling me. So what was it doing now, unasked and in secret? What new certainty was it getting ready to hit me with?

The puzzles of the conscious mind's relations with the unconscious and the creature's relations with the life-giving Spirit may not be the same puzzle, but perhaps they are close enough that one can illuminate the other.

The sin against the Spirit

There is a puzzling moment in the Gospel when Jesus promises forgiveness to anyone who says anything against the Son of Man (which is just what you would expect him to say) but then goes on to say that anyone who blasphemes against the Holy Spirit cannot be forgiven.* This goes so against the general impression of universal forgiveness that it stands out. Surely, we think, *no* sin, if repented of, is unforgivable?

It is indeed the case that any sin, once committed, can be repented of and, once repented of, can be forgiven. No sin is too great for this: not assassinating the Pope, not betraying Jesus. This principle has been at the core of the Church's teaching ever since sin was thought through systematically.

Sin covers two things: an act, and the state resulting from that act. It covers committing murder, and being a murderer. Absolution forgives the act and heals the state.

Although no sin is too great to be forgiven, it is possible to get into a state in which the Spirit, by definition, does not exist, and in such a state forgiveness becomes problematic. Theologians give several ways in which this can manifest itself. For instance, there is despair, a state which sees the sin as wholly unforgivable and unhealable: you can't ask for forgiveness if you are certain that forgiveness is impossible. Or there is the opposite state, complacency, in which it is impossible to ask for forgiveness because forgiveness is going to come automatically anyway.

Another way to make oneself proof against the Spirit and thus immune to the grace given by the Spirit is more structural than these. It is to exclude *life* as a principle, since if there is no such thing as life then Life cannot (by definition) intervene. For instance, you can exclude life by making sure you play the notes not the music, and you lock it out permanently by *defining* the word 'music' to mean 'the playing of the correct notes'.

If you list the commandments and avoid breaking each one of them because it is a commandment and for no other reason, then

---

* Luke 12:10.

you are performing some sort of act of love in that you are obeying the Law for the sake of the Law-giver, but you are still missing something. You are mistaking the signpost for the destination; you are the dog sniffing at its master's pointing finger. You are missing the point, and you are not fully living: you risk turning yourself into a programmed entity instead. If you ask, 'Who is my neighbour?', expecting a carefully worded definition of which houses are neighbouring ones and which aren't, then you have embarked on a way of not-being-alive that does not leave room for the Spirit of life to enter. If you ask, 'How many times must I forgive my brother?', expecting to hear something like, 'Seven times seven makes forty-nine,' then you have locked yourself away from a truly living answer.

And to move beyond the self: if in your dealings with others you deal with them purely as labels, as collections of identities and attributes by which they may be judged, then once more you are substituting calculation for encounter, and excluding the possibility of life and love.

What all these examples have in common is that, while the effects of an *act* can be segregated into the past and healed by forgiveness, once you have entered into a *state* in which the Spirit, life, plays no part, there is no way out, since you have excluded, by definition, the one way out there could have been.

Not that even this state of mind *necessarily* dooms the soul. God woos us with gentleness, even diffidence, always the still, small voice not the rushing mighty wind . . . until he doesn't. You can bar the windows against the Spirit and the Spirit will not come blowing in; you can build your house without a door so the Son can't come knocking; but you can never quite trust God the Father. Now and then he loses patience. He saves the soul by smashing it up and putting together the fragments to make something alive.

Sometimes the smashing is physical: a cannonball broke the leg of the soldier Ignatius of Loyola and set him on a path that led him to found the Society of Jesus. Sometimes it is professional: the successful young lawyer Alphonsus Liguori spectacularly lost a legal case, and the humiliation set him free to become a priest, an outstanding confessor and a great saint. Sometimes it is moral: falling in love will do it by turning the world upside down. But rather than getting distracted by the details, just remember that you can shut the windows and you can block the door, but you can't stop God ripping the roof off if he wants to.

33

Who proceeds from the Father and the Son

Qui ex Patre Filioque procedit

It is easy to make a wrong picture of God the Father. Actually, the wrong picture is quite a good place to start. 'Old man with a beard' or 'Celestial Artificer planning out his creation with a pair of dividers' are wrong pictures, but when the literal parts of them are cut away, what is left is something that means something. Everything is in our favour, anyway, because we are made in God's image, so if we start by making God in our image then we are starting with a shadow of a shadow of the truth. That is a lot better than starting with nothing.

It is easy to make a wrong picture of God the Son. The wrong picture is a good place to start. The human relationship of 'father and son' carries a fair amount of human baggage with it which the Creed is careful to carve away, one chisel-stroke at a time – light from light, true God from true God, and all the rest – but when all that is *not* the Son has been removed, what remains is the Son. It all works, and we have one thing in our favour throughout all this: the Son once took on our nature and walked the earth with us.

It is impossible to make a wrong picture of God the Spirit, because it is impossible to make any picture of the Spirit at all. The Breath of God cannot be pictured, so the technique of 'picture and then purify' will not work this time. There is nothing to start from. Imagining a dove minus its feathers, or a tongue of flame with the gas turned down, gets us nowhere because those were never pictures of the Spirit in the first place, only images of the Spirit's action. So when it talks about the Spirit, the Creed has to start from nothing rather than something, and add instead of subtracting.

The Spirit is Lord – which is to say, the Spirit is God: truly God, just as the Son is truly God, not simply an attribute or emanation of God.

The Spirit is Life-giver – and this, too, says that the Spirit is God, because looking deeply into what creation means, the giving of life is a necessary part of the notion of a Creator.

The Spirit proceeds, or comes out from the members of the Trinity whom we already know: the Father and the Son. Whether there is any real difference between the Spirit 'proceeding from' God and the Son 'being born of' God, I don't know. On the one hand, the choice of words may be the consequence of seeing the Spirit as a kind of breath and the Son as a kind of human son; but on the other hand, deeper minds may see a deeper distinction.

Both begetting and breathing make a certain point about the nature of the persons of God. The 'begetting not making' of the Son points to something that is not *an act* of the Father, which he might have chosen to do or not to do, but rather *a necessary relationship* between the Father and the Son. It is part of what it means for God to be God. And in the same way, the 'proceeding' of the Breath of God from the Father and the Son points to something that is not a voluntary act ('Shall we stop holding our breath now and see what happens?') but a necessary relationship among the members of the Trinity, a necessary part of God being God.

These three statements in the Creed add up to the following conclusion:

The Spirit is God – in the same sense as the Father is God and the Son is God.

Having got to 'The Spirit is God', we could stop here and have a nice short chapter. But people are people, and people wouldn't be people if they didn't quarrel, and 'proceeds from the Father and the Son' marks the battleground of a doctrinal disagreement which turned toxic and split the Church in half.

Proceeds from whom?

There were famous wars in the Church over whether the Spirit comes out from the Father alone or from the Son as well as the Father (the word at issue was *filioque*, 'and the Son'). Put like that, it can sound like the kind of futile technicality that can only amuse specialists, like asking how many angels can dance on the point of a pin.* But it was a lot more than a technicality. If enough people agree that a question is important enough for them to risk their careers and even their lives in disagreeing about it, the least we can do is pay them the compliment of believing in the importance of the question.

There are two ways of dealing with the *filioque* issue. One is to produce a magnificent detailed résumé of the whole unfortunate story from start to finish, not forgetting the ups and downs of the politics. That is the scholarly way. The other way is to ask oneself, 'What would make me, personally, *want* to believe or disbelieve this doctrine?' That is the way I shall take.

My reason for liking *filioque*, 'and from the Son', is that it fits in with the Being–Act–Life logic of the Trinity. The Life must come from the Act as well as the Idea which is thought by Being. Think about it: an idea cannot have life if it remains just an abstract concept. It can only have life if it is first given reality – 'en-acted', if you like – that is, if the Son is involved as well as the Father.

I can imagine not liking 'and from the Son' and wanting to deny it. My motive would be to preserve the utter oneness of God against any kind of anatomy or analysis. Of course, the doctrine of the Trinity doesn't really make God into three separate gods, but if you know there are people around who might misunderstand it like that, demoting the Son and making the Spirit dependent on the Father alone might be a useful bit of doctrinal insurance.

If protecting less-educated people from misunderstandings is a negative motive for removing *filioque*, the pursuit of high enlightenment is a positive one. Gnosticism and Neoplatonism both

---

* This is actually a perfectly reasonable question about whether non-material entities can be distinguished from one another if they don't have matter and don't have place: the word 'angels' is just a decoration attached to a serious philosophical question. The analogous question, 'How many fermions can dance on the point of a pin?', is a good way of discovering whether a first-year physics student has actually understood quantum mechanics.

loved to erect elaborate hierarchies of Powers, Beings, Aeons and the rest, to stretch between eternal perfect Being at the top of the cosmos and our temporal, temporary, might-have-been-otherwise world at the bottom.* In that kind of intellectual atmosphere, the 'geometry of theology' would be at its most elegant if God the Father were isolated at the top of it all, occupying the place of the Neoplatonists' eternal self-contemplating 'One', and the Son and the Spirit formed a Holy Dyad on the next level down. Deleting 'and the Son' from the Creed would be a step towards this higher elegance.

These are just a few suggestions. They show how one might want to be on one side or other of the question and also the way in which the question could turn out to be really important.

There is one thing that does have to be acknowledged before leaving this relaxed discussion behind and moving on, and that is that the real discussion at the time was not relaxed at all. It was political, poisonous and savage.

Odium theologicum

Odium theologicum, 'theological hatred', is the term used to describe the viciousness with which theological arguments are sometimes conducted. In itself, that viciousness is an unfortunate state of affairs: it is hard to see the truth through smoke. What is worse is that it can be used to discourage thinking about theology ('Don't think, but hug'), or even to discredit religion altogether ('If it makes people so nasty, better to ban it'). In any case, it is an embarrassment and a scandal.

The 'we should all just hug' tendency can be exploded quite easily by remembering that Christianity was founded by a criminal who stated from the outset that he had come to set the world on fire and bring a sword, not peace. This is true (although many Christians like to push it to one side), but while it is an adequate

---

* The gorgeous word 'ogdoad', meaning a group of eight, is in the dictionary because some of the Gnostics invented an Eighthood of beings for themselves – as you might say, a Holy Octonity.

refutation of, 'Let's hug,' it is not a sufficient excuse for hatred. It is perfectly possible to break eggs without making an omelette.

Theology is a science, so a slower and more enlightening answer is to look at the history of the sciences generally, not just at theology. And when you look, you will see that there really is such a thing as *odium scientificum*.

I am not going to go through the historical details because they are undignified and this is not the place for them. But throughout the sciences, the methods used to resolve the really big questions are, in order of priority:

1. Destroy your opponent's career.
2. Failing that, prove that your opponent is talking nonsense.
3. Failing that, establish the truth, but only if it is necessary to achieve 1 and 2.

Take any question and tick it off against that checklist. Racial or cultural hygiene, continental drift, climate change, string theory, cosmologies of all kinds: they all fit, to a greater or lesser degree.

It does not matter what the ultimate truth in any given case actually is. People on the 'wrong' side about fundamental physics have been publicly called 'terrorists'. People on the 'wrong' side about the weather have been prosecuted; people on the 'wrong' side about certain historical questions can be sent to prison.

In every such war of the sciences, money and political power have two key roles. They make the war possible, and they are reasons for fighting it. In the physical sciences, money and power may take the form of professorships and research grants. In church schisms, they may be bishoprics and the revenues arising from them. It has happened in Church history that a schism was on the verge of being settled to the satisfaction of the scholars until someone realised that healing it would put jobs at risk.

The viciousness with which the *filioque* war was fought does not mean that the question was unimportant. It does not mean that the final conclusion was unsound. It does not invalidate theology as a science either. On the contrary, it proves that the study of God is a science just like any other. Like all other sciences, it is pursued by fallen men who do not always remember that truth is the only good there is. But, despite their fallenness, the science is still worth pursuing. We need to know so that we can understand, and we need to understand so that we can live.

34

Is adored and glorified

Qui cum Patre et Filio simul adoratur et conglorificatur

There is a crystalline beauty about high theory in any science. It is pleasing to be able to reach higher and higher towards the perfect truth. But the higher you go, the thinner the air, and in the end there is nothing left for us ordinary mortals to breathe. Professors of physics may delight in hydrogen bonds and van der Waals forces; the rest of us are happy just knowing that ice floats.

The Creed is for everyone. Accordingly, having said what it had to say about the nature of the Holy Spirit, it turns to practical matters: what we do about the Spirit and what the Spirit does about us.

What we do about the Spirit is adore, or worship, him. We also glorify him – acclaim his glory – alongside the Father and the Son.

Adoration

'Adoration' is one of those words, like 'salvation', that get stuck in a corner of a church for too long while their meaning out in the world wanders off in strange directions.

I am not suggesting that we should try to find another word for 'adore' (the replacement would sooner or later lose its shape as well), but now and then it is good to clarify our understanding by looking directly at the meaning of the word.

Ad-orāre literally means 'to pray to', and by extension it means to show respect and reverence, to recognise authority, and all the other things that go with this. But the core remains prayer.

Outside church, the meaning of 'adore' has blurred. When we say a mother *adores* her son we do not mean that she prays to him: we mean she has excessive admiration for him even though he is a coward or a liar. If I were to say that I *adore* cream cakes, I would not mean that I am filled with awe and reverence when I think of them, but just that I am filled with greed.

Whether we 'ad-ore' or 'pray to' or 'worship', the Creed has just taken care to remind us yet again that the Spirit is God. When we adore (or worship) God, we do it to the Father *and* the Son *and* the Holy Spirit. One act of adoration or worship is directed at all three.

Acclaimed as glorious

The Creed says *conglorificatur*, 'is together-glorified', to emphasise yet again the unity of the Trinity.

A word is due on glorifying, because to someone who doesn't get its precise meaning it can sound like us awarding a prize to God, and that conveys rather a peculiar attitude of the creature towards its creator. 'Glory' on its own isn't that complicated. In the Old Testament it starts by meaning physical brightness or brilliance, and it broadens itself in a natural way to mean the brilliance of God in a wider sense, always bringing with it a sense of wonder and dazzlement. Glory in the physical and metaphorical sense is what the disciples saw at the Transfiguration. If there is any verbal awkwardness to be overcome, it is not in the word 'glory' but in the word 'glorified'.

'Glorifying' in the sense it is being used here is not an award but a recognition. That is why I have tried translating it as 'acclaimed as glorious' by way of a clarifying jolt. Our act is not to give God a prize for being glorious. It is to recognise that he *is* glorious and so to rejoice in his glory. Our act of glorification does nothing to or for God, but it does something for us, because to recognise God's glory means to open one's eyes to it and see it for what it is.

(There is a parallel here with canonisation. The Church has never *made* anyone a saint. She can't. All she does is *recognise* that someone is a saint. Sainthood is a gift for us, not a prize for the saint.)

The Creed is saying that when we recognise God's glory, we recognise the glory of the Father *and* of the Son *and* of the Holy

Spirit. The recognition may be sparked off by any one of the members of the Trinity. It may be the splendour of creation, pointing to the Father; it may be healing and love, the work of the Son; it may be the sheer aliveness of life, the work of the Spirit. Any of these may spark off the perception of God's glory, but the glory we rejoice in is always the glory of the whole.

35

Who has spoken through the prophets

Qui locutus est per prophetas

What we do about the Spirit is adore him: worship him as God. Now we turn to what the Spirit does about us, and the Creed starts with what the Spirit does about us as individuals. The Spirit is *spiritus*, the living breath who in-*spires* us, puts breath into us: and who in particular has in-*spired* the prophets.

Inspiration is not the same thing as dictation. A prophet is not possessed by the Holy Spirit in the way that a medium might be possessed by demons. God never dominates, and the Spirit does not dictate messages word by word using a person as a pen. A prophet is not a tool: for God, nobody is.

This turns out to be a useful way of distinguishing the work of the Spirit from its imitations. A cult can be distinguished from a true work of the Spirit because it subordinates its members to itself: they become less and less themselves and more and more members, limbs, tools of the cult. They smile the cult smile, and a deadly uniformity settles on them all.

On the other hand, a thriving community filled with the Holy Spirit is the opposite of a cult because its members become *more* themselves, not less. This is how it has to be, since the first action of God is to call us into being, into life, and the action of God the Spirit is to call us to more being, more life.

Moreover, God calls me to *my* life, not to anyone else's. I have seen this work of the Spirit in a monastery. The intellectual monk became more intellectual but was still kept free from the disdain that it is possible for intellectuals to feel for those whose minds are differently organised. The monk with a short fuse still exploded, but upwards rather than sideways, shooting sparks to the glory of God instead of injuring everyone round him with flying shrapnel.

The flame of the Spirit fuels the soul, and at the same time it purifies it by burning off the dross that clings to it. The soul remains the same soul, only more so.

Prophets

In the first instance, what the Creed means by the 'prophets' are the great prophets of the Old Testament after whom books of the Bible are named. Behind these there stand ranks of unnamed prophets, because being a prophet was a recognised calling in Israel, and prophets organised themselves into fraternities – thus establishing prophetic power as a sort of counterbalance to the structures of worldly power. Not that God pays much attention to institutions of any kind: some of the prophets whose names we know got into trouble precisely because they were not part of the recognised prophetical establishment and did not utter prophecies that conformed to the recognised pattern.

For the last four hundred years or so before the birth of Christ, the prophets fell silent and the Spirit operated in Israel in different ways. Then at the start of the New Testament came the last and greatest of the prophets, John the Baptist.* After that, everything changed.

Everything changed, but not in the sense of there being no more prophets. It is true that there are no more 'Books of' this prophet or that, but prophecy was not ended: it was distributed. No outstanding individuals were anointed as prophets, but that is only because today everybody who is baptised is anointed a priest, a prophet and a king.†

What is a prophet? Not just a forecaster – when we talk about 'prophecy' in terms of 'saying what is going to happen', it is a bit of a parody because talking about the future is only one aspect of

---

* Luke 7:26–8.

† 'As Christ was anointed Priest, Prophet, and King, so may you live always as a member of his body, sharing everlasting life.' And the priest anoints the child on the crown of the head with the sacred chrism (from *The Rite of Baptism for One Child*).

prophecy. The literal meaning of the Greek word *pro-phētēs* is one who speaks *for*, principally in the sense of speaking for or on behalf of a god. It would not be wrong to widen the meaning slightly and talk about someone who speaks *out*, who says something that has to be said. A prophet as a speaker-out has to know what to say when he speaks out, and therefore has to be someone who sees things clearly, clearer than the rest of us: clearer, often, than we would like to have them seen.

Some of the Old Testament prophets must, when not inspired, have been pretty awkward people to be around. They were not all poets like Isaiah or as endearingly full of human failings as Jonah. In that rebarbative passage of Ezekiel in which God explains and justifies his abandonment of the Jews, and then decides to be their God again not out of pity or mercy but because choosing a race and then abandoning it might look bad on his CV, one gets a sense of Ezekiel's own prickly personality, as angular as a room full of elbows. But the Spirit inspires everyone according to his nature, and to what other kind of personality could the Spirit have given a vision of a valley full of dead bones, dead and dry bones coming to life, a sign of hope for Israel?* It could not have been given to a prophet whose personality was soft, gentle and smooth.

Each prophet shines in his own particular colour. It is as if we were blind to the white light of God and had to put together 'white' by combining each separate colour of the spectrum: the reverse of what Newton did when he put a prism in a sunbeam and saw a whole spectrum of colours come out of it.

The prophets of the present time

You were anointed a prophet when you were baptised, and although it doesn't say so in so many words, the Creed implies that the Holy Spirit not only *has spoken* through the prophets but is also *speaking* through the prophets. He speaks through you.

The jump from knowing this to knowing what to do about it is such a big one that most people don't think about it. But we ought.

* Ezekiel 36:22; 37:1–14.

Prophecy is not the same thing as performance. Not only does that mean that we are not expected to be as big a nuisance as Jeremiah or as great a poet as Isaiah, but it also means that we ought not to try. Statistically, it is almost certainly not our vocation. Public prophecy is a gift and a calling, and most people aren't called to it. The madman on the bus telling everybody to be saved keeps more people from God, more effectively, than any number of insidious promoters of vice ever could.

Loving God with all one's mind has to include loving him with all one's common sense. We are to be as cunning as serpents, Jesus says.* We are not meant to insist on prophesying both in season and out of season.†

On the other hand, doing nothing at all is self-evidently not a way of living up to one's anointing.

There is one Spirit but there are many gifts, and that includes many ways of being a prophet. This is a matter for prayer and reflection leading to discernment, not something you can expect to get out of a book. Ask the Spirit, because a book is an inert collection of words on a page, but the Spirit is life.

A good way to start might be from the premise that you have been called to be a prophet to just one person, once in your life. After all, if each of us did only that much, a lot would get done. The 'just one person' is the important part of the exercise. I know a monk who wanted (one Lent) to get close in prayer to those in despair, but was wholly unable to do it until one day he was inspired to pray for one particular friend of his who had committed suicide. A group is only an abstraction, but an individual is a person.

If you are called to be a prophet just once, you do not know when that moment is going to come: but you can still make ready for it. That is, make yourself ready to be fully open to another person, and remove whatever barriers might stand in the way of that.

---

* Matthew 10:16.
† Paul tells Timothy to do this at 2 Timothy 4:1–2. But Paul knows Timothy and knows Timothy's situation. He does not know you.

Once in a lifetime is enough, and you may not know when or how it happens. Ronald Knox lived a public vocation as a priest and prophet, but quite separately there were moments such as this:

> I remember once getting a letter from a lapsed Catholic in Australia who said he was coming back to his religion as the result of a sentence, not bearing the smallest relation to theology, which he had read in one of my detective stories.*

The unusual thing about this event is not that it happened, but that the man wrote to Knox about it. Usually we never hear the effects of what we do.

It is really all a question of being ready. You don't have to do more than that, because the Spirit himself will choose where to blow and what to set on fire. Be ready and have your head and heart full of fuel – and dry fuel at that – and wait for the time and the place and the spark.

Learn, understand, know, love, and do not be afraid. The preaching bus maniac is not an example to follow, but neither is the confirmed under-bushel-hider who doesn't ever dare answer a serious question for fear of being derided or getting it wrong. When someone asks a question that you know is a deep question about belief (however well it may have been disguised: they often are), do not wriggle out of it from fear. If you think you know, say so; if you don't know, say so too, because that too is a channel of grace; but never be silent.

After all, making a fool of oneself is a valuable spiritual exercise, so pursue it. Derision hurts worse than martyrdom, so embrace it. God could have sent a doctor of theology into this moment, this situation, but he did not: he sent you instead. So do not be afraid.

---

* Ronald Knox, *A Retreat for Priests*, chapter 16. I wish I knew what the sentence was.

36

I believe in one, holy, catholic and apostolic Church

Et unam, sanctam, catholicam et apostolicam Ecclesiam

Looking back on the story so far, the Creed has said that the Spirit is the Life-giver in a general sense and then gone on to tell the story in terms of us as individuals, as prophets. This is as it ought to be. You and I are created individually by God. We make our profession of faith as individuals. We sin and we love as individuals, and as individuals we are saved, loved, judged and made immortal. But that is not yet the whole story. We are each of us 'I', but still in every human being there is not only an 'I' but a WE. Even a hermit hiding in the forest and never seeing anyone is still praying for, and praying as part of, the human race he never sees. Just as the Holy Spirit gives life to each 'I', so he gives life to every WE, and particularly – as the Creed now says – he gives life to the Church.

We are all of us part of many WEs, from family to club to group to nation to Church to the whole human race. Some of these are involuntary (like families), some are voluntary; some are formal and some less formal. Just as I and my works can have life or not have life, so too a WE can have life, or not. You can give a party and it never gets off the ground although everything about it is the same as the last one you had, which everyone said was such as success. There can be fifteen players* on the pitch or there can be one team: and the one team will beat the fifteen players any day. A school can be full of facilities and activities for its pupils and all they do is hang around saying, 'I'm bo-o-o-red,' while another, barer and poorer, is bursting with life.

The examples can be multiplied, but I hope the point is made. I am not claiming that the Holy Spirit is responsible for the success

---

* Some people say eleven, or thirteen, or eighteen.

of the next drinks party you hold: only that for every WE you can conceive there is a corresponding 'spirit of' which makes it alive rather than not alive, good rather than useless. That 'spirit of' is invisible and elusive, to be wooed rather than summoned. When St Teresa of Ávila shook up the Carmelite convents of her time (communities of ladies in which God was kept firmly in his place), it was the Holy Spirit who made it happen: the wind blowing where the wind wants to blow. Without the Spirit, for all her force of personality, St Teresa would (as I once heard a politician say) have been banging her head against a sponge.

Short of the human race itself, the biggest and oldest WE in the world is the Church.

St Paul portrays the Church as the mystical body of Christ, present on earth from Pentecost until the Second Coming. Jesus Christ is the head and the rest of us are the other parts. You can imagine hands, feet and fingers. You probably know one or two people who might be the gall bladder. St Jane Frances de Chantal writes sympathetically of the nobody-in-particular people 'of feeble hearts, little love and not much consistency': they could come under the heading of 'flesh (unspecified)'. Leaving metaphors aside, the important story is that whatever our qualities, we are all one in Christ. This is not just because we happen to be alive at the same time, but because the Holy Spirit unites the mystical body of Christ and the Holy Spirit gives it life.

One and universal

There are exactly as many Churches as there are Gods. As we know, God is one not in a numerical sense (as it might be, 'Let N be the number of Gods: then $N=1$'), but an intrinsic, 'not countable' sense. The same kind of reasoning applies to the oneness of the Church. The Church is a whole, not a set of units of which the count happens to be 1.

That the Church, as seen in the world today, appears fragmented and broken is a sad fact about the vicissitudes of history, about human nature and human error. Some people make the anatomy, analysis and history of the woundedness of the mystical body of Christ their life's work. I respect those whose vocation that is, but it is not mine, so I take care to respect them from a safe distance.

The Creed uses the word 'catholic',* which comes from the Greek word *cat-holikos*, which means 'covering the whole', 'all over the place', 'belonging to everywhere'. This ties in with oneness. It also points up one historical fact, which is that when, for whatever reason (it might be a good reason), a body detaches itself from the whole and calls itself 'the Church of *somewhere*', the currents of culture and history inevitably drag it to the point where that 'somewhere' becomes the very centre of its identity. The Church of Ruritania may start its life as 'the church whose centre is God and whose location is Ruritania', but with time it transforms into 'the church whose centre is Ruritania and Ruritanianness'.

Sanctam – holy

The first meaning of the adjective *sancta* is 'holy'. The Church is holy in that she is the channel through which the Holy Spirit has chosen to give his gifts to us. We human beings are amphibians. We are individuals, and at the same time we are also parts of a WE – and the WE through which the grace of God comes is the Church.

As an individual, I have a mind and a soul, and WEs, not being human, have neither. Nevertheless, my mind is not self-feeding. I can't think of everything for myself from first principles (even Descartes, who claimed to be doing it, was only pretending): I take most of what I know from one WE or another.

My soul is not self-feeding any more than my mind is. God is able to feed the soul directly in isolation, but he very rarely does. The grace of God does not all come to me as pure lightning from on high, as if I were a prophet on a mountaintop. Mostly it comes to me mediated, moderated, discerned through the medium of the Church. And the Church, by being the channel of that grace, becomes imbued with it herself.

---

* With a small 'c', of course: 'catholic' is an adjective, not a name.

The Church is a channel, not a source. Grace comes through her, not from her. It is false to say that 'all that is churchy must be holy': false, and dangerous.

To think of the Church as being intrinsically holy runs the risk of idolatry if it leads to reasoning like 'The Church is holy, therefore Father is holy, therefore whatever Father does or says is right.' Such a belief does harm to me because it makes me a slave. It does even more harm to Father because it disconnects him from the network of friction, collision, conflict and correction that is the inner structure of any collective organism, any WE.

Clerolatry is a deadly danger for both us and the clergy. I am not encouraging disrespect, but think how many of the saints had to overcome the opposition of the Church authorities before they could do what they had been sent here to do – and how the Church honoured them in the end.

Sanctam – set apart

The Church is *sancta* in another sense, in that she is consecrated, or set apart. This is something that dates from the first beginnings of the religious instinct in man, even before there were proper gods. Wars may be to the death, and defeated enemies eaten, but still there are sanctuaries, places set apart: in the sanctuary, you were safe. As Chesterton says, at the beginning of history people did not say to each other, 'We must not hit each other,' but 'We must not hit each other in the holy place.'*

In the Latin of the Creed, the same sense of set-apartness comes from the very word for 'Church', *ecclesia*, whose Greek root literally means 'called out', as in the Church being a community of people who have been called out from among the human race.

There are times and places where the set-apartness of the Church seems like a barrier that ought to be broken down for the good of everyone. But in every place and in every age, that is a disaster. It is very, very difficult to avoid using strength when it seems ready to hand, especially when the motive is (or starts off

* In *Orthodoxy*, chapter 5.

as being) to support the weak. At a time when something clearly needs to be done, you might be inclined to dismiss 'God's strength is manifested in weakness' as being just an excuse for doing nothing, but history shows us the terrible things that happen when the Church tries to be a power in the world. Then again, it also shows us the terrible things that happen when the world tries to be a power in the Church. Dante's *Paradiso* is full of outcries against both these disasters.

A clear example (which also has the merit of not getting bogged down in arguments about our own world) comes in *The Lord of the Rings*, where J. R. R Tolkien's angel-figure Gandalf says that he must not take the Ring of Power because, if he did, he would do good with it – and his doing good would in itself become a tyranny, all the more pernicious because of its very goodness.*

Apostolic

Finally, the Church is apostolic because she is founded on the Apostles and their successors and the successors of their successors, and so on up to the present day; and especially she is founded on the Apostle Peter.

If you had been Jesus, what would you have done? Whom would you have chosen? Looking round the Twelve, I am sure that most of us can see several more-qualified candidates than Peter. James and John, the Sons of Thunder, would have swept the world with a warrior religion resembling the Islam of a few centuries later. Judas Iscariot would have manipulated the power politics of the era and adroitly wielded the spiritual power which Jesus had brought into the world. John the beloved Apostle would have inaugurated an era of universal love and mysticism.

But we were given Peter the impulsive blusterer, Peter whose heart was several sizes bigger than his head, Peter who blurted out the deepest truths without thinking what he was saying, who saw himself doing heroic things for his Master but, when given the opportunity, instead behaved as unheroically as he possibly could.

* *The Fellowship of the Ring*, chapter 2, 'The Shadow of the Past'.

None of this is to criticise Jesus' judgement. The fact that he made the wrong choice according to our way of thinking shows the wrongness of our way of thinking, not his. It shows that the criteria we judge by are not God's. God's power is shown in imperfection rather than perfection,* but we are always surprised when he does it like that. We shouldn't be. The Father warned us that 'my thoughts are not your thoughts', and here the Son demonstrates the same thing.

The work of the Spirit

The Church is always defective, always sick, always (you might say) dying. The joy is that the Holy Spirit has always been present in the Church and always comes to the rescue. He acts, as he always acts, not by massive, definitive interventions, but by invisible means whose pattern is discovered (if at all) long after the event. Falling off a horse on the way to Damascus is the exception rather than the rule.

For your encouragement, here is a story of Boccaccio showing the invisible protection the Spirit gives the Church.†

John, a merchant in Paris, has tried hard to convert his fellow-merchant Abraham, a Jew. He has used all manner of theological and scriptural arguments, and in the end Abraham announces that he is almost persuaded: he will go to the centre to see what it is all about. He will go to Rome.

John is naturally terrified. He knows that if Abraham sees the corruption of Rome, the decadent cardinals willing to sell anything for money and pausing from their lusts only long enough to gorge themselves on rich and exotic foods, he will reject Christianity for ever. He tries to dissuade him, but to no avail: Abraham goes.

Abraham comes back from Rome. He has seen the corruption. He has seen decadent cardinals willing to sell anything for money and pausing from their lusts only long enough to gorge themselves

---

* 'My power is made perfect in weakness' (2 Cor. 12:9).
† *Decameron*, first day, second story.

on rich and exotic foods. And he says to John, 'If the Church has been like this for more than a thousand years, and survived, it can only be because of the power of the Holy Spirit. I want to be baptised!'

The Church blunders, like Peter. She flirts with infidelity, like the wife of the prophet Hosea; but somehow, without us quite seeing how, the Spirit guides her back: because the Spirit is in her. That is another sense in which the Church is 'holy'.

The sin against the Spirit again

It is possible to get a clearer picture of the work of the Spirit in the Church by looking at its opposite. This story might be called the parable of the vinaigrette; or again, the parable of the paint.

I take oil and I take vinegar and I add a spoonful of mustard and I shake it all up in a bottle. I started with two liquids that do not mix and I end up with an emulsion. Each drop of it is not *either* oil *or* vinegar, but *both* oil *and* vinegar. It is just right for salads.

Paint is flakes of solid pigment suspended in a viscous medium. Each drop of paint is liquid like the medium, and also opaque like the pigment: applied to wood, the medium dries and the flakes of pigment cover the surface. That is what paint is for.

The vinaigrette is a whole, and the paint is a whole: that is the key to this story. Now let time pass – years, in the case of the paint. You open the tin to touch up some chipped woodwork and you find a thick, strong-smelling, transparent liquid and, at the bottom of it, a layer of solid, coloured rock. The flakes of pigment have separated themselves out and stuck together. With a screwdriver you jab at the rock and get out a few gluey lumps, but breaking them all the way down into microscopic flakes is a hopeless task. In the end you have to leave the woodwork unpainted, or go out and buy another tin.

The vinaigrette version of this story can be left (as they say in the maths books) as an exercise for the reader: oily oil and sour water, and no way to blend them together again.

Any WE that grows big enough to be called an organisation has some kind of 'spirit' within it that gives it life; but any organisation that has developed beyond a certain point feels an urge to turn upon its own spirit and eliminate it. That is a kind of 'sin against its own spirit', and the Church is not immune to it.

Separation and specialisation are the foundation of the modern economy. I do not make gas. The gas board provides me with gas, which I consume. I do not make electricity. The electricity company provides me with electricity, of which I consume as much as I need, when I need it. They play their part; I play mine. We are producer and consumer.

It seems logical that the Church should not ignore the advances of the modern world in every field, including that of organisation. But if she really does embrace modern management, if the whole thing becomes a matter of arranging the efficient production of spiritual goods and services for the benefit of consumers, then the Church is no longer one, but two. There is the 'producing Church', staffed by specialists, which retails any of a wide range of things, from spiritual comfort to salvation; and there is the 'consuming Church', you and me, which consumes the goods and services produced.

That means that there is no Church. There is no WE any more because there is no longer anything that can say 'we' about itself. There are only a lot of individual consumers with their own demands, preferences and wishes; and producers with their management structures and even their trade unions.

A service-providing Church looks good on management diagrams. On one side of the chart there are the clergy, who are trained for the job of providing services to the laity. On the other side there are the laity, whose job is to know nothing (after all, we are not expected to know how to make electricity). The laity exist to obey the clergy and pay for them.

What could be better? What could be more efficient? It is certainly convenient for me as a layman because it demands no involvement from me, only a little cash. But both sides lose. The laity lose because they are no longer part of the Church: they can no longer say 'we' about the Church, but only 'it'. 'It' becomes an external service supplier that supplies goodness, enlightenment or whatever. As a supplier, the Church loses all authority, since one of the marks of a consumer is that he expects to receive what he wants rather than what he needs, and one of the marks of a supplier is that it supplies what the customer wants. After all, there are always other suppliers of uplift if you don't like the one you've got.

A 'church of two halves' can be successful in worldly terms – the cults thrive on this structure – but it is dead. It has taken deadness into itself. The Holy Spirit has no place in a well-organised Church because he cannot be drawn in a diagram on a management chart: how can you draw someone who is invisible? Without the rescuing power of the Spirit, all the Church's activities, however admirable, become (in Evelyn Waugh's phrase) 'a watch ticking on the hand of a dead man'.

There is no cure for this. I do not mean that it is incurable, but that there is no specific thing – no cure, prescription or formula – which, added to the diagrams, will make them into diagrams not of deadness but of life.*

This is not a reason for gloom but for hope – hope of the right kind. Looking back in history, there has never been any 'cure' for any state the Church has got herself into; and she has got herself into many. Rescue has come from people and from the Spirit. The only cure for a sick or dying WE is the life-giving power of the Spirit: in the Church and in each of us. It is the Spirit we must pray to, to keep the Church full of that life. And we too must do our part, because the Spirit works through us all.

To extend a well-known phrase, just as my relationship with God must be an 'I–thou' relationship, so my relationship with the Church must be an 'I–we' relationship. No other way has life.

---

* If there were such a cure, someone would summarise it as one more bullet point in one more slide in one more management meeting, and we would be back where we started.

37

I confess one baptism

Confiteor unum baptisma

Baptism comes just here in the Creed, after the Spirit and the Church, because it is the work of the Spirit and is administered by the Church. Baptism comes from the Church, and the Church comes from baptism: if there were no baptised then the Church would have no members.

Baptism is **one** in that it is done once. Once you have been baptised you *are* baptised. To repeat the process would do nothing, because you cannot become something you already are: it wouldn't make sense.

One of the symbols accompanying baptism is death, death by drowning in water. This reinforces the point. In taking one symbolically through death into new life, baptism echoes Jesus' death and resurrection. As you die and are resurrected once only, so you can only be baptised once.

Baptism is **one** in another sense because all Christians share the same baptism. However many schisms and excommunications may stand between us, my baptism is your baptism and your baptism is mine. Official Church documents exist that tabulate which baptisms count as baptisms and which do not. That would be dismal if it came out of some kind of high-level diplomacy – 'We'll recognise yours if you recognise ours' – but the enchanting fact is that it doesn't. The question asked when making the list is a much simpler one: the simplest possible. Do these people baptise in the name of the Father and the Son and the Holy Spirit? If they do, then their baptism is a baptism. If they don't, it isn't.

There is a further bit of legalism that is equally enchanting because it emphasises how serious we are about the absolute oneness of baptism. It can happen that one isn't sure whether one has been baptised at all. Possibly there is no one alive who remembers. In that case, a different rite is laid down. Paraphrasing it, the priest says, 'If you have not been baptised then I now baptise you in the name of the Father and the Son and the Holy Spirit,' meaning, 'If you *have* been baptised, then I am now pouring water on you for no reason.'

Once the connection between water and cleansing has been made, it holds. A good person can baptise; a bad person can baptise; a layman can baptise; probably even an atheist can. The high theologians, the technicians of theology will, true to their vocation, fill in the details to fit what computer scientists call the awkward 'corner cases'. There is a theology, for instance, of the 'baptism of desire', and there have been times in the world's history when people have even had the generous custom of receiving baptism on behalf of their dead pagan forebears.

The birth of the sacraments

The Creed proclaims baptism, but it does not go on to say anything about any other sacrament. This is partly a historical accident in terms of what the Creed needed to say at the time it was written, but it also reflects the fact that the Creed has now said everything that needs saying. It has said that God can establish a causal connection between a physical act and a spiritual effect. We call these connections 'sacraments'. What sacraments exist and how many of them there are is an additional detail, and the Creed does not feel the need to go that far: the foundation is established.

It is a law of our being, a physical and biological law, that water administered internally relieves thirst. It is a law of our being, a spiritual law established by God, that water applied externally cleanses from sin. God has created this particular connection between act and effect, and once the connection has been created, it becomes a law. God does not decide afresh to confer a grace each time someone is sprinkled with water any more than God decides afresh, each time you drink a glass of water, to relieve your thirst.

The result of all this is that anyone who does something by administering a sacrament really does do it. A sacrament gives a human being the quality of *agency* on the spiritual level: the power to act and, by that act, to make something happen.

The sacraments show once again that matter matters. A sacrament happens when something done in the material world has a spiritual effect. In a sense, it is an echo of the fact that our redemption happened because the Son's becoming incarnate in the material world had a spiritual effect.

It took time for the sacraments we know to grow from that root and take their final form, and it is right that this should have been so. Sacraments are the work of God, not of the Church. The Church cannot make a sacrament: she had to discover them by a long process of discernment and coming to understand.

Doctrine does not happen all at once, as if we had been given a set of stone tablets like the ones Moses brought down from Sinai. As in all the sciences, there is an interplay of 'theory of' and 'practice of' which leads to understanding, and thence to discovery. The Creed establishes the concept of a sacrament and establishes the principle of the forgiveness of sins. That is the foundation on which understanding is built. The actual building takes time, as it does in every science. Some of the building work had already been done;* more of it took place later.†

---

* The first step in this direction, in AD 251, was accompanied by a brief schism. Were there sins (such as giving in to persecution) that could never be forgiven, so that all the Church could do would be to pray to God for mercy on the sinners at the Last Judgement? To say Yes would be to abandon the sinners; to say No would be to disrespect those who had remained firm in the persecutions and suffered for it. A century filled with savage and thorough persecutions was a very good time to be addressing this question. See, for example, the story of Novatianism in Henry Chadwick, *The Early Church* (1967).

† This whole theme is treated with great thoroughness by Newman in *An Essay on the Development of Christian Doctrine* (1845).

38

For the forgiveness of sins

In remissionem peccatorum

Baptism is the first and greatest of the sacraments. This is because to be baptised is to be washed clean of one's sins.

Sin is the greatest contribution Christianity has made to the health and happiness of the human race. Sin means that a bad act can be performed by someone who is essentially good. If there were no sin, then good people would only ever do good things, and anyone who ever did anything bad would himself be bad through and through.

Life without sin

Let's imagine what it would be like if there were no such thing as sin.

Suppose I have done something wrong. Suppose, for instance, that I have wheedled my way into the house of a poor widow and stolen the savings she keeps in the tea caddy on the shelf in her kitchen. When taxed with this crime, what do I say?

My response has to be one of the following:

1. I was struck by a sudden overwhelming impulse – in other words, **I didn't do it**, not in the full sense of performing a completely voluntary act.
2. She would have wanted me to have the money if she had known how much I needed it – in other words, **it wasn't stealing**.
3. It isn't fair that people like her hold on to all the money in the world without using it, while people like me, who could use it, don't have any – in other words, **stealing itself is not a crime** but an act of justice.
4. I am nothing but a sneaky little thief – **I am a bad person**.

If there is no such thing as sin, no other answer is possible.

I cannot realistically believe that I am, deep down, a bad person. That eliminates the fourth option. For any of the remaining three, I can, if pressed, elaborate an argument worthy of any trial lawyer. But, not being a lawyer, I cannot bring myself to believe my own lies. Three options are incredible, and the fourth is intolerable. I am stuck.

This is an impossible problem, but in a world without sin there is no avoiding it. Often the contradiction resolves itself in scapegoating. If *someone else* does exactly the same thing I did, the same four options are available, but this time the fourth one is not intolerable at all. The culprit is a bad person, is a very bad person indeed, and I join in jumping up and down on him as a substitute for jumping up and down on myself.

And all this, because of saying there is no such thing as sin.

Liberation in the acknowledgement of sin

Accepting that there is such a thing as sin is a liberation. It is a liberation that comes in two stages.

The first stage is simply to believe that even someone good can do a bad thing. This lifts the immediate burden because you don't have to believe you did right every time you did wrong, and you don't have to believe you are bad just because you did a wrong thing.

The first stage is good, but on its own it is not enough. You are not bad, which is a relief; but although you are good, there is something wrong with you. That is not a good place to be. If you believe in sin but not in healing, then you both know that you need to be healed and know that you can't be. A soul in that position understandably turns tail and flees back to the lie that there is no such thing as sin. The lie may be deadly, but at least it hurts less.

Here is where the Creed is a liberation. By asserting that sin can be healed, it makes it psychologically possible to believe the truth: that sin exists.

The 'protection racket'

There is a difficulty with sin and religion which needs to be addressed very early on. It is not a difficulty anyone has naturally, but it is a favourite attack on believers, and one that needs answering. It goes like this. The Church (or God) tells us we are sinners and the Church (or God) offers to heal us of being sinners. Isn't this a kind of protection racket? The accusation of sin and the offer to get rid of the sin come from the same source.

Look around the world and you will see examples of this protection racket. The 'holistic practitioner' tells you both that your humours need rectifying (whatever that means) and that he can rectify them for a fee. The climatist tells you both that going on holiday is evil and that buying indulgences from him will make the evil good. Progressive forces of all kinds will identify you as a deviationist (or a racist or a capitalist roader or whatever name they want to use), and also kindly send you to courses and re-education camps to cure you.

The beginning of an answer is this: there are cases where telling you there is something wrong with you and offering to cure it does not add up to a protection racket. Take a cancer specialist, for example. He will diagnose the disease and he will also offer to treat it. So the pattern alone does not automatically imply dishonesty.

So, looking at sin, is the whole business a protection racket, or honest?

The question boils down to whether the 'bad thing' we are being cured of is real. In the case of the quack, he is himself inventing the thing he plans to charge you for curing. In the case of the cancer, it is objectively there and the specialist is not inventing it, only diagnosing it.

The question is transformed into, 'Does sin exist objectively, like cancer, or is it defined?'

The answer to this question is very definite. A sin is a sin solely because it *is* a sin. Sin has the same objective reality as cancer. Nothing is a sin purely as a result of someone defining it to be one. God did not choose between 'shalt' and 'shalt not' when composing the Ten Commandments: the Ten Commandments are not a definition of right and wrong, but a description of them. If the Church says that a particular act is a sin, she is not saying, like a legislator, 'This *shall* be a sin,' but, like a doctor or a scientist deducing from observation, 'This *is* one.'

There are theologies that deny this. Some of them call themselves Christian. They say not that God forbids certain actions because they are sins, but that certain actions are sins because God forbids them. They imply that God might really have said 'shalt' rather than 'shalt not' and we might really have found ourselves in a world in which we could be condemned for *not* coveting each other's asses.

This is a profoundly anti-human doctrine. It denies the power of human reason to know the truth: in this case, to know right from wrong. Human beings, on this view, are mere slaves whose duty it is to do whatever they are told to do, and to be grateful for being told. I will not pursue the matter further except to say that this is not how orthodox Christianity operates. God has not *made* right and wrong. Right and wrong *are*, just as the truths of arithmetic *are*.

Healing from sin

God cannot make a sin be a sin. God also cannot make a sin not have happened: when I sin, the statement, 'I have sinned,' becomes true and it stays true. This is where the second side of the story of sin comes in, the side without which the first side (the existence of sin at all) would be intolerable.

The second side of the story of sin is that although sin cannot be un-happened, it can still be healed, just as the Resurrection does not cancel the Crucifixion but does transmute it. And God does have complete power here. Assuming a degree of consent to the treatment, even a tiny degree, God can heal sin. One cannot un-break bones, but broken bones can heal.

There is a whole theology of all this, of course. What the Creed says is only the root from which it all grows.

39

I look forward to the resurrection of the dead

Et exspecto resurrectionem mortuorum

The Creed began before the creation did, and it reaches its conclusion after time has ended: our present kind of time, at least. Although its final statements are immeasurably far away in time, they are surprisingly earthy. There is no soaring up into pure spirituality, all angels and clouds and harps. 'Heaven,' someone once said of that angelic kind of future, 'is an acquired taste,' and he was right and more than right. It would take *twice* the length of eternity to acquire a taste for an anaemic existence like that.

But the Creed does not expect us to look forward to a purely spiritual future. Instead, it insists on the resurrection of the dead, which means resurrection of body and soul. A risen body and a risen soul, but body and soul nonetheless.

As for the nature of this risen state, all we really have is a set of indications. We know that it must involve becoming *more* ourselves, not *less*. What that means, we don't really know. There is a tradition that sees the condition of man after the Fall as being not a punishment but an act of mercy. Just as when a doctor puts a patient into an induced coma to let a brain injury heal, so God separates us from our full powers until we are healed of the Fall and capable of handling them.

Whatever the truth of that idea (Dante certainly makes good use of it), the joys of the next world are reincarnate joys: not bodiless and bloodless ones. They are the smell of a bonfire or gunpowder or a good cigar. They are the taste of a top-notch cassoulet. They are 'eating *pâtés de foie gras* to the sound of trumpets'. Or rather, those bodily pleasures are shadows of the joys to come.

The Creed has implied over and over again that we are not body with a soul squeezed in like a ghost in a machine, and not soul inexplicably burdened with a dead weight of flesh. Nobody *has* a body. Nobody *has* a soul. We *are* both body and soul. This is a good part of what the Incarnation is about (and it is what some heretics love to get wrong about the Incarnation).

Now the Creed stops implying and comes right out and says it in so many words: 'I believe in the resurrection of the dead.' Before death we were one, body and soul, but at odds within ourselves; at death we were cut in half. In our resurrection we are made whole, and we are made one.

The resurrection of the dead

Man is body and man is soul, so the real problem with being both body and soul comes when we lose one of the two. Who or what is left?

> John Brown's body lies a-mouldering in his grave:
> His soul goes marching on.

I die. My body moulders one way or another, so what arrives at the Pearly Gates is not me, not the whole me, but only a disembodied spirit. The first thing I will say to St Peter is, 'Where is the rest of me?'

Heaven is a place of multiplied joys. All the same, in heaven I am not all there because man is not only soul, but also body. It is through the body that all our sensations come, and our experience and our knowledge. It is through the body, and not the soul alone, that we encounter other people.

I can believe in the abstract joys of heaven, the bliss, rejoicing and freedom from suffering. I am told to believe it, and I do. But still I can't call this living, not when half of me isn't there. A heaven of disembodied spirits cannot be our final home because disembodied spirits is not what we are.

So the resurrection of the dead must happen. Jesus taught it, and the Creed proclaims it.

As to how it happens, and what the resurrected body is like, even clever and holy people don't know. St Paul himself could not say it clearly when he was pestered by the curious (the Greeks always preferred to know the truth rather than to try to live it).

There are some things that can be said, all the same. This is not a 'same all over again' reincarnation of the kind some eastern religions believe in. Being reincarnated into the same mode of being over and over again is no part of Christian belief.

The trouble is that human language wasn't adequate for what Paul wanted to say: a once-and-for-all resurrection into our final, whole and definitive mode of being with all our powers restored. Paul was forced to talk about being 'raised up a spiritual body',[*] and that in turn gave unintentional encouragement to the kind of people who didn't approve of matter and preferred us to be just disembodied souls.

It is hard to blame Paul, because Greek doesn't have a word for 'a body made out of something that transcends matter'. Dante came up with the word 'transhumanised',[†] but even he had to admit that the word couldn't really mean anything because he had only just invented it himself.

As we go blundering about trying to describe the Resurrection, perhaps our blunders are themselves the best answer. As Dionysius says, when it comes to God, all our assertions fail and we end up only able to say what God is *not*. He could have said the same thing about our resurrected selves.

Impossibility of description is not a failure. Finding truths that cannot be specified or pinned down, but only pointed at, happens in every science, and there is nothing shameful about it. The truths we can grasp are only shadows. But they are truthful shadows:

> All truth is shadow except the last truth. But all truth is substance in its own place, though it be but shadow in another place. And the shadow is a true shadow, as the substance is a true substance.[‡]

[*] 1 Corinthians 15:44.
[†] *Paradiso*, I.70.
[‡] Isaac Penington (1616–79), quoted in Dorothy L. Sayers, *Introductory Papers on Dante* (1954), 'Dante's Imagery: I – Symbolic'.

40

And the life of the world to come

Et vitam venturi sæculi

If the human condition can be said to involve a constant coming to terms with our own mortality, the Christian condition goes one step further. We need to come to terms with our own immortality.

Mortality, such as the pagans believe in, has poignancy to it and a high puzzled sadness. One and the same night awaits us all, says the poet Catullus to his mistress.* At the end of the *Iliad*, King Priam of Troy visits the hero Achilles, who killed his son, and together they contemplate the nothingness that awaits them both.†

Mortality is all those sad things, but it brings us a great gift. That gift is meaninglessness. If nothing really matters in the end, then it doesn't matter what I do. To party as if there were no tomorrow is easy when there really is no tomorrow. As Virgil says, bringing his narration of a sonorous splendid battle to its climax, 'Throw a little dust on it, and all will be quiet.'‡

This gift of meaninglessness is denied to us Christians. Everything we do matters. Whatever I do now, at this moment, changes what I am, even if it does so infinitesimally. Doing it means that I will be in a state of 'having done it', not just until I die, but for ever. All our acts are definitive and irreversible.

If this life is about becoming, and the next life is about being what one has become, then that is all the answer to 'Why be good?' that anyone ever really needs.

I commend the contemplation of immortality to you as an exercise worth doing. I cannot tell you how to do it. After all, I am

---

* 'Let us live, my Lesbia, and love . . .' Catullus 5.
† Homer, the *Iliad*, 24.477ff.
‡ '*Pulveris exigui iactu compressa quiescent*', Virgil, *Georgics*, IV.86–87.

not in a position to say anything factual about the next world. Nobody is. Even the Apocalypse deals in visions rather than descriptions.

The next world

Beyond knowing that we are resurrected as whole beings, body and soul, we can't say anything authoritative about the life of the world to come. But that doesn't stop us having questions, and being distracted by them.

Some people have imagined that the risen body will be of the perfect age (thirty?) or of the perfect shape (a sphere?). Some people say that the blessed are no longer capable of sin; others that to be incapable of *anything* is to constrain one's freedom and turn one into an automaton, and that the state of the blessed must be more like 'can sin, but able not to'. Perhaps Mary can be our guide here because she could have said No, but didn't.

Time in the next world is another question. At present the time we can conceive of is the all-at-once Nowness of the eternal Father or the moment-after-moment nowness of our own lives. But the first of these seems too alien to us; and as for the second, what if we get bored after the first million centuries?

To all these questions there can be no answer, except to say, 'If these thoughts seem counterproductive, go and think about something else.' We know now as much as we need to know now, and that is enough to be getting on with. We are not designed to know everything in advance.

Someone once compared the mourners at a funeral to caterpillars gathered sadly round a chrysalis. So imagine St Francis preaching to the caterpillars. What could he say about butterflies that they could ever understand? Even if they did understand, what would they find desirable in such a state of life?

To add to the unanswered questions, here is a puzzle which has come to me recently. We are not talking, thank goodness, about a washed-out 'spirit only' heavenly existence, all clouds and harps. That is good, because we are both body and soul. But let's look further into it. We spend a lot of time in this world avoiding

hunger and thirst and heat and cold and death. A first approximation to imagining the next world could be to imagine all those
evils gone.

But wait. Will there really never be any frosty mornings in
heaven? Will nobody ever be cold, even for a moment? Or think of
a warrior who has experienced the joy of defending his family
against attackers at the risk of his own life: in the next world, how
will that joy come, with no enemies and no death?

The answer to every question is to remember what the Red
Admiral caterpillar thought when St Francis preached metamor-
phosis to it. It couldn't see much point in a future state in which
one couldn't crawl over nettle leaves, munching.

The next world will be like a surprise in a theo-drama. It is
unimaginable in advance, but once it has happened it will all fit in
with everything, and fit in so well that it will be impossible to
imagine, looking back, that things could have turned out any
other way.

Until then, I hope that the time spent reading this book has not
been wasted. The time spent writing it certainly hasn't been. Love
as you are loved, live as if you were immortal because you are –
and see you there.

Further reading

This does not pretend to be a complete bibliography. Its purpose is to suggest a few of the directions from which the ideas in this book came, and directions in which they might usefully lead.

C. S. Lewis, *Mere Christianity* and *The Four Loves*. If you have not tried understanding religion before, these books are an excellent introduction. Their value is their simplicity and the thoroughness with which they eliminate misconceptions and establish the basic foundations.

Dante Alighieri, *The Divine Comedy*. This is the greatest poem in the whole of Christian literature (and the second greatest epic poem ever). Its whole being is filled with passion about the world: politics, science, astronomy, philosophy and the presence of God in all things. The translation I found best the first time I read Dante is the one by Dorothy L. Sayers (*Hell*, 1949; *Purgatory*, 1955; *Paradise*, 1960). Sayers brings the freshness and vigour of Dante to a modern reader without specialist knowledge, and her introductions and notes explain not only the people portrayed and the images used, but also the theology that underlies the poem. As a way of learning theology in its wholeness as a living way of thought, it is unparalleled.

Another translation worth mentioning is the one by Robin Kirkpatrick (*Inferno*, 2006; *Purgatorio* and *Paradiso*, 2007). The verse translation itself is more modern than Sayers', and it has the Italian text on the facing page. The notes do not explain everything and everyone, as Sayers does, but they go into more scholarly detail on the poem as a literary work.

Charles Williams, *The Figure of Beatrice* (1943). *The Divine Comedy* is a poem structured around love, and this book lays out a theology of the Way of Affirmation, which lies in using created things as an approach to God rather than avoiding them as a distraction. It is a masterwork of what one could call 'Romantic Theology', and is far too little known.

G. K. Chesterton, *Orthodoxy* (1908) followed by *The Everlasting Man* (1925). Chesterton takes the opposite of an intellectual approach. In a series of striking images he describes how he tried to quarry sanity out of the weary decadence of his age, and how, having finished, he discovered it had all been done already:

> I tried to be in advance of the truth; and I found that I was eighteen hundred years behind it. When I fancied that I stood alone I was really in the ridiculous position of being backed up by all Christendom. I did try to found a heresy of my own; and when I had put the last touches to it, I discovered that it was orthodoxy.

Henry Chadwick, *The Early Church* (1967). To the extent that the present book is an attempt to come to terms with doctrine by trying to work it out from first principles, 'Why would I want to believe or disbelieve this?', Henry Chadwick's book is the perfect complement because it portrays the Church actually in the process of working all these things out. Anybody can tabulate the details, but Chadwick tells the story up to the fifth century as if these questions really mattered to real people like you and me – which, of course, they did.

Julian of Norwich, *Revelations of Divine Love* (1393). The great rediscovery of Julian came with Grace Warrack's edition of 1901, which removed words and grammar that had gone out of use since the fourteenth century, gently and without disturbing Julian's characteristic voice. An edition published by Universalis (2020) takes this process forward by one more century: the quotations in this book are taken from it. Actual translations into fully modern English do exist, but to me it seems a pity to lose the sense that the real Julian is talking to one in her own language. Her personality shines across the centuries.

G. K. Chesterton, *St Thomas Aquinas* (1933). This book gives the essence of Aquinas' teaching without any of the technicalities. Etienne Gilson, in his time the world's most highly esteemed

Thomist scholar, wrote:

> Chesterton makes one despair. I have been studying St Thomas
> all my life and I could never have written such a book ... It is
> without possible comparison the best book ever written on St
> Thomas. Nothing short of genius can account for such an
> achievement ... Chesterton has said all that which the scholars
> were more or less clumsily attempting to express in academic
> formulas.

R. C. Zaehner, *Mysticism Sacred and Profane* (1957) and *At
Sundry Times* (1958). Zaehner was Spalding Professor of Eastern
Religion and Ethics at the University of Oxford and deeply read
and learned in Hindu, Buddhist, Islamic and Zoroastrian mysticism and theology, all of which he could read in the original.
Zaehner's strength is that his study of comparative religion is not
of the superficial stamp-collecting kind: he thinks deeply into
each religion (and into its conflicting schools) and sees each of
them more clearly because he knows intimately how the others
have tackled the same basic questions.

Joseph Ratzinger (Pope Benedict XVI), *Jesus of Nazareth, Part
Two: Holy Week* (2011). This is a scholarly but accessible work.
It aims to put into practice the principles of biblical exegesis
formulated by the Second Vatican Council, and it goes systematically through all the events narrated in the Gospels from Palm
Sunday to the Resurrection, asking questions about their meaning
and significance and, of course, about Jesus himself, and summarising all strands of current thinking on the subject.*

Homer, the *Iliad*. The reason for citing the *Iliad* here is that this
book is about life and the *Iliad* is the first poem in history that
speaks about what it is to be fully alive and also mortal. As

---

* The German Protestant theologian Joachim Ringleben has written *Jesus*
(2008) on similar principles, starting from the opposite end theologically
but still, as Ratzinger says, 'reaching a profound unity in the essential
understanding of the person of Jesus'. Unfortunately, this book has not
been translated into English and I have not been able to read it.

Chesterton says in *The Everlasting Man*, 'If the world becomes pagan and perishes, the last man alive would do well to quote the *Iliad* and die.' As for translations, the power of Homer will always shine through, so find one that suits you and go through it. Adam Nicolson's *The Mighty Dead* (2014) is a fitting companion, as is Gilbert Murray's *The Rise of the Greek Epic* (1934); but no companion is really needed.

IN GLORY TO JUDGE THE LIVING AND THE DEA
THE HOLY SPIRIT, THE LORD, THE GIVER OF LI
WHO WITH THE FATHER AND THE SON IS ADO
PROPHETS. I BELIEVE IN ONE, HOLY, CATHOLIC .
THE FORGIVENESS OF SINS AND I LOOK FORWA
OF THE WORLD TO COME. I BELIEVE IN ONE G
AND EARTH, 48 OF ALL THINGS VISIBLE AND
THE ONLY BEGOTTEN SON OF GOD, 71 BORN C
LIGHT FROM LIGHT, TRUE GOD FROM TRUE GC
FATHER; 78 THROUGH HIM ALL THINGS WERE
100 HE CAME DOWN FROM HEAVEN, 112 AND B
MARY, 121 AND BECAME MAN. 133 FOR OUR SAK
SUFFERED DEATH 178 AND WAS BURIED, 181 AN
WITH THE SCRIPTURES. 191 HE ASCENDED INT
THE FATHER. 204 HE WILL COME AGAIN IN GL
HIS KINGDOM WILL HAVE NO END. 234 I BELIE
LIFE, 242 WHO PROCEEDS FROM THE FATHER A
IS ADORED AND GLORIFIED, 260 WHO HAS SF
HOLY, CATHOLIC AND APOSTOLIC CHURCH. 2
OF SINS 280 AND I LOOK FORWARD TO THE R
WORLD TO COME. 287 I BELIEVE IN ONE GOD,
OF ALL THINGS VISIBLE AND INVISIBLE. I BEL
SON OF GOD, BORN OF THE FATHER BEFORE A
FROM TRUE GOD, BEGOTTEN, NOT MADE, CONSU
WERE MADE. FOR US MEN AND FOR OUR SALV
SPIRIT WAS INCARNATE OF THE VIRGIN MARY,